CREATIONISM IN TWENTIETH-CENTURY AMERICA

Volume 1

ANTIEVOLUTIONISM BEFORE WORLD WAR I

ANTIEVOLUTIONISM BEFORE WORLD WAR I

Edited by
RONALD L. NUMBERS

LONDON AND NEW YORK

First published in 1995 by Garland Publishing, Inc.

This edition first published in 2022
by Routledge
4 Park Square, Milton Park, Abingdon, Oxon OX14 4RN
605 Third Avenue, New York, NY 10017

Routledge is an imprint of the Taylor & Francis Group, an informa business

© 1995 Introductions Copyright Ronald L. Numbers

All rights reserved. No part of this book may be reprinted or reproduced or utilised in any form or by any electronic, mechanical, or other means, now known or hereafter invented, including photocopying and recording, or in any information storage or retrieval system, without permission in writing from the publishers.

Trademark notice: Product or corporate names may be trademarks or registered trademarks, and are used only for identification and explanation without intent to infringe.

British Library Cataloguing in Publication Data
A catalogue record for this book is available from the British Library

ISBN: 978-0-367-43553-0 (Set)
ISBN: 978-1-00-314991-0 (Set) (ebk)
ISBN: 978-0-367-40776-6 (Volume 1) (hbk)
ISBN: 978-0-367-40778-0 (Volume 1) (pbk)
ISBN: 978-0-367-80903-4 (Volume 1) (ebk)

DOI: 10.4324/9780367809034

Publisher's Note
The publisher has gone to great lengths to ensure the quality of this reprint but points out that some imperfections in the original copies may be apparent.

Disclaimer
The publisher has made every effort to trace copyright holders and would welcome correspondence from those they have been unable to trace.

New Preface to the Re-issue of 2021

This anthology of primary documents related to the early history of creationism in the United States first appeared a quarter century ago, in 1995. My interest in the topic had been aroused by my years of research on creationism, which resulted in *The Creationists* (New York: Alfred A. Knopf, 1992). In the meantime, a former student of mine, Edward J. Larson, had published an excellent legal survey, *Trial and Error: The American Controversy over Creation and Evolution* (New York: Oxford University Press, 1985). The philosopher of science Michael Ruse had published the edited volume *But Is It Science? The Philosophical Question in the Creation/Evolution Controversy* (Amherst, NY: Prometheus Books, 1988); and the anthropologist Christopher P. Toumey had just released *God's Own Scientists: Creationists in a Secular World* (New Brunswick, NJ: Rutgers University Press, 1994). Led by Willard B. Gatewood's *Preachers Pedagogues and Politicians: The Evolution Controversy in North Carolina, 1920–1927* (Chapel Hill: University of North Carolina Press, 1966), local studies had also begun to appear. Nevertheless, few, if any, research libraries had begun collecting creationist literature; and not one, to my knowledge, possessed even a complete run of the *Creation Research Society Quarterly*, launched in 1964.

During the past quarter century the landscape of creationism has changed dramatically. Since 1995 the institutional heart of creationism has shifted from the Institute for Creation Research, founded by Henry M. Morris in southern California in 1972, to Ken Ham's Answers in Genesis, headquartered in northern Kentucky. In 2007 the charismatic Australian-born Ham opened a $27-million Creation Museum in Petersburg, Kentucky, across the Ohio River from Cincinnati. Forty-five miles away, in Williamstown, Kentucky, Ham in July 2016 opened an Ark Encounter featuring a "life-size" replica of Noah's ark, at a projected cost of $150 million.

Such growth has attracted considerable attention, such as Susan L. Trollinger and William Vance Trollinger Jr., *Righting America at the Creation Museum* (Baltimore: Johns Hopkins University Press, 2016), and James S. Bielo, *Ark Encounter: The Making of a Creationist Theme Park* (New York: New York University Press, 2018).

The literature on the general history of creationism in the twentieth century has exploded, symbolized most dramatically by Edward J. Larson's Pulitzer Prize-winning volume *Summer for the Gods: The Scopes Trial and America's Continuing Debate over Science and Religion* (New York: Basic Books, 1997). Other significant contributions include Michael Lienesch, *In the Beginning: Fundamentalism, the Scopes Trial, and the Making of the Antievolution Movement* (Chapel Hill: University of North Carolina, 2007); Adam Laats, *Fundamentalism and Education in the Scopes Era: God, Darwin, and the Roots of America's Culture Wars* (New York: Palgrave Macmillan, 2010); Jeffrey P. Moran, *American Genesis: The Evolution Controversies from Scopes to Creation Science* (New York: Oxford University Press, 2012); and Adam R. Shapiro, *Trying Biology: The Scopes Trial, Textbooks, and the Antievolution Movement in American Schools* (Chicago: University of Chicago Press, 2013).

Still, access to creationist sources before the early 1960s remains patchy. To help remedy this condition, Routledge has agreed to reissue the 10-volume set of *Creationism in Twentieth-Century America*. I thank them for their continuing interest.

Ronald L. Numbers
April 2021

CREATIONISM IN TWENTIETH-CENTURY AMERICA

A Ten-Volume Anthology of Documents, 1903–1961

Series Editor
RONALD L. NUMBERS
University of Wisconsin–Madison
William Coleman Professor of the
History of Science and Medicine

A GARLAND SERIES

SERIES CONTENTS

1. ANTIEVOLUTIONISM BEFORE WORLD WAR I

2. CREATION-EVOLUTION DEBATES

3. THE ANTIEVOLUTION WORKS OF ARTHUR I. BROWN

4. THE ANTIEVOLUTION PAMPHLETS OF WILLIAM BELL RILEY

5. THE CREATIONIST WRITINGS OF BYRON C. NELSON

6. THE ANTIEVOLUTION PAMPHLETS OF HARRY RIMMER

7. SELECTED WORKS OF GEORGE McCREADY PRICE

8. THE EARLY WRITINGS OF HAROLD W. CLARK AND FRANK LEWIS MARSH

9. EARLY CREATIONIST JOURNALS

10. CREATION AND EVOLUTION IN THE EARLY AMERICAN SCIENTIFIC AFFILIATION

VOLUME

1

ANTIEVOLUTIONISM BEFORE WORLD WAR I

Edited with introductions by
RONALD L. NUMBERS
University of Wisconsin—Madison
William Coleman Professor of the
History of Science and Medicine

GARLAND PUBLISHING, INC.
New York & London
1995

Introductions copyright © 1995 Ronald L. Numbers
All rights reserved

Library of Congress Cataloging-in-Publication Data

Antievolutionism before World War I / edited with introductions by Ronald L. Numbers.
    p.   cm. — (Creationism in twentieth-century America ; v. 1)
    Contents: The other side of evolution / Alexander Patterson—At the deathbed of Darwinism / Eberhard Dennert—Collapse of evolution / Luther Tracy Townsend—The passing of evolution / G. Frederick Wright.
    Includes bibliographical references.
    ISBN 0-8153-1802-2 (alk. paper)
    1. Evolution (Biology)—Religious aspects—Christianity—Controversial literature.   2. Evolution—Controversial literature. 3. Creationism—History of doctrines—20th century.   4. Bible and evolution.   I. Numbers, Ronald L.   II. Title: Antievolutionism before World War I.   III. Series.
BT712.A57   1995
231.7'65—dc20   94-45044
                                                                                   CIP

Printed on acid-free, 250-year-life paper
Manufactured in the United States of America

Contents

Series Introduction	vii
Volume Introduction	ix
The Other Side of Evolution *Alexander Patterson*	1
At the Deathbed of Darwinism *Eberhard Dennert*	177
Collapse of Evolution *Luther Tracy Townsend*	323
"The Passing of Evolution" *George Frederick Wright*	387
Acknowledgments	403

SERIES INTRODUCTION

In recent years creationism has enjoyed a stunning renaissance both in the United States and around the world. Public opinion polls show that 47 percent of Americans, including one quarter of college graduates, believe that "God created man pretty much in his present form at one time within the last 10,000 years." In the early 1980s two states, Arkansas and Louisiana, passed laws mandating the teaching of "creation science" whenever "evolution science" was taught in the public schools. The United States Supreme Court subsequently overturned these laws, but creationists actively—and often successfully—continue to promote their cause in local schools and churches.

Since the early 1960s creationism has become increasingly identified with a particular nonevolutionary belief known as "scientific creationism" or "creation science." Scientific creationists believe that all life on earth originated no more than 10,000 years ago, and some argue that the entire universe is equally young. To explain the appearance of age suggested by the fossil record, they typically invoke Noah's flood, which, they claim, deposited virtually the entire geological column in the span of a year or so.

Before the 1960s relatively few Americans, including religious fundamentalists, subscribed to such restrictive views of earth history. At the height of the antievolution controversies of the 1920s, for example, most creationists who expressed themselves on the subject embraced interpretations of the book of Genesis that allowed them to accept the evidence of historical geology for the antiquity of life on earth. They generally did so in one of two ways: either by assuming that the "days" of Genesis 1 really meant "ages" or by interposing a gap of perhaps hundreds of millions of years between the creation "in the beginning" and the relatively recent Edenic creation (or restoration, as some would call it) associated with Adam and Eve. Only a few fundamentalists at the time, mostly Seventh-day Adventists, insisted on the recent appearance of life and on the geological significance of the deluge. In recent years, however, through the influence of books such as John C. Whitcomb, Jr. and Henry M. Morris's *The Genesis Flood* (1961), organizations such as the Creation Research Society (1963) and institutions such as the Institute for Creation Research (1972), the so-called flood geologists, now known as scientific creationists, have co-opted the very name creationist for their once peculiar views.

Despite the undeniable importance of antievolutionism in American cultural history, few libraries, academic or otherwise, have collected more than the odd book or pamphlet on creationism, and early creationist periodicals are almost impossible to find. Whether the result of prejudice or indifference, such neglect has made it difficult for students and scholars to explore the development of creationist thought in the twentieth century. This collection of reprinted documents from the first six decades of the century makes available some of the most widely read works on creationism by such stalwarts as Arthur I. Brown, William Bell Riley, Harry Rimmer, Byron C. Nelson, George McCready Price, Harold W. Clark, and Frank Lewis Marsh. It also reprints, for the first time, three of the earliest and rarest creationist journals in America: the *Creationist*, the *Bulletin of Deluge Geology*, and the *Forum for the Correlation of Science and the Bible*.

INTRODUCTION

Within fifteen or twenty years of the publication of Charles Darwin's *Origin of Species* (1859), scientific defenders of special creation could scarcely be found on the North American continent. The nearly unanimous acceptance of evolution within the American scientific community was highlighted in 1879 when the editor of the *Independent*, after surveying the teaching of evolution in the colleges of the North, challenged a rival religious weekly, the *Observer*, to name just "three working naturalists of repute in the United States—or two (it can find one in Canada)—that is not an evolutionist." But besides the Canadian John William Dawson of McGill University, only one could be identified: Princeton's Arnold Guyot.[1] Although many American biologists questioned the ability of natural selection to explain the origin of species, most of them came to see evolution as a scientific fact. Thus criticism of evolution in the early twentieth century came largely from nonscientists increasingly concerned about the growing popularity of evolution among the general public.

Turn-of-the-century debates within the scientific community over the role of natural selection in evolution encouraged such critics to speak out. By the early twentieth century skepticism about the Darwinian emphasis on natural selection had swelled to such proportions, especially in Germany, that the Stanford biologist Vernon L. Kellogg opened his book *Darwinism To-Day* (1907) with a chapter called "The 'Death-Bed of Darwinism.'" He took his title from a recent German work, Eberhard Dennert's *Vom Sterbelager des Darwinismus* (1903), which he described as "an intemperate and unconvincing but interesting brief against the Darwinian factors, *i.e.*, the selection theories, in evolution." Like many of his scientific colleagues, Dennert accepted evolution but not Darwin's particular explanation of it. Kellogg valued Dennert's contribution for bringing together "the anti-Darwinian opinions and declarations of numerous, mostly well-known and reputably placed biologists." He thought that some German biologists might quarrel with Dennert's interpretations of their views but that "for the most part the anti-Darwinian beliefs of these biologists are unmistakably revealed by their own words." A year after its appearance in Germany, Dennert's work came out in an American edition, published in Burlington, Iowa, under the title *At the Deathbed of Darwinism*.[2]

Luther T. Townsend, one of the most visible of the clerical opponents of evolution at the turn of the century, conveyed a similar message to the American public in his booklet *Collapse of Evolution* (1905). In this frequently reprinted (and sometimes expanded) tract Townsend told of the mounting anti-Darwinian sentiment in Europe and challenged American evolutionists to be "as honest and manly" as their German colleagues in admitting the failure of Darwinism. To support his claim that evolution was collapsing, Townsend assembled one of the earliest—and most frequently cribbed—lists of alleged nonevolutionists in order to prove that "the most thorough scholars, the world's ablest philosophers and scientists, with few exceptions, are not supporters, but assailants of evolution." In addition to such late creationists as Louis Agassiz, Guyot, and Dawson, Townsend cited the English physiologist Lionel S. Beale and the German pathologist Rudolf Virchow, both of whom had expressed doubts about the evidence for human evolution, as well as a dozen or so lesser lights, including Dennert.[3]

A graduate of Dartmouth College and the Andover Theological Seminary, Townsend served as pastor of several Methodist Episcopal churches before becoming, in 1868, professor of Hebrew and New Testament Greek at the Boston Theological Seminary, which later became the Boston University School of Theology. He remained at the seminary in various capacities until 1893, when he resigned his professorship in order to devote full time to writing and lecturing. Active in the Chautauqua movement, he also served on the board of directors of the Bible League of North America, founded in 1903, which claimed to be "the only Organized Movement of any kind . . . that stands for the Defense and Confirmation of the Faith of the People in the Bible as the inspired and authoritative Word of God."[4]

In such works as *Evolution or Creation* (1896), *Adam and Eve* (1904), and *Collapse of Evolution,* Townsend defended the first chapters of Genesis as "a simple, straightforward narrative of the facts as they actually occurred." His interpretation, however, was anything but straightforward. In order to accommodate the findings of geologists with a literal reading of the word "day," he argued that "the six vast geological epochs which science describes are types and prophecies of the six ordinary days of which Moses writes, a thousand years being as one day and one day as a thousand years." In other words, "in six literal days, and in the order given in the Bible, the Creator brought the world out of the chaos of the glacial wreck, made it habitable, created modern flora and fauna and gave them life and power to propagate themselves until the end of time." Unlike some creationists who could not imagine being wrong, Townsend modestly acknowledged that time might necessitate the revision of some of his conclusions, that paleontological research, for example, might require the modification of his views on early humans and missing links.[5]

As word spread of the alleged demise of Darwinism, some American antievolutionists came to suspect that perhaps liberal Christians had capitulated to evolution too quickly. In view of the recent turn of events it seemed likely to one observer that those who had "abandoned the stronghold of faith out of sheer fright will soon be found scurrying back to the old and impregnable citadel, when they learn that 'the enemy is in full retreat.'"[6]

Encouraging this return to orthodoxy was the Presbyterian evangelist and sometime lecturer at the Moody Bible Institute, Alexander Patterson, who contributed *The Other Side of Evolution* (1903) to the growing body of antievolution literature. Like many evangelical Christians, Patterson believed that a historical hiatus had occurred between the first and second verses of Genesis 1:

> In that interval lies all geology tells us of. This includes all up to the beginning of the Six Days' Creation. Here is where the fossil creatures lived and died. All this is passed over in silence in the Bible account.

Although inclined toward a literal reading of the Bible, he did not think it necessary to interpret the days of creation as "our short days of twenty-four hours" or to insist on the universality of Noah's flood. And whether or not the Edenic creation had made use of preexisting species was of little concern to him—so long as there was no connection between humans and brutes, which he regarded as "the central point" of the doctrine of evolution. Adopting what the historian Jon H. Roberts has called the "populist conception of validation," he demanded the right to participate in the evaluation of evolution because "the questions involved are too important to be left to the scientist alone." Evolution, he insisted, must appear "before the judgment seat of Christian Common Sense," where "the best juryman will be the intelligent non-scientific mind." In this respect he found it heartening to remember "that there are thousands of quiet thinkers who have never given in their adhesion to this startling theory, and more, that the great masses of the church at least, have no confidence in it." Nevertheless, he feared that evolution was sweeping the country, and he predicted ominously that "if this theory is accepted, we much look for widespread lapse from all Christian faith and, as conduct follows belief in all intelligent creatures, we shall see also great moral declension."[7]

When William Jennings Bryan launched his crusade against evolution in the early 1920s, he borrowed (without acknowledgment) from Patterson's account of the development of the eye to show that Darwinism was nothing but "guesses strung together," and poor guesses at that. "The evolutionist guesses that there was a time when eyes were unknown—that is a necessary part of the hypothesis," Bryan began.

> A piece of pigment, or, as some say, a freckle appeared upon the skin of an animal that had no eyes. This piece of pigment or freckle converged the rays of the sun upon that spot and when the little animal felt the heat on that spot it turned the spot to the sun to get more heat. The increased heat irritated the skin—so the evolutionists guess, and a nerve came there and out of the nerve came the eye!

"Can you beat it?" Bryan asked incredulously—and that it happened not once but twice?[8]

The Other Side of Evolution so impressed the influential pastor of the Moody Church in Chicago, A.C. Dixon, that Dixon arranged for the Bible Institute Colportage Association, forerunner of the Moody Press, to purchase the plates for a revised edition, which students from the Bible institute would then sell from their horse-drawn "Gospel Wagons." Dixon considered Patterson's treatise to be "about the best thing" he had read on the subject, and he thought that the book would "do an immense amount of good if sent to all the preachers, theological professors, theological students, Y.M.C.A. secretaries and Sunday School superintendents of the English-speaking world."[9]

When Dixon laid plans for *The Fundamentals* (1910–1915), the series of twelve mass-produced booklets that launched the fundamentalist movement, he asked the cleric-geologist George Frederick Wright for a chapter that would discredit both materialistic and theistic varieties of the theory. In making his pitch as editor, Dixon noted the strengths and weaknesses of other candidates for the job. He greatly admired Patterson's *The Other Side of Evolution* for the factual evidence it presented, but he recognized that no one would consider the Chicago evangelist authoritative on the subject. Townsend had proved himself to be "strong along these lines," but he, too, had no scientific qualifications. The same was true of James Orr, the conservative Scottish theologian from Glasgow who occasionally addressed scientific issues. In view of

Introduction

these impediments, Dixon thought Wright, who possessed both scientific and theological credentials, might be just the person to contribute an article that would "make the matter so clear that the vagaries of Evolution shall be driven from the minds of thousands."[10] Ironically, Dixon had picked to be the first "fundamentalist" spokesman a man who just a few decades earlier had been one of Darwin's most enthusiastic American advocates.[11]

In the 1870s Wright, a Congregational clergyman, undertook a study of the glacial deposits in New England that won him recognition as a geologist and brought him to attention of the Harvard botanist Asa Gray, Darwin's leading American champion. The eminent botanist, then in his sixties, became "like a father" to young Wright, tutoring him in the ways of science and sharing his vision of a Christianized Darwinism. Together they sought to fashion "a right *evolutionary teleology*" that would provide an alternative interpretation to that offered by the "infidel class of Darwinian expositors" on the one hand and such antievolutionists as Dawson and the Princeton theologian Charles Hodge on the other. Both Wright and Gray derived great comfort from Darwin's inability to explain the origin of the variations preserved by natural selection because this limitation seemed to open the door for divine intervention. In Wright's view, it "rob[bed] Darwinism of its sting," "left God's hands as free as could be desired for contrivances of whatever sort he pleased," and preserved a "reverent interpretation of the Bible."[12]

In 1881 Wright left New England to return to Oberlin as professor of New Testament language and literature in the theological seminary. Back in Ohio, he slowly shifted the thrust of his efforts from defending evolution and the scientific enterprise against biblical literalists to defending the historical accuracy of the Bible against critics who applied evolution to the making of the Bible itself. At the same time, his attitude toward science changed from enthusiasm to skepticism. By the early 1900s he had allied himself with the conservative religious movement that came to be known as fundamentalism. Symbolic of his shifting views was a complimentary, though cautious, introduction he wrote in 1903 for Patterson's *The Other Side of Evolution*. "While not saying that all the points in this little volume are well taken, I can say that I disagree with fewer things in it than with those in almost any other on the subject, and that it is fitted to serve as a very needful tonic in these days of the confusion of bad Philosophy and fragmentary Science." By this time he had achieved such prominence as a spokesman for conservative Christianity—as editor of *Bibliotheca Sacra* and as a contributor to such staunchly antimodernist journals as the *Sunday School Times* and the *Homiletic Review* —that he was invited to serve as a director (along with Townsend) of the newly formed Bible League of North America, which engaged "in an active warfare against unbelief in many of its most dangerous forms."¹³

Although Wright came to regard the Genesis story of creation as scientifically accurate, he followed Guyot in interpreting the Mosaic "days" as representing six great epochs of cosmic history. At a time when the leading Darwinists were expanding the scope of evolution to embrace all living things, Wright insisted on limiting Darwinism, as its founder had done in 1859, to the origin of species from perhaps four or five primordial forms, presumably created by God. Wright also began to emphasize the unproven status of natural selection and to repeat Darwin's description of himself—in the context of his continuous efforts to explain away the difficulties of his theory—as the prince of "wrigglers." Despite his conservative swing, Wright continued his geological investigations (sometimes with the support of the U.S. Geological Survey) and in 1889 brought out his magnum opus, *The Ice Age in North America: And Its Bearing upon the Antiquity of Man,* which passed through five editions before his death.¹⁴

In his essay for *The Fundamentals,* titled "The Passing of Evolution," Wright lashed out at contemporary evolutionists while emphasizing the creationist elements in Darwin's own early writings. Unlike his modern disciples, who were irresponsibly teaching that all forms of life had arisen by strictly natural processes from one primordial speck, Darwin, said Wright, had postulated a Creator who breathed the force of life into several forms of plants and animals "and at the same time endowed them with the marvelous capacity for variation which we know they possess." And instead of attributing "all the differences between animals or between plants" to natural selection, the great English naturalist had taught "simply that species may reasonably be supposed to be nothing more than enlarged or accentuated varieties, which all admit are descendants from a common ancestry." Man, continued Wright, differed so greatly from the higher animals it was "necessary to suppose that he came into existence as the Bible represents, by *the special creation of a single pair,* from whom all the varieties of the race have sprung."¹⁵

Although concerned Christians such as Townsend, Patterson, and Wright sounded warnings about evolution in the years before World War I, most of the militant evangelicals who soon marched under the banner of fundamentalism perceived a greater threat to orthodox faith than evolution: higher criticism, which treated the

Bible more as a historical document than as God's inspired Word. Their relative apathy toward evolution is evident in *The Fundamentals*, the manifesto of fundamentalism. Dixon, who founded the series, confessed to feeling "a repugnance to the idea that an ape or an orang-outang was my ancestor," but expressed a willingness "to accept the humiliating fact, if proved." Reuben A. Torrey, who brought out the last two volumes, took an even more conciliatory position. Although he himself had given up believing in evolution "for purely scientific reasons," he acknowledged—to the consternation of some of his less tolerant fundamentalist friends— that a man could "believe thoroughly in the absolute infallibility of the Bible and still be an evolutionist of a certain type."[16] The essays in *The Fundamentals*, roughly one-fifth of which touched on the issue of evolution, covered the entire spectrum of evangelical opinion: from Wright's progressive creationism and James Orr's admission of "some genetic connection of higher with lower forms" of life to one author's identification of evolution as "the inspiration of the Higher Criticism" and the enemy of the Christian faith. But despite frequent disapproval of the theory of evolution and premature celebration of its imminent death, the collection as a whole lacked the strident attacks that would soon characterize the fundamentalist movement. Fundamentalists may not have liked evolution, but at this time few, if any, saw the necessity or desirability of launching a crusade to eradicate it from the schools and churches of America.[17]

Notes

Most of this introduction is extracted (with the permission of the publisher) from Ronald L. Numbers, *The Creationists* (New York: Alfred A. Knopf, 1992), pp. 7, 15–17, 20–23, 25, 28–29, 32–34, 36–39, 42–43, 51.

1 [William Hayes Ward], "Do Our Colleges Teach Evolution?" *Independent* 31 (December 18, 1879): 14–15. For a summary of the *Independent-Observer* debate, see "Scientific Teaching in the Colleges," *Popular Science Monthly* 16 (1880): 556–59.

2 Vernon L. Kellogg, *Darwinism To-Day* (New York: Henry Holt, 1907), pp. 1–9, quotations on p. 7; Eberhard Dennert, *At the Deathbed of Darwinism*, trans. E.V. O'Harra and John H. Peschges (Burlington: IA: German Literary Board, 1904).

3 L.T. Townsend, *Collapse of Evolution* (New York: American Bible League, 1905), pp. 48–53. For one instance of unacknowledged

indebtedness to Townsend, see T.T. M[artin], "The Three False Teachings of President Poteat of Wake Forest," *Western Recorder* 95 (February 5, 1920): 5.

4 "Luther Tracy Townsend," *Dictionary of American Biography*, 18: 618–19; "Abstract of the Annual Report of the Education Committee of the Bible League of North America," *Bible Student and Teacher* 10 (1909): 372–73.

5 Luther Tracy Townsend, *Evolution or Creation: A Critical Review of the Scientific and Scriptural Theories of Creation and Certain Related Subjects* (New York: Fleming H. Revell, 1896), pp. 13, 133–34, 154; L.T. Townsend, *Adam and Eve: History or Myth?* (Boston: Chapple, 1904), p. 83; Townsend, *Collapse of Evolution*.

6 G.L. Young, "Relation of Evolution and Darwinism to the Question of Origins," *Bible Student and Teacher* 11 (1909): 41.

7 Alexander Patterson, *The Bible as It Is: A Simple Method of Mastering and Understanding the Bible* (Chicago: Winona Publishing, 1906), pp. 55–77, 103; Alexander Patterson, *The Other Side of Evolution: An Examination of Its Evidences*, 3d ed. (Chicago: Bible Institute Colportage Association, 1912), pp. ix–xii, 11, 60; Jon H. Roberts, *Darwinism and the Divine in America: Protestant Intellectuals and Organic Evolution, 1859–1900* (Madison: University of Wisconsin Press, 1988), p. 96. Although Patterson's career remains obscure, his connection with Dwight L. Moody and the Moody Bible Institute is documented in a letter to A.P. Fitt, including "Recollections of D.L. Moody," November 14, [?], Moody Bible Institute Library. The *Minutes of the General Assembly of the Presbyterian Church in the United States of America* first show Patterson as an evangelist in Chicago in 1884; in 1904 he is identified as the pastor of a small church in Morgan Park.

8 William Jennings Bryan, *In His Image* (New York: Fleming H. Revell, 1922), pp. 94, 97–98. See Patterson, *The Other Side of Evolution*, pp. 32–33, for a similar description. Bryan recommended Patterson's book in his popular lecture "The Bible and Its Enemies," reprinted in Bryan, *The Dawn of Humanity* (Chicago: Altruist Foundation, 1925), p. 69.

9 A.C. Dixon to G.F. Wright, May 5, 1910, G.F. Wright Papers, Oberlin College Archives.

10 A.C. Dixon to G.F. Wright, May 16 and 24, 1910, G.F. Wright Papers.

11 See Ronald L. Numbers, "George Frederick Wright: From Christian Darwinist to Fundamentalist," *Isis* 79 (1988): 624–45.

12 G. Frederick Wright, *Story of My Life and Work* (Oberlin, OH: Bibliotheca Sacra, 1916), pp. 116, 133–40; G.F. Wright to Asa Gray, June 26, 1875, Archives, Gray Herbarium, Harvard University; Asa Gray to G.F. Wright, August 14, 1875, and June 1, 1876, G.F. Wright Papers; George F. Wright, "Recent Works Bearing on

the Relation of Science to Religion: No. II—The Divine Method of Producing Living Species," *Bibliotheca Sacra* 33 (1876): 474, 487, 492–94.

13 George Frederick Wright, introduction, *The Other Side of Evolution*, pp. xvii–xix; William Phillips Hall to G.F. Wright, October 13, 1904, Wright Papers.

14 G. Frederick Wright, "Editorial Note on Genesis and Geology," *Bibliotheca Sacra* 54 (1897): 570–72; [G.F. Wright], Review of *The Life and Letters of Charles Darwin,* ed. Francis Darwin, *Bibliotheca Sacra* 45 (1888): 366–72; [G. Frederick Wright]. "Transcendental Science," *Independent* 41 (October 3, 1889): 10; G. Frederick Wright, *The Ice Age in North America: And Its Bearings upon the Antiquity of Man*, 5th ed. (Oberlin, OH: Bibliotheca Sacra, 1911).

15 George Frederick Wright, "The Passing of Evolution," *The Fundamentals*, 12 vols. (Chicago: Testimony Publishing Co., n.d.), 7:5–20. The exact meaning of Wright's phrase "by the special creation of a single pair" is unclear; see Numbers, *The Creationists*, pp. 34–36.

16 A.C. Dixon, *Reconstruction: The Facts against Evolution* (n.p., n.d.), p. 18, from a copy in the Dixon Collection, Dargan-Carver Library of the Historical Commission of the Southern Baptist Convention, Nashville, Tennessee; "Dr. R.A. Torrey Replies to Dr. O.E. Brown," *Moody Bible Institute Monthly* 26 (1925): 162.

17 James Orr, "Science and Christian Faith," *The Fundamentals*, 4: 101–02; J.J. Reeve, "My Personal Experience with the Higher Criticism," ibid., 3: 99. On the death of evolution, see "Evolutionism in the Pulpit," ibi ., 8:30; David N. Livingstone, *Darwin's Forgotten Defenders: The Encounter between Evangelical Theology and Evolutionary Thought* (Grand Rapids, MI: William B. Erdmans, 1987), p. 161, tentatively identifies the author of this piece as Frank E. Allen of Winnipeg, Canada. I am indebted to Rennie B. Schoepflin's unpublished manuscript "Anti-Evolutionism and Fundamentalism in Twentieth-Century America" (M.A. paper, University of Wisconsin—Madison, 1980), for my quantitative statements.

The Other Side of Evolution

Its Effects and Fallacy

BY

REV. ALEXANDER PATTERSON

Author of
"The Greater Life and Work of Christ," "The Bible As It Is,"
"Bird's-Eye Bible Study" and "The Bible Manual."

CHICAGO
THE BIBLE INSTITUTE COLPORTAGE ASSOCIATION
826 NORTH LA SALLE STREET

COPYRIGHT, 1903
BY
THE BIBLE INSTITUTE COLPORTAGE
ASSOCIATION OF CHICAGO

TABLE OF CONTENTS.

PREFACE.

Claims of Evolution.—Interest in subject.—Effect on Christian belief.—Opinion of eminent scholars.—Effect on the common man.—Evolution being accepted on exparte evidence.—Question too important to be left to science.—The average man capable of understanding the arguments.—The court of last resort. vii

INTRODUCTION.

Meaning of Evolution.—Conversational and scientific use of the word.—Le Conte's definition.—Spencer's Spheres of Evolution.—Theistic and Atheistic Evolution.—The origin of man, the vital point.—The Bible account and Darwin's. xix

CHAPTER I.

EVOLUTION IS AN UNPROVEN THEORY.

Nearly all evolutionists admit this.—Citations from Tyndall, Spencer, Huxley, Prof. Conn, Whitney, Dr. J. A. Zahm, Dr. Rudolph Schmidt, and others.—Evolution rejected by many and opposed.—Complaint of Prof. Haeckel on this.—Prof. Virchow's opposition.—List of scientists who do not advocate Evolution.—Discarded theories of the past.—Uncertainty of scientific theories in general. ...   5

Table of Contents

CHAPTER II.

THE EVOLUTION OF THE UNIVERSE AND EARTH.

The four problems facing Evolution, the origin of matter, of force, the formation and orderly adjustment of the universe and the origin of life.—Evolution makes no attempt at the first two.—Spencer admits it is the unknowable.—Lord Kelvin's testimony.—Prof. George Frederick Wright on the Nebular Hypothesis.—The solar system unique.—The firemist and its wonderful contents.—Failure as to origin of life.—Le Conte's theory.—Testimony of Tyndall, Wilson, Conn, against spontaneous generation. 17

CHAPTER III.

EVOLUTION OF SPECIES.

Evolution's great field.—No case of evolution known.—No cause of evolution known.—How evolution originated species.—Argument from Geology.—Geologists opposing it; Sir J. W. Dawson, Sir R. Murchison, Barrande.—Prof. Conn's admissions.—Haeckel's admissions.—The argument from Morphology.—Rudimentary parts.—The Eohippus, "Old Horse."—Argument from classification of species.—No agreed classification.—Evolution's phantom tree.—No changes in Egypt's 4,000 years or prehistoric man's longer time.—Distribution of plants and animals.—Argument from Embryology.—The threefold argument of Evolution.—Facts opposing Evolution. 26

Table of Contents

CHAPTER IV.

THE EVOLUTION OF MAN.

The vital question.—All evolutionists agree here.—The two accounts of Bible and Evolution.—Arguments from origin of species.—Argument from similarity of structure.—Argument from human characteristics. —Rudimentary organs in man.—The "gill-slits."— How the brute became man.—Prof. Edward Clodd's account of "The Making of a Man."—Edward Morris' description of primeval man.—The Theistic Evolutionist's Adam and how he fell.—The Missing Link.—The Calaveras skull.—Neanderthal skull.— Haeckel's "Pithecanthropus-Erectus."—The Colorado monkey's skeleton.—Croatia skeletons.—Argument from the brain.—Prof. Clodd's story of how man got his brain.—Argument from language.— Prof. Max Mueller's protest.—Argument from prehistoric man.—Antiquity of man.—Testimony as to man's recent origin from Prof. George Frederick Wright, S. R. Pattison, Prof. Friedrich Pfaff, Winchell, Dr. J. A. Zahm.—Argument from uncivilized races.—Argument from history of limits of man's history.—Evolution and religion.—Evolution's ethics. —Christian experience.—Christ and evolution. . 60

CHAPTER V.

EVOLUTION UNSCIENTIFIC AND UNPHILOSOPHICAL.

Four steps necessary to proof, Facts, Classification, Inferences, Verification.—Fails to account for facts.— Has no classification.—False in inferences and has

Table of Contents

no verification.—Rests on imagination.—Tyndall's "Scientific Use of the Imagination."—Evolution the Doctrine of Chance revamped and clothed in scientific terms. 112

CHAPTER VI.

EVOLUTION AND THE BIBLE.

Evolution has no scriptural argument.—The two accounts mutually exclusive.—Bible account appealed to by all Scripture writers as Fact.—Evolution's interpretation of Scripture.—Christ's testimony to the facts of Scripture.—Evolution and Bible doctrines.—Importance of Adam as basis of Scripture doctrine.—Man's state and remedy as given by Evolution and by the Bible.—The future of the Bible and of Evolution.—Evolution in its logical form is Atheism.—Evolution a relic of heathenism.—Testimony of James Freeman Clarke, Sir J. William Dawson. 120

CHAPTER VII.

THE SPIRITUAL EFFECT OF EVOLUTION.

Must affect the spiritual state.—Effect on candidates for ministry.—Latent effect on faith.—On experimental religion.—Evolution as a state of heart.—A comfortable theory to the impenitent.—Prepares for "isms."—Weakens pulpit power.—Eliminates faith in the supernatural and eternal.—Education's place in modern giving.—Is this the last form of unbelief?—The common people and the Gospel of the Cross. 137

PREFACE.

Evolution is claimed by its advocates to be the greatest intellectual discovery of the past century, and, by some, the greatest thought that ever entered the mind of man. In the words of its greatest philosopher, Herbert Spencer, "It spans the universe and solves the widest range of its problems, which reach outward through boundless space, and back through illimitable time, resolving the deepest problems of life, mind, society, history and civilization." It has woven into one great philosophy the history of the material universe, the entire organic creation, man and all his faculties, the whole course of human history and the origin and progress of all religion.

It also undertakes to account for the Bible, for what is popularly called higher criticism represents the biblical branch of Evolution. It has reconstructed the Bible and remanded its miraculous narratives to the realm of myth. It has formulated a theology in which the most sacred doctrines of evangelical belief are discarded. In its central theory of the origin of man, it vitally affects the doctrines of the nature of man, of sin

Preface

and penalty, man's need and the work of Christ. It even touches the person of Christ, for many of its advocates say that He too comes within its scope. In its radical and most consistent form, it utterly discards belief in God. Most of the great teachers of Evolution, such as Ernst Haeckel of Jena, are and have been atheists.

It is true that many evolutionists are theistic. But it is not enough to be theistic. The devil is "theistic," so was Thomas Paine. Christianity is far more than theism. It is the grossest sophistry to teach that because a belief has some truth in it we must therefore tolerate it. All false doctrine is sugarcoated with truth. That we are not overstating the dangerous nature of the theory will appear from the following opinions of competent scholars and observers.

Prof. George Frederick Wright, the eminent geologist, says of Evolution: "It is the fad of the present, which is making such havoc and confusion in the thought of the age, leading so many into intellectual positions, whose conclusions they dare not face and cannot flank, and from which they cannot retreat except through the valley of humiliation." (*Bibliotheca Sacra,* April, 1900.)

Prof. George Howison sounds this alarm: "It is a portent so threatening to the highest concerns of man, that we ought to look before we leap and

Preface

look more than once. Under the sheen of the evolutionary account of man, the world of real persons, the world of individual responsibility, disappears; with it disappears the personality of God." (*Limits of Evolution*, pp. 5, 6.)

There is a vital connection between Facts, Doctrines, Experiences, Conduct and Prospects. These successively flow from each other. Christianity rests on facts, from these we derive doctrines and from doctrines come experiences, which give rise to conduct and that ends in suitable prospects. Facts form the basis of Christianity. When, therefore, Evolution attacks the Facts of the Bible, it attempts to undermine the very basis of all Christianity. President Francis L. Patton has said: "You may put your philosophy in one pocket and your religion in another and think that, as they are separate, they will not interfere, but that will not work. You have to bring your theory of the universe and your theory of religion together. This is the work of this age."

While all do not go the length of the radical evolutionists, yet such is the natural working of the human mind, that this will be its logical conclusion. If this theory is accepted, we must look for widespread lapse from all Christian faith and, as conduct follows belief in all intelligent

Preface

creatures, we shall see also great moral declension.

To the ordinary man, the matter appears in this light: If we cannot believe a man's statements we will not take his advice. If we cannot believe the Bible's narratives why should we believe its religion? If it is not trustworthy as to facts of this world, why depend upon it as to the other world? If it cannot teach correctly the nature of insects and animals, why should it be able to tell us the nature of God? The common man reasons rightly. The Bible must stand or fall by its reliability all along the line of truth of every kind.

Evolution is being taught, or taken for granted to-day in high schools, academies, colleges, universities, and seminaries. It meets the Sunday School scholar at the first chapter of Genesis. A busy city pastor says he has been asked about it every day in the week. It is a living question and must be met. In every free library are the works of Spencer, Darwin, Tyndall, Huxley and others, and these are read continually.

It does seem as if the other side of such a question ought to be given and considered, if there be another side, and there certainly is.

The theory of Evolution is being accepted to-day upon ex-parte evidence. The books on Evolution are numbered by hundreds, those giving

x

Preface

the other side are few. Many do not even read for themselves but rely upon the weight of noted names, or the supposed "consensus of scholarship."

It is even asserted that none but scholars have the right to discuss the subject. Dr. Lyman Abbott says in his "Evidences of Christianity" that "those who are not scientists must be content to await the final judgment of those who are experts on this subject, and meanwhile accept tentatively their conclusions." Not to notice this demand that we rest on an unfinished theory, might we not ask permission to accept, "tentatively" at least, the Bible as it is, while awaiting the conclusions of scientists as to what we shall think or believe about it; especially in view of the fact that all that has been done so far by Christianity on earth has been effected by the conservative belief in the Bible.

But non-scientific people are able to comprehend Evolution. The scientist to-day is able to state conclusions in language the non-scientific can readily understand, and the evolutionist himself tells us we can understand his facts and arguments. So we who are not scientists may proceed to investigate a subject in which we have so much at stake. The questions involved are too important to be left to the scientist alone. The scientist is

Preface

mainly a witness as to the facts of nature. It is the duty of the whole body of the intelligent Christian community, lay and clerical, to generalize and draw conclusions. These form, as they have in the past, the court of last resort in such discussions. The best generalizer will be, not the scientist whose labors are necessarily confined to a single science, or even to a department of it, and who may be even more or less biased by his environment, but the best juryman will be the intelligent non-scientific mind. It is before the judgment seat of Christian Common Sense that this and all other theories must appear. It is the man in the pew who says to this pastor, Come, and he cometh, and to that professor, Go, and he goeth.

Nor is this examination premature. Evolution has been now for many years before the public and its writings fill libraries. We may assume that the evidence is now before us and, if not all in, at least enough is given us by which to judge its nature and probable outcome. This we may further assume in view of the fact that the advocates of the theory admit that an increasing number of facts are not giving increasing evidence but that their case is more beset with difficulties than in the day of Darwin, the father of the

Preface

hypothesis, or rather, its step-father. So we may proceed with our examination.

The author of this book makes no claim to being a scientist. He is simply one of the great jury to whom this theory appeals. He has, therefore, here simply considered the evidence and given herein his conclusions. The facts and arguments of evolutionary writers will form the chief source of the examination. Nearly one hundred writers and works are cited. Out of its own mouth we will condemn it.

The citations in a book as small as this must be brief but care has been taken that they are fair as to the points they are given to show. It is not claimed that the citations from evolutionary writers exhibit their opinion on the whole subject but that they do show their fatal admissions and their general uncertainty on the whole subject.

It will be shown that Evolution is not accepted by all scientists and scholars; that it is rejected by some of the greatest of these; that it is admittedly an unproven theory; that it has never been verified and cannot be; that not a single case of evolution has ever been presented, and that there is no known cause by which it could take place. Its arguments will be considered one by one and their fallacy shown. It will be shown to be, by its own principles, unscientific and unphilosophical, and

Preface

simply a revamping of the old doctrine of Chance clothed in scientific terms. Finally, it will be shown that it is violently opposed to the narrative and doctrines of the Bible and destructive of all Christian faith; that it originated in heathenism and ends in atheism.

Much of the material in this book has been presented by the author in lectures upon the Bible during Bible institutes and conferences, and he has been frequently requested to put it in printed form. He hopes that where the arguments do not convince, they will at least bring the reader to what Mr. Gladstone called "that most wholesome state, a suspended judgment."

Among others, the following writers are cited: Agassiz, Abbott, Argyle, Askernazy, Balfour, Brewster, Ballard, Bruner, Barrande, Bunge, Brown, Bowers, Bixby, Bonn, Clodd, Conn, Cope, Clarke, Cooke, DeRouge, Dana, Dawson, Dubois, Etheridge, Fovel, Fiske, Gladstone, Galton, Gregory, Hilprecht, Huxley, Howison, Haeckel, Haecke, Harrison, Herschel, Hartman, Harnack, Heer, Humphrey, Hoffman, Hamann, Ingersoll, Jones, Kelvin, Koelliker, Liebig, Lecky, LeConte, Lang, Meyer, Max Mueller, Monier, Murchison, Naegeli, Paulsen, Pfaff, Petrie, Pattison, R. Patterson, Pfliederer, Patton, Parker, Ruskin, Romanes, Reymond, Renouf, Schlie-

Preface

mann, Sayce, Starr, Schultz, Sully, Spencer, Schmidt, Sedgwick, Stuckenberg, Snell, See, Townsend, Thomas, Tyndall, Thomson, Virchow, Von Baer, Wallace, Winchell, Warfield, Wright, Whitney, Wagner, Woodrow Wilson, White, Wiseman, Zahm, Zoeckler.

I especially acknowledge indebtedness to Prof. George Frederick Wright, of Oberlin College, in revising this book and for his valuable suggestions and corrections, and especially his favorable introduction. To his works confirming many of my conclusions I refer the reader, as follows: The Logic of Christian Evidence, The Scientific Aspects of Christian Evidences, The Ice Age in North America, Man in the Great Ice Age.

ALEXANDER PATTERSON.

PREFACE TO THIRD EDITION.

In issuing a third edition of this book it is proper to state what changes, if any, have occurred in the discussion.

While the belief in Evolution is wide-spread, no known cause or causes have yet been discovered by which the supposed changes in species occurred, for "Evolution" is not a force or energy of any kind, but only the name of a theory

Preface

by which the present order of nature is supposed to have come. The method Darwin proposed was by Natural Selection arising from the prodigality of production, the small variations that occur in living things, the struggle for existence and the survival of the fittest, aided by environment and other causes all of which by slow degrees during infinite ages have produced the progressive order of species.

This has been decided to be insufficient and has been abandoned by evolutionary writers. It is now agreed that the changes must have occurred in variations originating in the embryo or in the germ, or in the very substance of which that is composed. But all this is far beyond human ken as all writers admit, as follows: "We are ignorant of the factors which are at work to produce evolution. We do not even know whether the life processes are conducted in accordance with the principles of chemistry and physics, or are in obedience to some more subtle vital principle." (Metcalf, *Organic Evolution.*) President David Starr Jordan and Prof. Vernon Lyman Kellogg, both of Stanford University, say: "These changes or variations, if they do occur, cannot be explained." (*Evolution and Animal Life, p. 112.*)

This is universally admitted by scientific

Preface

writers and the search is now for some proof for Evolution along these lines. But as President Jordan makes the still greater confession that "science does not comprehend a single elemental fact of nature," and such writers as the late Lord Kelvin, president of the British Association for the Advancement of Science, agree thereto, the required proof seems far off.

So the discussion is in even a less tangible state than in Darwin's time, for that had a theory supposed to be sufficient, but now there is no known cause which can be demonstrated or offers the slightest explanation, as admitted above by these leading writers.

The facts which are advanced to support the theory are dealt with in this volume and their fallacy shown, that all may be explained without reverting to such an unproven theory as Evolution.

ALEXANDER PATTERSON.

Chicago, April 15, 1912.

INTRODUCTION

BY PROF. GEORGE FREDERICK WRIGHT
OF OBERLIN COLLEGE.

The doctrine of Evolution as it is now becoming current in popular literature is one-tenth bad Science and nine-tenths bad Philosophy. Darwin was not strictly an Evolutionist, and rarely used the word. He endeavored simply to show that Species were enlarged varieties. The title of his epoch making book was, "The Origin of Species by Natural Selection." On the larger questions of the origin of genera and the more comprehensive orders of plants and animals, he spoke with great caution and only referred to such theories as things "dimly seen in the distance."

Herbert Spencer, however, came in with his sweeping philosophical theory of the Evolution of all things through natural processes, and took Darwin's work in a limited field as a demonstration of his philosophy. It is this philosophy which many popular writers and teachers, and some thoughtless Scientific men have taken up and made the center of their systems. But the most of our men of Science

Introduction

are modest in their expressions upon such philosophical themes. Herbert Spencer does not rank among the great men of Science of the day. Lord Kelvin's recent remarks upon the subject are most truthful and significant. (See below pp. 18, 24.)

Mr. Patterson does well to emphasize the fact that *orderly succession* does not necessarily imply *evolution from resident forces*. The orderly arrangements of a business house proceed from the activity of a number of free wills, each of which might do differently, but act in a definite manner, through voluntary adherence to a single purpose. God is all wise and good as well as all powerful. His plan of Creation will therefore be consistent whatever be the means through which he accomplishes it.

Mr. Patterson, also, does well to dwell upon the "uncertainties of Science." Inductive Science looks but a short distance either into space or time, and has no word concerning either the beginning of things or the end of things. Upon these points the Inspired Word is still our best and our only authority. While not saying that all the points in this little

Introduction

volume are well taken, I can say that I disagree with fewer things in it than with those in almost any other on the subject, and that it is fitted to serve as a very needful tonic in these days of the confusion of bad Philosophy and fragmentary Science.

GEORGE FREDERICK WRIGHT.
Oberlin, Ohio, Aug. 10, 1903.

FOREWORD.

Before entering upon the discussion we need to enquire as to the meaning of the word "Evolution" as applied to the theory. We must also ask a definition of the theory as given by its best-known writers; and also enquire as to the spheres it claims to cover. To clearly state a question is often half the task of solving it.

MEANING OF EVOLUTION.

We must distinguish between the ordinary conversational sense of the word Evolution and the technical use of the term as designating a theory by that name. We speak of the evolution of the seed into the plant and the further evolution of the flower and the fruit, meaning by our words merely the natural progressive action of the life within the plant. This principle the evolutionist applies to the whole universe which he says came in a similar way.

Again we use the word Evolution to describe any succession of things which show progress. Such an instance is given us in the change in appliances for the use of steam from the time when

Foreword

its power was first observed in the lifting lid of the tea-kettle to the time when it drives the latest ocean liner. This is, however, simply the succession of a series of things in advancing order, but without vital connection. Their real relation is outside of themselves in the minds of the inventors who, in turn, may be many and widely separated. Succession is not Evolution nor does it prove or imply such a process. That demands an intimate and genetic connection between the things as they appear, the higher growing out of the substance of the lower in physical things and the intellectual likewise.

The theory of Evolution asserts that from a nebulous mass of primeval substance, whose origin it never attempts to account for, there came by natural processes, as a flower from a bud, and fruit from the flower, all that we see and know in the heavens above and the earth beneath.

Tyndall's statement of the scope of the theory is as follows: "Strip it naked and you stand face to face with the notion, that not only the ignoble forms of life, the animalcular and animal life, not only the more noble forms of the horse and lion, not only the exquisite mechanism of the human body, but the human mind with its emotions, intellect, will and

Foreword

all their phenomena, were latent in that fiery cloud." *(Christianity and Positivism, p. 30.)*

Dr. Lyman Abbott further defines its application to man thus: "Evolution is the doctrine that this life of man, this moral, this ethical, this spiritual nature has been developed by natural processes." *(Theology of an Evolutionist.)*

Herbert Spencer's celebrated definition is as follows: "Evolution is a progress from the homogeneous to the heterogeneous, from general to special, from the simple to the complex elements of life." But we deny the right to apply this definition exclusively to the theory of Evolution. Creaton also proceeds on the same order, so also does manufacture or any other intelligent operation.

The clearest account of the theory is that given by Prof. Le Conte, as follows: "All things came (1) by continuous progressive changes, (2) according to certain laws, (3) by means of resident forces." *(Evolution and Religious Thought.)* It is the latter clause in which the real meaning of the theory lies. These "resident forces" include exterior influences such as food, climate, etc.

The theories of Evolution are as many as the respective writers. Each one has his own theory

Foreword

as to the scope and cause and operation of it all. Theistic Evolution allows the intervention of God at the creation of the primeval "fire-mist" and at the origin of life and the production of man's spiritual nature. The atheist denies any interference of a Creator at all. Haeckel says the best definition of Evolution is "the non-miraculous origin and progress of the universe." He and many others say that if the Creator is admitted at any point, He may as well be admitted all along. This is consistent Evolution.

The theistic and the atheistic evolutionist however agree in saying that man was descended from the brute, as to his body at least, and some even, as above shown, claim this descent for the whole man. This doctrine as to man is the vital part of the whole theory and in this all evolutionists are practically agreed. So that so far as their effect on Christian doctrine and Bible fact is concerned, all may be classed together.

CHAPTER I.

EVOLUTION AS AN UNPROVEN THEORY.

With perhaps the exception of Prof. Ernst Haeckel of Jena, all evolutionists admit that Evolution is unproven. One of the latest writers, and most impartial, is Prof. H. W. Conn, who says in his "Evolution of To-day:" "Nothing has been positively proved as to the question at issue. From its very nature, Evolution is beyond proof. . . . The difficulties offered to an unhesitating acceptance of Evolution are very great, and have not grown less since the appearance of Darwin's *Origin of Species,* but have in some respects grown greater." (pp. 107, 203.) He makes many such admissions. Dr. Rudolph Schmidt writes, "All these theories have not passed beyond the rank of hypotheses." *(Theories of Darwin, p. 61.)* Prof. Whitney, of Yale University, says, "We cannot think the theory yet converted into a scientific fact and those are perhaps the worst foes to its success who are over-hasty to take it and use it as a proved fact." *(Oriental and Linguistic Studies, pp. 293-4)* Tyndall said: "Those who hold the doctrine of

5

The Other Side of Evolution

Evolution are by no means ignorant of the uncertainty of their data, and they only yield to it a provisional assent." *(Fragments of Science,* p. 162.) Dr. J. A. Zahm writes: "The theory of Evolution is not yet proved by any demonstrative evidence. An absolute demonstration is impossible." *(Popular Science Monthly,* April, 1898.) Huxley said, "So long as the evidence at present adduced falls short of supporting the affirmative, the doctrine must be content to remain among the hypotheses." *(Lay Sermons,* p. 295.) Down to the end of his life, he said the evidence for Evolution was insufficient. *(Quarterly Review,* January, 1901.)

This universal admission will be a surprise to the non-scientific, especially in view of the astounding and sweeping claims the theory has made. It will seem strange that a confessedly unproven theory should be made the basis of all "modern thinking," the foundation of a universal philosophy, the cause of a revolution in theology, and the reason for rejecting the narratives of the Bible, and, on the part of some, of abandoning Christianity and launching into atheism. Yet such is the case. Well may we draw a long breath here and say, Is this Science? Is it scientific to accept as true an unproven theory and make it the basis of all belief? We have even more start-

6

The Other Side of Evolution

ling facts to present as to this amazing form of unbelief.

In discussing Evolution, we must also continually distinguish between fact and theory, between things proven and assumed. For the writers continually intermingle these in a confusing way. We need ever to ask concerning its statements, Is this proven or assumed? The jury have a right to ask that everything be proved absolutely before rendering a verdict for Evolution.

EVOLUTION IS NOT ACCEPTED BY ALL SCIENTISTS AND SCHOLARS.

The statement is often made that Evolution has "the Consensus of Scholarship." This carries force to the non-scientific, indeed to all, for we must rest our faith, for facts at least, on the opinion of scientists. But while many have followed it, there remain many scholars who have not bowed the knee to Baal. Prof. Haeckel, its greatest living advocate, complains bitterly of the opposition of many of the scientists of Europe, and that many once with him have deserted him.

The late Dr. Virchow, the great pathologist and the discoverer of the germ theory, was an active opponent of Evolution. He says: "The reserve which most naturalists impose on themselves is

7

supported by the small actual proofs of Darwin's theory. Facts seem to teach the invariability of the human and the animal species." *(Popular Science, pp. 50, 52.)* Dr. Groette, in his inaugural address as rector of the University of Strasburg, rejected Evolution.

Dr. D. S. Gregory of New York, editor of the Homiletic Review and in a position to know the facts, vouches for the statement, that, "It is a strange fact that no great scientific authority in Great Britain in exact science, science that reduces its conclusions to mathematical formulae, has endorsed Evolution."

The late Dr. J. H. W. Stuckenberg, of Cambridge, wrote me, that many of the scientists of Germany reject the extreme views of Evolution, and the inferences which men like Prof. Haeckel, of Jena, have drawn from Darwinism. He quotes Dr. W. Haecke, a zoologist of Jena, the home of Prof. Haeckel, as saying: "We the younger men must free ourselves from the Darwinian dogma, in which respect quite a number of us have been quite successful." Prof. Paulsen, of Berlin, has exposed some of Haeckel's fallacies and regards his reasoning as "a disgrace to Germany." He said the mechanical theory for which Darwinism was held to stand, is rejected by such scientists as Naegeli, Koelliker. M. Wagner, Snell, Fovel,

The Other Side of Evolution

Bunge, the physiological chemist, A. Brown, Hoffman and Askernazy, botanists; Oswald Heer, the geologist, and Otto Hamann, the zoologist. Of Carl Ernst von Baer, the eminent zoologist and anthropologist, Haecke affirms, that in early years he came near adopting the hypothesis of Evolution into his system, but that at a later date he utterly rejected it. The same change occurred in the late Du Bois Reymond and Prof. Virchow, the eminent scientist of the University of Berlin. (See also articles of Dr. Stuckenberg in *Homiletic Review,* January, 1901, May, 1902.)

Sir J. William Dawson, the great geologist of Canada, utterly rejected it and says: "It is one of the strangest phenomena of humanity; it is utterly destitute of proof." *(Story of the Earth and Man,* p. 317.) Dr. Etheridge, examiner of the British Museum, said to Dr. George E. Post, in answer to a question, "In all this great museum, there is not a particle of evidence of the transmutation of species. This museum is full of proofs of the utter falsity of these views." Thomas Carlyle called Evolution "the gospel of dirt." Ruskin said of it, "I have never yet heard one logical argument in its favor. I have heard and read many that are beneath contempt." *(The Eagles Nest,* p. 256.)

Prof. Zöckler writes: "It must be stated that

The Other Side of Evolution

the supremacy of this philosophy has not been such as was predicted by its defenders at the outset. A mere glance at the history of the theory during the four decades that it has been before the public shows that the beginning of the end is at hand."

Such utterances are now very common in the periodicals of Germany, it is said. It seems plain the reaction has commenced and that the pendulum that has swung so strongly in the direction of Evolution, is now oscillating the other way. It required twenty years for Evolution to reach us from abroad. Is it necessary for us to wait twenty years more to reverse our opinions? Why may we not pass upon facts for ourselves without awaiting the "Consensus of European Scholarship," which is after all so subject to perplexing reversals? It makes plain people dizzy to attempt to follow leaders of opinion who change with every wind that blows across the ocean.

Many citations will appear in the following pages which show the strong exceptions taken by leading scholars against the theory in whole or in part. Indeed, as said already, the arguments to be given herein against Evolution are drawn from the statements of leading evolutionists themselves. Some of these are earlier opinions and some their latest utterances. In every case the state of the discussion will be shown to be far from that "Consensus of Scholarship" so airily claimed by the writers on the subject and so unhesitatingly accepted by their followers.

It may be objected that some of these authorities are dead and that later scholars differ from them. Not to mention the names of still living writers named above, let us remark that all wisdom is not left to our day. Socrates and Bacon are dead, yet their opinions are still of value. Moses is dead, yet the Ten Commandments are still believed if not obeyed. Our present evolutionary writers will also one day be dead, yet they hope even then to be given some credit for sense and science. The "consensus of scholarship" ought to include wisdom past as well as present.

It is also to be remembered that there are thousands of quiet thinkers who have never given in their adhesion to this startling theory, and more, that the great masses of the church at least, have no confidence in it. Those preparing to launch their ships upon this current had better, as a matter of common prudence at least, wait a while at least till the mists have rolled away.

The Other Side of Evolution

DISCARDED THEORIES OF THE PAST.

Prof. George Frederick Wright says, "The history of science is little else than one of discarded theories. . . . The so-called science of the present day is largely going the way so steadily followed in the past. The things about which true science is certain are very few and could be contained in a short chapter of a small book." *(The Advance, May 12, 1902.)*

It is sometimes charged to the church that it has held theories which the discoveries of science have shown to be untrue. But it must be borne in mind that these false theories were just as firmly held by the scientists of the day as by the church.

Dr. Andrew White has written two great volumes on the warfare between science and theology. He might write many and larger volumes on the wars between the theories of science. Every one of these discarded theories, and they are numbered by thousands, has been the center of terrific conflicts.

Galileo's discovery of the satellites of Jupiter was opposed by his fellow astronomers, who even refused to look at them through his telescope. Dr. J. A. Zahm quotes Cardinal Wiseman as saying that the French Institute in 1860 could count

The Other Side of Evolution

more than eighty theories opposed to Scripture, not one of which has stood still or deserves to be recorded. At a meeting of the British Association, Sir William Thomson announced that he believed life had come to this globe by a meteor. His theory lived less than a year. Mr. Huxley said that the origin of life was a sheet of gelatinous living matter which covered the bottom of the ocean. This theory had even a shorter life. Among the most recent reversals of this kind is that of a universally held theory, namely, that coral reefs are built up by the coral insects in their desire to keep near the surface as the ocean's bottom sinks. Prof. A. Agassiz has just demolished this theory.

Scholars were unanimous a short time ago that Troy was a myth. But Dr. Schliemann's great discoveries have overthrown that "consensus of scholarship." Prof. Harnack, one of the greatest of critics in his great work, *The Chronology of the Christian Scriptures,* admits that science, meaning Higher Criticism, has made many mistakes and has much to repent of. Joseph Cook said, "Within the memory of man yet comparatively young, the mythical theory of Strauss has had its rise, its fall, its burial."

The thirty thousand citizens of St. Pierre on Martinique, trusting in the assurances of the

13

The Other Side of Evolution

scientists, remained in their fated city and the next day were overwhelmed in the most awful calamity of modern times.

We may consider in this connection the dissatisfaction of some of the greatest minds of evolutionary circles with the results of their own theory.

Mr. Herbert Spencer is thus quoted, writing in his eighty-third year: "The intellectual man, who occupies the same tenement with me, tells me that I am but a piece of animated clay equipped with a nerve system and in some mysterious way connected with the big dynamo called the world; but that very soon now the circuit will be cut and I will fall into unconsciousness and nothingness. Yes I am sad, unutterbly sad, and I wish in my heart I had never heard of the intellectual man with his science, philosophy and logic." *(Facts and Comments.)*

Prof. Frederic Harrison, the agnostic, thus writes: "The philosophy of evolution and demonstration promised but it did not perform. It raised hopes, but it led to disappointment. It claimed to explain the world and to direct man, but it left a great blank. That blank was the field of religion, of morality, of the sanctions of deity. It left the mystery of the future as mysterious as ever and yet as imperative as ever. Whatever

The Other Side of Evolution

philosophy of nature it offered, it gave no adequate philosophy of Man. It was busy with the physiology of Humanity and propounded inconceivable and repulsive guesses about the origin of Humanity." *(North American Review,* December, 1900, p. 825.)

From the opposite side of the field, President Woodrow Wilson writes: "This is the dis-service scientific study has done for us; it has given us agnosticism in the realm of philosophy, scientific anarchism in the field of politics. It has made the legislator confident that he can create and the philosopher sure that God cannot." *(Forum,* December, 1896.)

UNCERTAINTY OF SCIENTIFIC THEORIES IN GENERAL.

Another feature which strikes the non-scientific mind curiously is the wide differences among great scientists as to the facts of nature. The age of the earth is variously declared to be ten million years by some, and by others equally able, a thousand million years. The temperature of its interior is stated to be 1,530 degrees by one, and 350,000 degrees by another. Herschel calculated the mountains on the moon to be half a mile high, Ferguson said they were fifteen miles high. The

15

height of the Aurora Borealis is guessed from two and a half to one hundred and sixty miles, and its nature is still more widely described. The delta at the mouth of the Mississippi was calculated by Lyell to have been 100,000 years in forming. Gen. Humphrey, of the United States survey, estimated it at 4,000 years, and M. Beaument at 1,300 years.

The deposits of carbonate of lime on the floor of Kent Cavern in England have been estimated by different scientists to have been from a thousand to a million years in forming.

The discovery of radium and other similar substances, it is said, is almost revolutionizing the theories of the constitution of matter and affecting all physical science.

These facts are not cited to discredit science. No one in his senses would fail to acknowledge our great debt to the earnest and laborious workers in these varying fields. But these instances of many such are cited to show that there is need for caution in accepting proposed theories.

CHAPTER II.

EVOLUTION OF THE UNIVERSE AND EARTH.

In undertaking to account for the universe, Evolution faces four problems. 1. The origin of matter. 2. The origin of force. 3. The formation and orderly arrangement of the universe. 4. The origin of life. In all of these it fails; it confesses its failure in the first two and last, and makes ludicrous attempts to explain the third. We will consider each in turn.

1. Evolution fails to account for the origin of matter. Spencer says this is the Unknowable. So that Spencer's great philosophy rests on what he doesn't know and cannot find out. Darwin said as to the origin of things, "I am in a hopeless muddle." Prof. Edward Clodd wrote: "Of the beginning of what was before the present state of things, we know nothing and speculation is futile, but since everything points to the finite duration of the present creation, we must make a start somewhere." *(Story of Creation,* p. 137.) Science is what we know. Therefore Evolution rests upon an unscientific foundation. Nor is there any other account conceivable than that the Bible

The Other Side of Evolution

gives. As long as this first and fundamental fact is not solved, the theory must be content to be at most a limited one, and far from being that sweeping discovery which its advocates assert it to be.

2. Evolution fails to account for the origin of Force. The great forces which animate the universe, such as gravity, heat, motion and light, must be accounted for by this theory to give it the standing it demands. It makes no attempt to do this. Evolution is silent when we ask, Whence came these mighty forces? Calling them Laws of Nature does not answer the question. Laws need law makers and enforcers also. Laws do not enforce themselves. As forces, they show the ceaseless giving out of energy. Where is the dynamo from which this perpetual energy originated and still proceeds?

In this connection, let us notice the reticence and limitations of really great scientists as to the nature of these energies. Lord Kelvin, the greatest living scientist, said at the meeting of the British Association for the Advancement of Science, of which he was president: "One word characterizes the most strenuous of the efforts for the advancement of science that I have made perseveringly for fifty-five years. That word is failure. I know no more of electric and magnetic

The Other Side of Evolution

force, or of the relation between ether, electricity and ponderable matter, or of chemical affinity, than I knew and tried to teach to my students of natural philosophy fifty years ago in my first session as professor."

Haeckel himself, the greatest living evolutionist, admits: "We grant at once that the innermost character of nature is just as little understood by us as it was by Anaximander and Empedocles 2,400 years ago. . . We grant that the essence of substance becomes more mysterious and enigmatic the more deeply we penetrate into the knowledge of its attributes." *(Riddle of the Universe.)*

3. Evolution fails to account for the orderly movements of the heavenly bodies which have the accuracy of a chronometer, aye, which are the standards by which all chronometers are regulated, so that the astronomer can calculate to a second when the heavenly bodies shall pass any particular point of view or form their many conjunctions. There is no collision, no noise. "There is no speech nor language, their voice is not heard."

Our Solar System is unique in the heavens. Prof. See tells us there is no other like it in the regularity of its orbits, and in its distant position from the powerful attractions of the mighty sys-

The Other Side of Evolution

tems of the heavens. The earth, too, is the only world so far known to be advanced enough for the production of life. Its situation is far enough from the sun to be beyond its powerful heat and electric energy and yet near enough to preserve and continue all life. The arrangement of its surface into land and water proportions gives the requisite amount of moisture over the land areas. The atmosphere is mixed of gases in just the right proportions for life. All this speaks as loudly as any mechanism can speak, of intention and benevolence and control and careful adjustment; far from that haphazard effect which comes from the undirected working of "resident forces."

Evolution declares the universe began with a nebulous mass, which Tyndall says was "fire-mist," and contracted as it became cold; but Spencer says it was a cold cloud which became heated as it contracted. We are left to the perplexity of deciding for ourselves which theory we will accept. This is only one of many such contradictions we shall meet. But however, or whatever it was, it organized itself into the wonderful universe of stars by a rotary motion which the contraction produced, and this threw off portions as a carriage wheel throws off mud, each portion taking up a similar motion and cooling in a sim-

The Other Side of Evolution

ilar fashion until it became cool enough for living things.

Proof for all this is supposed to be seen in a nebula which is seen in the constellation Orion, which has a spiral form and is supposed to be a world in the making.

But in February, 1901, a new star appeared surrounded by a nebula and this in rapid motion from the center. This sudden appearance of a world in a nebulous state seems like the reversing of the evolutionary process or indeed like a world being destroyed and reduced to its first estate. Other facts are also contradictory, such as the motion or revolution of some of the satelites in a reverse order from that demanded by the theory.

Indeed the whole nebular theory is now being called in question.

Prof. George Frederick Wright of Oberlin University, thus writes of it:

"The nebular hypothesis, which all forms of evolution now assume for a beginning, involves the supposition that the molecules of matter composing the solar system were originally diffused through space like the particles of mist in a vast fogbank, and that then, under the action of gravitation, they began to approach each other and to collect in masses, which began to revolve about

21

The Other Side of Evolution

their axes and to move in orbits around the center of attraction. Every step in this supposition involves an added mystery. The existence of the molecules in their original diffused state is but the beginning of the mystery, though that is utterly incomprehensible.

"The power of gravitation which compels the separated particles to approach each other is an utter mystery, which has completely baffled all efforts at explanation by scientific men. The revolution of the various masses of the solar system on their axes and in their orbits is another mystery for which there is no solution.

"Thus is the thorough-going evolutionist at every point confronted with an insoluble mystery, and he deceives himself if he fancies that he has discovered anything which will take the place of the Christian's conception of God as the creator, sustainer and ruler of all things." *(Record-Herald,* Chicago, Dec. 24, 1902.)

Other facts are even more perplexing to this theory. The moon is moving from her place at an increasing rate and astronomy cannot account for it. The earth's axis of revolution has varied from time to time. Only one star in a thousand has ever been catalogued. Of only about a hundred is the calculation of the parallax possible, so distant are they.

The Other Side of Evolution

As to our earth, a well-known writer says: "No one of standing in the scientific world of to-day is willing to go on record as having a theory of his own regarding the internal fires of this planet or attempting to account for their origin."

In view of this state of uncertainty, it seems to the non-scientific mind hazardous to project across these vast ages a guess as to what the conditions were and how the universe originated. And above all to found on this guess a vast philosophy of the universe affecting all we hold precious for this life and that to come. Well may we hesitate before such demands.

4. The origin of life is a problem Evolution has sought in vain to solve or account for by its natural or resident forces.

Prof. Le Conte labors hard to show that it might have come from the union of the four gases, carbon, hydrogen, nitrogen and oxygen, under some peculiar circumstances. If he had said under the direct act of the Creator we could assent cheerfully. For these do enter into the substance which forms the bodies of living things. But the claim of Evolution is that all came by "resident forces," self-operating. Once admit the direct act of the Creator, and, as Haeckel says, they might as well admit it along the whole process, for the argument for a single instance is valid for the whole. So they will have none of it.

Prof. Le Conte labors to show that protoplasm might be self-originating, but Prof. Conn says, "Protoplasm is not a chemical compound but a mechanism. . . . Unorganized protoplasm does not exist. . . . It could never have been produced by chemical process. Chemistry has produced starches, fats, albumens, but not protoplasm." *(Method of Evolution.)*

Lord Kelvin, in writing to the *London Times,* said:

"Forty years ago I asked Liebig, walking somewhere in the country, if he believed that the grass and flowers which we saw around us grew by mere chemical forces. He answered, 'No, no more than I could believe that a book of botany describing them could grow by mere chemical forces.'"

Tyndall, after laborious experiments during eight months, thus candidly states the result, in an address before the Royal Institute, London: "From the beginning to the end of the inquiry, there is not, as you have seen, a shadow of evidence in favor of the doctrine of spontaneous generation. . . . In the lowest, as in the highest of organized creatures, the method of

The Other Side of Evolution

nature is, that life shall be the issue of antecedent life."

And Mr. Huxley also admitted, "The doctrine that life can only come from life is victorious all along the line." Prof. Conn states, "There is not the slightest evidence that living matter could arise from non-living matter. Spontaneous generation is universally given up." *(Evolution of To-day, p. 26.)*

Wilson, the great authority on the cell says, "The study of the cell has seemed to expand rather than narrow the enormous gap that separates even the lowest forms of life from the inorganic world." *(The Cell in Development and Inheritance, p. 330.)*

Here then, is the greatest chasm of all: Evolution fails at the very start in the story of life. Yet this is its chosen field. On this depends the whole theory. If there was a Creator at the origin of life, why not at the origin of all living things? It is simply a question of degree. The making of a single cell, the simplest creature that lives, is as great a mystery as that of man. Conceptually the one is as possible as the other.*

---
* See these points discussed more fully in Wright's Scientific Aspects of Christian Evidences.

25

CHAPTER III.

THE EVOLUTION OF SPECIES.

This is Evolution's great field of labor. It was this which mainly occupied Darwin's labors and is the basis of the whole sweeping theory. This suggested man's animal origin and all that follows as to man's history and religion and civilization. So that this is the basal part of Evolution. Yet against this fundamental argument, two great charges are made and admitted: First, not a single case of evolution of species is known, and, second, no law or force by which such changes could take place has been discovered. We will consider these two fatal defects.

NOT A SINGLE INSTANCE OF EVOLUTION IS KNOWN.

In support of this assertion we might quote the admissions of nearly every evolutionary writer. Prof. Winchell writes upon this point as follows:

"The great stubborn fact which every form of the theory encounters at the very outset is, that notwithstanding variations, we are ignorant of a single instance of the derivation of one good

The Other Side of Evolution

species from another. The world has been ransacked for an example, and occasionally it has seemed for a time as if an instance had been found of the origination of a genuine species by so-called natural agencies, but we only give utterance to the admissions of all the recent advocates of derivation theories, when we announce that the long-sought *experimentum crucis* has not been discovered." *(The Doctrine of Evolution, p. 54.)*

Prof. Conn, in one of the most recent works upon Evolution, says: "It is true enough that naturalists have been unable to find a single unquestioned instance of a new species. . . . It will be admitted at the outset on all sides, that no unquestioned instance has been observed of one species being derived from another. . . . It is therefore impossible at present to place the question beyond dispute." *(Evolution of To-day, p. 23.)*

Here then is a fatal defect. The world has been ransacked for evidence, the museums are full of specimens, the secrets of nature have been explored in every land, the minutest creatures discovered and analyzed. We have the remains of animals and plants of many kinds thousands of years old, such as the mummied remains from Egypt, and yet not a single instance of the change Evolution asserts has ever been known! Yet this change of species is the fundamental argument of Evolution. On this rests its theory of the origin of man and all that flows from that assertion, and this basal assertion is absolutely without an actual instance of fact.

The changes in certain species such as roses, primroses, tomatoes, pigeons and dogs, are not new species, but only varieties, having none of the traits of species, easily intermingling, propagating, and readily reverting to their original forms, changes which true species are not susceptible of. Darwin admitted that the continued fertility of these varieties was one of his greatest difficulties. One of the definitions of species is that they will not interbreed and propagate. So that hybrids are sterile. "After its kind," is the primal law of nature, and as Dr. Jesse B. Thomas says, "The stubborn mule still blocks the way of Evolution."

NO CAUSE OF EVOLUTION IS KNOWN.

Evolution is not a force. There is no power or cause which is known as Evolution. The word simply describes the order in which things have been supposed to come. We must draw a clear line of distinction between Cause and Order of Appearance. There is a certain order in the suc-

The Other Side of Evolution

cession of living things as they came, but what caused that order is the very question at issue. The Duke of Argyle warns against confusing these when he says, "Evolution puts forward a visible order of phenomena as a complete and all-sufficient account of its own origin and cause." *(Theories of Darwin.)*

The absence of an agreed cause is admitted by evolutionists. Huxley says, "The great need of Evolution is a theory of derivation." *(Man's Place in Nature.)* Darwin admits, "Our ignorance of the laws of derivation is profound." *(Descent of Man.)* "The laws governing inheritance are for the most part unknown." *(Origin of Species.)* Prof. Conn in *Evolution of To-day*, says, "No two scientists are agreed as to what is the cause of the supposed changes of species." (p. 337.) Prof. Clodd traces it to the protoplasm which forms the germ and ends his exhaustive treatise by saying the cause is still unknown. *(Method of Evolution.)*

Darwin's theory was Natural Selection. It is this which is technically called "Darwinism," although some writers apply that name to the general subject of Evolution. Natural selection is the theory that inasmuch as minute variations occur in the struggle of living things for existence, the variations which would prove favorable to the welfare of the animal would be transmitted to its progeny and be increased and so, in many generations, the accumulating effects, aided by climate, food, sexual selection, and other causes, would amount to a new species. Prof. Conn says of this theory, "Natural selection is almost universally acknowledged as insufficient to meet the facts of nature, since many facts of life cannot be explained by it." (p. 243.)

Mr. Huxley said long before: "After much consideration, and with assuredly no bias against Mr. Darwin's views, it is our clear conviction that as the evidence now stands it is not absolutely proved that a group of animals, having all the characteristics exhibited by species in nature, has ever been originated by selection, whether natural or artificial." *(Lay Sermons, 295.)*

The theories as to what produced the supposed changes are as many as the writers on Evolution. Prof. Conn says, "All agreement disappears. Each thinker has his own views." And adds, "Thus far we have seen no indication of the manner in which this evolution has been manifested." (p. 20.) Prof. J. Arthur Thomson, lecturer on zoology in the School of Medicine, Edinburgh, said: "Unless we can give some theory of the origin of variations we have no material for further consideration. Unfortunately we are very ignorant about the whole matter." The various writers ascribe the changes to food, climate, sexual selection, extraordinary births, isolation and many other supposed causes. All these have been in turn combatted by other evolutionist writers, and the war goes on and has produced libraries of volumes. It is around this that the conflict rages and the war is a merry one.

HOW EVOLUTION ORIGINATED SPECIES.

It is when Evolution gives the particulars of these changes that it becomes especially interesting. We will, by way of lighting up the examination, consider a few of the stories it tells us as to how things came.

Spencer tells us how the backbone came to be, for the primitive animals had none. Prof. Conn quotes his account as follows: "He thinks the segmentation, the division of the spinal column into vertebrae, arose as the result of strains. Originally the vertebrate was unsegmented, but in bending its body from side to side in locomotion through the water, its spinal column became divided by the action of simple mechanical force." (*Evolution of To-day,* p. 65.) Thus what we usually consider a serious calamity, the breaking of one's backbone, became one of the greatest

The Other Side of Evolution

blessings, for what would we be without flexible backs, with which to follow the meanderings of Evolution?

Evolution also tells us how legs originated. The earliest animals were without legs. Some animal in this legless state found on its body some slight excrescences or warts, which aided materially its progress as it wiggled along, and thus it acquired the habit of using these convenient warts. This habit it transmitted to its posterity and they increased the habit until the excrescences, lengthened and strengthened by use, became legs of a rudimentary kind, which by further use developed a system of bones and muscles and nerves and joints such as we have ourselves.

Spencer's account of the origin of quadrupeds is that the earliest animals propagated by dividing into two parts, and in some of these the division was not perfectly made, and so the animal had duplicated ends, each of which had legs, forming finally the present quadruple arrangement.

Eyes originated from some animal having pigment spots or freckles on the sides of its head, which, turned to the sun, agreeably affected the animal so that it acquired the habit of turning that side of its head to the sun, and its posterity inherited the same habit and passed it on to still other generations. The pigment spot acquired

The Other Side of Evolution

sensitiveness by use and in time a nerve developed which was the beginning of the eye. From this incipient eye came the present wonderful combination of lenses, nerves and muscles, all so accurately adjusted that, of the sixteen possible adjustments of each part, only once in a hundred thousand times would they come together, as they now are, by chance.

Land animals began thus, according to Evolution: In a time of drought some water animals, stranded by the receding waters, were obliged thenceforth to adopt land manners and methods of living. Although, strangely, the whale by the same cause was forced to the water, for it was once a land animal, but in a season of drought was obliged to seek the water's edge for the scant remaining herbage, and, finding the water agreeable, remained there and its posterity also, and finally, the teeth and legs no longer needed, became decadent and abortive as we see them now. Darwin inferred the history of the whale's marine career from seeing a bear swimming in a pool and catching insects with its wide-open mouth as it so skimmed the water's surface.

The same drought produced another and wonderful change, for it is to this that the giraffe owes his long legs and neck. The herbage on the lower branches withering up, he was obliged to

The Other Side of Evolution

stretch his neck and legs to reach the higher branches. This increased, as all such changes increased, in his posterity, and finally after many generations produced the present immense reaching powers of the giraffe. So that the same drought deprived the whale of his legs and conferred them upon the giraffe.

The mere recital of these speculations will be enough for all who have not surrendered their judgment to the keeping of others. It seems scarcely necessary to assure readers unacquainted with the theory, that this is not exaggeration or caricature. We have simply abbreviated, and rendered into untechnical language, the accounts of evolutionary writers given in all seriousness and with high-sounding scientific terms. Any such work will give many specimens of similar accounts. Reply seems unnecessary, yet must be made.

1. All this is pure speculation. Not a single such change is known, or has been observed.

2. All is based on Natural Selection, which evolutionists have themselves discarded; yet for want of any other theory they are constantly obliged to fall back upon it.

3. Such acquired traits are not transmitted, as Prof. Thomson of Edinborough, tells us. Only characteristics inherited, or congenital in the fer-

34

tilized egg cell, are so transmitted. *(Outlines of Zoology,* p. 66.) The "sports" such as the white robins and crows occasionally seen, disappear as individuals and do not propagate as distinct types.

Let us pause here to contemplate the spectacle of a theory, which its own advocates admit is unproven, and which has been opposed by some of the greatest minds, a theory which has not a single direct fact of evidence, and has no way of accounting for the changes which it declares have taken place; such a theory accepted as the basis of every science, the foundation of a universal philosophy, taught in educational institutions to youth as if demonstrated, demanding immediate and universal submission, undertaking to revise Scripture, to revolutionize theology, and to prescribe what we must do to be saved and to save others! Surely it is safe to hesitate before such demands.

We will not discount the great service done humanity in the patient research in the realms of nature by laborious students. All this should be given weight. We also admit the value of a theory as a means to the ascertaining of truth. But we cannot consent that the vast interests affected by Evolution shall be decided by "the balancings of probabilities," or the mooted value of a theory. This is no place for theories, which must be held tentatively, if at all. This is a matter which affects the belief and lives and hopes of millions, their welfare here and hereafter. Religion is too sacred to be made a shuttlecock tossed about in the arena of intellectual amusement.

Sir J. William Dawson said of some writers and their theories· "To launch a clever and startling fallacy, which will float a week and stir up a hard fight, seems as great a triumph as the discovery of an important fact or law; and the honest student is distracted with the multitude of doctrines and hustled aside by the crowd of ambitious groundlings." *(Story of the Earth and Man, 313.)*

Evolution has much to say for itself, but, as we see, it is all of the nature of circumstantial evidence. This seems to the non-scientific mind as strange for anything called science, which we have been accustomed to think means something known or proven. We have been accustomed to see cases thrown out of court when presenting no evidence and to fare badly in general on mere circumstantial evidence. However, as Evolution is so persistent for a hearing, we must examine what it has to advance for our consideration. Its arguments are drawn from Geology, Classification, Distribution of Plants and Animals, Morphology and Embryology.

The Other Side of Evolution

THE ARGUMENT FROM GEOLOGY.

The argument from this science is that the fossils appear in the strata of the earth in advancing order, the simplest first, and more complex afterwards. The assumption is that the higher came from the lower, by a chain of infinitesimal changes, through a long series of ages. Now the facts are not as claimed. We will show this later. But admitting that they are, the argument is wanting.

1. All this is pure assumption. No such changes are known in existing species to have ever taken place, and the assumption that these changes took place in geologic ages is wholly unwarranted. If it cannot be predicated of the animals we see and know, how can it be asserted of a period millenniums ago?

2. Mere succession is not evolution. The coming in orderly succession is evidence of some plan but not necessarily of evolution. An intelligent Creator would work in the same way, especially if he had intelligent beings to instruct thereby, at the time or afterwards.

3. Evolution in comparing the successive comings of the rocky strata and the fossil creatures, compares two kinds of things that cannot be made analogous. Rocks are not produced by evolution,

the higher growing out of the lower, as is claimed of species. That certain species appeared with the lower rocks and strata, and higher orders with later rocks and strata only proves of one, as of the other, an advancing order of production but tells nothing of the cause of either.

4. We are supported in these doubts as to the value of Evolution's argument from Geology by the fact, that many of the most eminent geologists deny any proof of evolution in their chosen science.

Sir Roderick Murchison said, "I know as much of nature in her geologic ages as any living man, and I fearlessly say that our geologic record does not afford one syllable of evidence in support of Darwin's theory." The great Swiss geologist, Joachim Barrande states, "One cannot conceive why in all rocks whatever and in all countries upon the two continents, all relics of the intervening types should have vanished. . . . The discordances are so numerous and pronounced, that the composition of the real fauna seems to have been calculated by design for contradicting everything which the theories (of Evolution) teach us respecting the first appearance and primitive evolution of the forms of life upon the earth." (Quoted by Winchell, in *Doctrine of Evolution*, p. 142.)

The Other Side of Evolution

Prof. Conn, an evolutionist, admits the presence of many facts disclosed by geology which oppose the theory of Evolution. He says, "In the earliest records geology discloses, we find not a few generalized types but well differentiated forms, nearly all the sub-kingdoms as they now exist, five-sixths of our orders, nearly an equal proportion of sub-orders, a great many families and some of our present species. All this is a surprise and an unexplained problem." Such a result, he says, is not what Evolution would lead us to expect. All the important classes of animals made their appearance without warning. *(Evolution of To-day,* pp. 6. 100, 103, 118.*)*

Haeckel writes, "We cannot shut our eyes to the fact that various groups have from the time of their first appearance, burst out into an exuberant growth of modification of form, size and members, with all possible, and one might almost say, impossible shapes, and they have done this within a comparatively short time, after which they have died out not less rapidly. *(Last Link,* p. 144.*)*

The testimony of geology, as adduced by geologists and even by evolutionists, is that it does not sustain the claims of Evolution. Species existed in present form from the earliest times. Geologic species came in suddenly and went out suddenly. Some of the simplest remain unchanged through all earth's transformations to the present time. (Dr. Robert Patterson, *Errors of Evolution,* p. 221.) The great fossil cemeteries show that the living creatures fell in serried ranks, overtaken by cataclysms, in every act of life. Le Conte tries to explain this by saying that there were "paroxysmal" eras, but what the paroxysms were, or whence they came, he does not say. The whole testimony is against Evolution and reverts to proof of the Bible story of Creation. Professor Adam Sedgwick says: "At succeeding epochs, new tribes of beings were called into existence, not merely as the progeny of those that had appeared before them, but as new and living proofs of creative interference."

THE ARGUMENT FROM CLASSIFICATION OF SPECIES.

This is one of the strong points of Evolution. It is claimed that plants and animals can be so classified in an ascending order that it is evident the higher came out of the lower. We object as follows:

1. There is no classification agreed upon by scientists. This comes largely from want of agreement as to what a species is. Scientists

40

The Other Side of Evolution

differ widely and radically. Spencer presents a review of all these schemes of classification and ends by saying, "It is absurd to attempt a definite scheme of relationship." His own plan of the scheme he says is the figure of a "laurel bush squashed flat by a descending plane." *(Principles of Biology,* p. 389.) This agrees with his statement as to the absurdity of such schemes. Some arrange the whole in a continuous straight line from the lowest up.

Darwin thought the whole came from half a dozen germinal forms. Where these came from he did not say. Dr. J. Clark Ridpath said, "The eagle was always an eagle, the man always man. Every species of living organism has I believe come up by a like process from its own primordial germ." (*Arena,* June, 1879.) Haeckel insists that the theory demands but a single primeval germ as the ancestor of all living things. He presented a tree, showing twenty or more stages between primeval protoplasm and man, but this has been now rejected by evolutionists. Prof. D. Kerfoot Schults represents the classification as follows: "If all the animals that have ever existed on the earth be represented by a tree, those now existing on the earth will be represented by the topmost twigs and leaves, and the extinct forms

The Other Side of Evolution

will be represented by the main trunk and branches." *(First Book on Organic Evolution, p. xiv.)*

But the source of all, the primeval protoplasm, is wanting. The missing primeval germ or germs leaves the tree without a root, and Prof. Conn tells that even the sub-kingdoms are not united by fossils. Spencer admits that not a single species has been traced to its source or its family tree completed, and even the ancestors of our living species are wanting.

Prof. Dana admitted as follows, "If ever the links (upon which the doctrine of Evolution depends) had an actual existence, their disappearance without a trace left behind is altogether inexplicable." Here then is a tree without root or trunk or branches, and having only the tips of outer twigs and leaves, in other words, a phantom tree, a fit representation of the theory for which it stands.

The present orders of plants and animals give a strong argument against Evolution. It has been seen that Succession is not Evolution. The mere coming of animals in orderly succession shows only plan, but the means of executing that plan is not shown thereby. But further, while in the geologic ages there was Succession, here in our age is Simultaneousness of species, two very

42

The Other Side of Evolution

different and contradictory phenomena. Why has Succession ceased? Why have not the higher orders pushed the lower out, as in the geologic ages, if Evolution was the cause? Yet here they all exist quietly together as if they knew nothing of Evolution or its requirements.

Nor have any such changes occurred in thousands of years, as the mummied remains of cats and crocodiles and ibises in Egypt show. Surely 4,000 years would show some evolution if there had been such a thing; but it is not seen in all the 4,000 years, or even in the more distant period since primeval man existed, for we have the remains of animals found with man in his early history. Out of 98 species, 57 are the same as we have to-day unchanged, and still others, as the lingula, the same as in ages past. Thus Evolution's trusted argument from Classification utterly fails of demonstration.

DISTRIBUTION OF PLANTS AND ANIMALS.

The distribution of plants and animals is another favorite argument of this theory. Certain animals are said to be found only in certain regions, the bison only in North America, the kangaroo only in Australia, the armadillo only in Mexico. Evolution triumphantly asks, Were they

The Other Side of Evolution

created only in these places? We now simply remark that difficulties as to Creation do not prove Evolution. Evolution says the ancestors of these came from other parts ages ago and by long isolation and environment became what they are.

Facts again are against the theory. Huxley himself says that in the neighborhood of Oxford are animal remains like those of Australia; that Britain was once connected with the continent, and so these animals passed over. The same is true he says of the isolated fauna of New Zealand and South America. (Address in *Daily Post*, March 27, 1871.)

This argument might be used against Evolution as well as the previous arguments. Two islands in the Pacific, only fifteen miles apart, have the animals of Asia in one and of Australia in the other. One of the Bermudas has lizards like those of Africa and another like those of America. In fact it is evident that animals and plants have scattered widely.

THE MORPHOLOGICAL ARGUMENT.

The comparative study of plants and animals presents another argument for Evolution. It is found, for example, that there is a similarity of plan in the fin of the fish, the wing of the bird,

The Other Side of Evolution

the flipper of the whale, the leg of the animal and the arm of the man. So also in a measure with all other corresponding parts. This Evolution says, shows that all these animals are genetically connected and all came from the same ancestors.

Huxley himself replies to this argument in these words, "No amount of purely morphological evidence can suffice to prove that things came into existence in one way rather than another." *(Study of Zoology, p. 86.)* Another great scientist, Prof. Quatrefages, professor of anthropology in the Museum of Natural Sciences, Paris, writes on this as follows: "Without leaving domain of facts, and only judging from what we know, we can say, that morphology itself justifies the conclusion that one species has never produced another by derivation." Prof. Conn admits, after going through the whole subject with the latest facts, that unless some further explanation can be found, homology does not prove descent. *(Evolution of To-day, p. 76.)*

This resemblance of parts is just what we should expect in things originating from one intelligent operator, whether Creator or manufacturer. It is found in every factory. The wheel is the same in the wheelbarrow, the cart, carriage and locomotive. In fact, uniformity of plan proves unity in the cause, and not the diversity

The Other Side of Evolution

of chance causes claimed by Evolution. If Evolution were true, there would be as much diversity among organs as there is among the forms of organs. If the operation of chance conditions has resulted in radical changes in the forms of organs, why then is there not this similar diversity among the organs themselves? Evolution has no reply. Creation has such reply; God is one and his plan one. Why should not the forms of all these things be alike, seeing they are to live in the same climates, eat the same food and propagate in the same manner?

The rudimentary, abortive and discarded parts found in some animals form one of the strongest arguments Evolution advances. The favorite instance it presents is found in the horse. The horse walks on one toe and has splints further up the leg, which they tell us are the remains of the other toes, and the callosities on the leg are the remains of thumbs. The remains have been found of an animal as large as a dog which resembles the horse and has two toes, and another older animal, as large as a fox, which has four toes. Putting these side by side, Evolution calls them all horses, and says the one-toed animal came from the two-toed, and he from the four-toed, and that this proves the evolution of the horse from the Eohippus (Old Horse) as it is called.

The Other Side of Evolution

1. Bearing in mind that this conclusion is pure assumption, and only inference at best, let us remark that it violates the primal law of evolution laid down by Spencer, that of evolution from the simple to the complex. It should have shown first the one-toed horse, then his development into a two-toed animal, and so on up to a horse having five toes. This would be evolution. As it is, we see the opposite of evolution, degradation, which often occurs in nature, and we see few if any instances of any subsequent restoration to primal conditions.

2. Besides all this, that most necessary thing to a good horse, a pedigree, is wanting. The connecting links are all missing in his ancestral tree. For the ancestors of that first of horses are unknown. But he is not alone in this, for even his owner has the same sad want of proven descent, as we will see later. Just how the horse lost his appendages, and why he dropped toe after toe in this extraordinary manner the story leaves untold.

3. But another great objection exists. It takes time to breed horses. It required all of the Tertiary period to produce the one-toed animal from the four-toed ancestor and much longer time was required to develop him from a totally different animal, where more than a mere question

47

The Other Side of Evolution

of toes comes in. For we have to face the difficulty, and the time necessary, to develop a good horse, say from an alligator, and the still greater task of producing him from an animal without toes at all, or even legs, or anything to hang legs on, and simply a bag of jelly-like substance, which the evolutionist assures us was the ancestor of all horses and their riders. If it appears to the reader that life is too short for such business we can say the geologist agrees with him, for he tells us the age of the old earth itself was not one tenth long enough to produce Evolution's horses, and still less their riders.

Another instance of Evolution's proofs is the swim-bladder of fishes. This Evolution sometimes states is an incipient lung, and that the fish learned in a drought to breathe air. Sometimes, as the need of the theory demands, the swim-bladder is claimed as the relic of a discarded lung. These however are two different and opposing claims. Either as a prophecy or a relic the swim-bladder is fatal to the claims of Evolution. If it is an incipient lung, then here is intention, which Evolution rejects. If a relic, here is retrogression, the opposite of evolution. The abortive organ is one of the difficulties of the theory which Darwin admitted, and Prof. Conn tells us, is not yet answered. Prof. Huxley said, "Either these rudiments are of no use to the animal, in which case they ought to have disappeared, or they are of some use to the animal, in which case they are arguments for teleology." *(Darwinism, p. 151.)*

THE ARGUMENT FROM EMBRYOLOGY.

Evolution derives its greatest argument from the study of the embryo. It makes three claims. First, that the germ of everything, plant and animal, is the same, neither chemical analysis nor the microscope showing any difference. If therefore, such vast variety could come from origins so alike, why could not all we see come from a similar origin, the primitive animal, which was also such a simple cell? Second, in the growth of the embryo it recapitulates the ancestral history of that particular organism. Third, all this when compared with the geologic record, and the present orders of living things as classified, presents the full succession of the forms of life, the one supplying what the other lacks.

These claims must be examined separately.

1. The claim that the germs of all living things are alike is not true. The resemblance is only superficial. Protoplasm, of which the germ is composed, differs and is not homogeneous material. That which builds the muscles is one kind,

and that which builds brain and nerves is entirely different. Prof. Clodd tells us it is not a chemical compound but a mechanism. Nor could the germs be alike. For the plant breathes carbon, the animal oxygen. The one oxidizes, the other deoxidizes. There are still greater and deeper differences.

Tyndall says, "Under the most homogeneous material, there lie structural energies of such complexity, that we must question whether we have the mental elements with which to grapple with them. . . . The most trained and disciplined imagination retires in bewilderment from the problem. In that realm, inaccessible to everything but mind, the wonders of Creation are wrought out. . . . Here is determined the germ and afterwards the complete organization." *(Fragments of Science, p. 153.)* So that these cells or germs, which appear so alike, contain each in itself the entire plan and life of the coming creature, to the color of a feather, the trick of a hunting dog and the smile and dimples of a child.

2. The second claim that the course of each embryo traverses its ancestral history, is not nearly so vociferously made as some years ago. Prof. A. Agassiz writes, "Anything beyond a general parallelism is hopeless." Prof. Conn admits "Embryology alone is not a safe guide, and only

The Other Side of Evolution

when verified by the fossils can it be relied upon. It seldom gives a true history. . . . The parallel is largely a delusion. . . . It often gives a false history." *(Evolution of To-day,* pp. 125, 134, 137, 150.*)* Prof. Thomson writes, "Recapitulation is due to no dead hands of the past, but to physiological conditions which we are unable to discover." *(Outline of Zoology,* p. 63.*)* He also says that the young mammal was never like a worm, a fish, or reptile. It was at the most like the young of these in their various stages. So far from the course of all being alike, Baer says he can tell the difference between the embryo of the common fowl and duck on the second day. *(Principles of Biology,* p. 1.*)* So far as this claim holds good, it forms an argument against evolution. For here is a goal or ideal to which all things strive. This is intention, and plan and purpose, all of which is opposed to the main idea of Evolution. It is in line with Creation.

3. The culminating argument for Evolution is given by arranging in ascending classification the geologic orders of life (which we have seen do not appear as Evolution demands), and placing alongside of these the classification of present animals (which we have seen is not agreed upon, and is as diverse as the writers themselves), and then laying alongside of these two artifical ar-

51

The Other Side of Evolution

rangements, the embryonic recital (which is now doubted and is often false to the past history), and triumphantly pointing to the three-fold combination. The gaps geology shows are thus filled by present forms and what both lack, by the embryonic recital.

Here are compared three things which radically differ. The geologic record shows progress from lower to higher, although not that complete nor unvarying record necessary to the theory, while the present orders of life exist simultaneously. Both show the existence of separate things having no individual connection. The embryo is a single individual, designed from its conception on a predetermined plan, animated by internal forces, and limited to a certain end and life. It is as Dawson says, a "closed series." The worlds of living and fossil creatures consist of myriads of individuals, under many widely different conditions, and aimed at widely different ends and lives. The two are contradictory for the uses of Evolution.

What we do see in these three facts are three marks of personal intelligence. In embryonic growth we see the plan of production. In the coming of the fossil creatures we see the progress of the plan in historical appearance. In the present display of nature we see the ultimate purpose of the whole. It all forms one great consistent plan and bears all the marks of personal and creative work.

So that summing up the argument from comparison of the three facts, the geologic order, the present classification, and the embryonic growth, we find in the first absolute separation of species, in the second no genetic connection as already shown under that argument, and in the third different phenomena having no points in common with the other two. The whole argument then fails of conclusion and reverts as the former do, to proof against Evolution.

FACTS OPPOSING EVOLUTION OF SPECIES.

A theory to be proven must meet the facts and account for them. The theory in question fails lamentably in this. There are countless facts not only unaccounted for but diametrically opposed to it and antagonizing it. We cite some of these:
1. *Degeneration in nature.* Nature shows a constant tendency downward. Prof. E. D. Cope, an eminent evolutionist, writes: "The retrogradation in nature is as well or nearly as well established as evolution." The wild varieties of plants and animals are far inferior to the cultivated kinds. The older species are far superior to the present.

The Other Side of Evolution

The saber-toothed tiger is far superior to the present animal. So also is the Mammoth as compared with the elephant. Plants show degeneration in colors. The order of superiority is from yellow, the lowest, to white, pink, red, purple and blue, the highest. When they drop from blue to yellow, it is degeneration. Some now having green flowers once had colored blossoms. Progress is not seen to be upward in the flowers. So also parasitism is degeneration both in plants and animals. The course of nature is not, as it has not been, constant development upward. The scripture statement "The whole creation groaneth and travaileth in pain," describes accurately the condition of nature *(Ro. 8:22.)*

2. *Continued unchanged species for ages.* The crustacea, for example in Lake Tanganyika, Africa, remain as the receding ocean left them ages ago.

3. *Species instead of increasing in number have decreased.* There were 500 species of trilobites. They have all disappeared. There were 900 species of ammonites; all are gone. Of the 450 species of nautilus, only three remain. Indeed whole families have become obliterated. All this is antagonistic to Evolution.

4. *Species continue the same under the most diverse environments.* Environment is claimed

54

The Other Side of Evolution

as a cause of the changes demanded by Evolution. But the same species exist in the most diverse regions, e. g., mosquitoes, whales and oaks.

5. *Adaptation of one species to another.* Darwin says that a single case of the adaptation of one species to another would be fatal to his theory. Yet he himself gives the data for hundreds of such adaptations. He adduces the fact that a hundred head of red clover produced 2,700 seeds. A similar number protected from insects produced none. The fertilization of plants by insects is well known. The Smyrna fig is said to owe its value to its fertilization by the piercing of an insect. Some of these insects have been introduced into California for that purpose. There is an orchid which can be fertilized only by an insect falling into a cup of liquid which the flower has, and escaping through a side opening in which it touches the pollen.

Dr. Andrew Wilson writes: The colors of flowers—nay, even the little splashes of a hue or tint seen on a petal—are intended to attract insects that they may carry off the fertilizing dust, or pollen, to other flowers. It is to this end also that your flowers are many of them sweet-scented. The perfume is another kind of invitation to the insect world. The honey they secrete forms a third attraction—the most practical of all.

The Other Side of Evolution

6. *Complex adjustments of nature.* "Evolution in vain attempts to account for the wonderful complex adjustments we see in nature, such as the mimicry of animals and plants; the walking stick so closely resembles a twig that it deceives the closest observer. The withered leaf butterfly, with spots and wrinkles, is exactly like the thing it imitates. This is true also of the leaf butterfly and of another which exactly resembles a bird's dropping. Evolution cannot account for the ventriloquism of insects, such as the cricket and tree toad; the battery of the electric eel; the beauty of insects and fish and shells and birds and flowers, especially the harmony of their colors. Edible insects are plainly colored, the poisonous kinds highly colored. Some butterflies have "scareheads" on their wings, exactly resembling an owl's head, and other insects have similar frightful appearances which they thrust out when attacked. All this tells of design and interest and often has the appearance of humor in the creation of these numerous creatures.

7. *The mathematical adjustments of nature are as exact as the multiplication table.* Illustrations of this are the accuracy of the orbits of the heavenly bodies and the law of gravitation. The growth of the cell proceeds on geometrical progression in the division of parts into 2, 4, 8, 16,

56

The Other Side of Evolution

etc. The climbing plants form their coils with mathematical accuracy and proportion. The proportions in which chemicals will mix is mathematically fixed.

Prof. Tyndall thus calls our attention to crystallization: "By permitting alum to crystallize in this slow way we obtain these perfect octahedrons; by allowing carbonate of lime to crystallize, nature produces these beautiful rhomboids; when silica crystallizes we have formed the hexagonal prisms capped at the end by pyramids; by allowing saltpeter to crystallize, we have these prismatic masses, and when carbon crystallizes we have the diamond." *(Fragments of Science,* p. 357.) "Looking at it mentally we see the molecules [of sulphate of soda] like disciplined squadrons under a governing eye, arranging themselves into battalions, gathering around distinct centers and forming themselves into distinct solid masses, which after a time assume the visible shape of the crystal now held in my hand. Here then is an architect at work, who makes no chips nor din, and who is now building the particles into crystals similar in shape to these beautiful masses we see upon the table." *(Belfast Address.)*

8. *The structure of living things shows the true principles of architecture.* A Mr. McLaughlin, a noted Scotch mathematician, tried by mathe-

The Other Side of Evolution

matical calculation to ascertain the shape of a building which would contain the most room with least material and yet embody the greatest architectural strength in its retaining walls. After many laborious calculations, he found after he had arrived at a conclusion that the honey bee had long before given the same plan of structure in its cell. The human skull is a true dome, and the spinal column a true pillar. The ribs of the ship are copied from the fish, the yacht from the duck, and its deep fin from the fish.*

Evolution pretends to account for every one of these facts by chance changes, extending through countless ages as has already been shown in its amazing account of the origin of legs, eyes, backbones and other members. Surely this is an appeal to credulity! The faith of the Christian is sometimes taxed but what shall we say of the faith of the evolutionist? Which is more credible, the simple account of miraculous creation or this long, involved and absolutely unseen and unknown process?

9. *The age of the earth.* Prof. George Frederick Wright, the geologist, tells us that geologic time is not one-hundredth part as long as it was supposed to be fifty years ago, and the popular writers who glibly talk of the antiquity of man

*See "Number in Nature," Hastings, Boston, for further illustrations of this.

58

The Other Side of Evolution

are behind the times and ignorant of the new light which as a flood has come from geology.*

Summing up the case, Prof. Francis M. Balfour tells us: "All these facts that fall under our observation contradict the crude ideas of those socalled naturalists, who state that one species can be transmitted into another in the course of generations." So also Sir David Brewster declares: "We have absolute proof of the immutability of species, whether we search for it in historic or geologic times."

Dr. Etheridge, the famous English authority on fossils, says: "Nine-tenths of the talk of evolutionists is sheer nonsense, not founded on observation and wholly unsupported by fact. Men adopt a theory and then strain their facts to support it. I read all their books, but they make no impression on my belief in the stability of species. Some men are ready to regard you as a fool if you do not go with them in all their vagaries, but this museum is full of proofs of the utter falsity of their views."

*See Man in the Glacial Period, by Prof. Geo. Frederick Wright.

CHAPTER IV.

THE EVOLUTION OF MAN.

The central point in the whole theory is the descent of man from the brute. It is this which, as stated, gives it importance to the Christian. But for this, the hypothesis would be but a curious scientific theory. It is a matter of comparatively minor interest how the universe or the various species came. It is only because these theories are used to assert the animal origin of man that they are dealt with here.

It is in this claim as to the origin of man that all the various theories of Evolution agree, however they may vary in other matters, and, as this is the vital point, these theories are considered as one in this discussion. This is a question merely of fact. Did or did not man descend from the brute or was he specially and divinely created? This is the question in a nut-shell. The two accounts are as follows placed side by side. Darwin's account is accepted substantially by all evolutionists.

The Other Side of Evolution

THE BIBLE ACCOUNT.	EVOLUTION'S ACCOUNT.
(Gen. 1:26, 27; ii: 7. v: 1, 2.)	(From Darwin's Descent of Man, ii, 372.)

THE BIBLE ACCOUNT.
(Gen. 1:26, 27; ii: 7. v: 1, 2.)

"And God said, Let us make man in our image, after our likeness.... And God created man in his own image, in the image of God created he him; male and female created he them.... And the Lord God formed man of the dust of the ground and breathed into his nostrils the breath of life and man became a living soul.... In the day that God created man, in the likeness of God made he him: male and female created he them; and blessed them and called their name Adam

EVOLUTION'S ACCOUNT.
(From Darwin's Descent of Man, ii, 372.)

" Man is descended from a hairy quadruped, furnished with a tail and pointed ears, probably arborial in its habits and an inhabitant of the Old World. This creature, if its whole structure had been examined by a naturalist, would have been classed among the Quadrumana, as surely as would the common and still more ancient progenitor of the Old and New World monkeys. The Quadrumana and all the higher mammals are probably derived from an ancient marsupial animal, and this through a long line of diversified forms, either from some reptile-like, or some amphibian-like creature, and this again from some fish-like animal. In the dim obscurity of the past, we can see that the early progenitor of the Vertebrata must have been an aquatic animal, provided with branchia, with the two sexes united in the same individual."

61

The Other Side of Evolution

The Bible account is circumstantial, with mention of places and rivers of undoubted historical character. It is accepted by subsequent Scripture writers and made the basis of their historical and spiritual teachings. The evolutionary account is lacking in all of this. There are no exact data nor any attempt to give any. No description save an imaginary one is ever given. As no one was there to see, the whole is fanciful.

The two accounts are utterly irreconcilable. Whatever the Scripture account means it does not mean Evolution, and literary justice demands that we do not impose upon a writer a meaning he did not intend or give.

Prof. Pfliederer writes, "There is only one choice. When we say Evolution we definitely deny Creation. When we say Creation we definitely deny Evolution." Prof. James Sully says, "The doctrine of Evolution is directly antagonistic to that of Creation." *(Bible Student,* July, 1901, quoted by Prof Warfield.*)*

How anyone can accept both accounts passes all understanding. The late Dr. John Henry Barrows, president of Oberlin University, tells of meeting a Hindu boy in his visit to India, who had attended the mission schools and learned there the shape and situation of the earth. He had of course previously been taught the Hindu

The Other Side of Evolution

cosmogony that the earth was surrounded by salt water and that by a circle of earth and that by successive circles of buttermilk, sweet cane juice, and other "soft drinks" with intervening circles of land. Dr. Barrows asked the boy which belief he would hereafter hold. He replied that he would believe both. This might be possible to the Hindu boy, but it surpasses all previous intellectual feats that any intelligent person can accept both the Bible account and Darwin's account of the creation of man.

We will review the arguments for and against the evolutionary account of the origin of man from the following spheres and subjects:

1. The Argument from the Evolution of Species. 2. From Similarity of Structure in Animals and Man. 3. Rudimentary Organs in Man. 4. Human Characteristics in Animals. 5. History of the Evolution of Man from the Brute. 6. The "Missing Link." 7. The Brain. 8. Man's Mind and Consciousness. 9. Language. 10. Pre-historic Man. 11. Antiquity of Man. 12. Savage Races. 13. History of Mankind. 14. Religion. 15. Ethics. 16. Christian Experience. 17. Christ.

The Other Side of Evolution

I. ARGUMENT FROM THE ORIGIN OF SPECIES.

On this argument rests the theory of man's animal origin. But for the desire to prove that such is man's origin, the argument would never have been conceived. We introduce it here again to call special attention to this fact. We have seen that there is decided difference of opinion on this theory; that many object to it; that there is not a single case of such origin of species known; that there is no law or force or cause agreed upon or known by which such origin of species could take place; that there are countless objections and facts against it; that its arguments are confessedly insufficient; and they are at best but inferences and only "the balancing of probabilities."

If therefore the proofs of the Origin of Species are wanting the whole theory of Evolution falls in ruins to the ground. There would seem no need to proceed further. Yet Evolution lightly steps over the ruins of its previous claims and proceeds to further assertions. Some of the greatest of the exact scientists stop here. Prof. Dana, the great geologist, says: "Man's origin has thus far no sufficient explanation from science. The abruptness of transition from preceding forms is most extraordinary and especially because it occurs so near the present time." *(Elements of Geology.)*

Prof. Virchow, the most eminent pathologist of Europe, wrote as follows: "There always exists a sharp line of demarcation between man and the ape. We cannot pronounce it proved by science that man descends from the ape, or from any other animal. Whoever calls to mind the lamentable failure of all attempts made very recently to discover a decided support for the '*generatio aequivoc*' in the lower forms of transition from the inorganic to the organic world will feel it doubly serious to demand that this theory, so utterly discredited, should be in any form accepted as the basis of our views of life."

Many more such expressions might be quoted from eminent scientists to the same effect. But as we will use these under the respective heads of the foregoing order of argument, we pass on here to the arguments as stated.

2. SIMILARITY OF STRUCTURE IN ANIMALS AND MAN.

It is well known that the internal and external form of man is like that of the lower animals. This, Evolution claims, is an argument for

The Other Side of Evolution

genetic connection. The same argument would prove that a locomotive was born from a stage coach, and that from a cart, and that from a wheelbarrow. Similarity of structure proves only uniformity of design. An intelligent maker of any nature would so operate, and man himself so manufactures now. Why should not God make man on the model of the lower animals, seeing he is to live in the same world, under the same conditions, eat the same food and propagate in the same way? There is no reason for departure from a form which has proved useful and appropriate. All the parts in the human form have been thus tested in the lower forms and found right for their purpose and are now, as we would expect, applied to man. Man is the climax of all. All is for his use in the lower worlds of plants and animals; then why not use their frame and inner organs also? The mechanic uses the same appliance such as the wheel in his most complex construction as well as in the simplest engine.

But there are parts in the human frame not found in the lower orders. Wallace, one of the greatest evolutionists, says the soft human skin cannot be accounted for by natural causes, nor the valves in the human veins which are in different position from those of the brute, nor the human foot nor larynx, nor the human voice, espe-

The Other Side of Evolution

cially the female voice, nor the absence of hair on the body, nor why man is short armed and long legged, while his ape-man ancestor is the reverse. Many more such problems vex the evolutionist. Creation accounts for all this, and does so by one simple, sweeping argument in place of Evolution's complex and bewildering maze of speculations.

Ruskin teaches us in this extract that God works by law and does not deviate therefrom even where it seems to us that He might have wrought differently: "But God shows us in Himself, strange as it may seem, not only authoritative perfection, but even the perfection of obedience, an obedience to his own laws; and in the cumbrous movement of those unwieldiest of His creatures, we are reminded, even in His divine essence, of that attribute of uprightness in the human creature, 'that sweareth to his own hurt and changeth not.'" *(Seven Lamps of Architecture, II., p. 78.)*

3. RUDIMENTARY ORGANS IN MAN.

Evolution points to certain features in man which it claims came from his brute ancestry, such as the long hairs in the eyebrow, which they say came from the ape-man, the tips of the ear, and

The Other Side of Evolution

the hair on the forearm, which slants from the hand to the elbow. The whole outside ear is also claimed as a relic from that brute and is unnecessary for hearing. So also of the five toes when a solid foot would have been better, although most of us think not. They also point to some evidences of a tail which they say was rubbed off when the ape-man learned to sit down. This, however, many apes do now with no signs of decreasing tails. Many internal members and organs are pointed to, which are too numerous here to mention. One instance is as good as the whole catalogue, and one reply also.

All this proves too much for the theory. Here is the loss of useful organs and the survival of others not needed. This is not evolution, at least not the kind we have been asked to build our hopes upon for progress. Further, these so-called "relics of the brute" are counted as having no use save to support Evolution. The "gill-slits" in the neck of the human embryo are the favorite instance of this kind of fact. Haeckel and, after him others, picture the forms of fish, dog and man in embryonic state, and say in triumph, There is proof of the descent of the man from the dog and of him from the fish; and this resemblance has survived to tell the tale, there being no other use for it. But this is not the only feature that "survives." Heads and mouths and eyes also "survive." Why are these not pointed to as proofs of descent? Because we can see use for them, while there appears to be no use for the "gill-slits" except to prove Evolution. If we could see some use in the "gill-slits" in the neck of the embryo, the argument of Evolution would fall to the ground. Evolution's argument from the gill-slits and all other "relics of the brute" rests therefore on ignorance, a very unsafe foundation for a scientific theory, for knowledge is constantly increasing, especially of the human frame, and there is not the slightest doubt, reasoning from analogy and past experience, that there is use for these peculiar embryonic features.

We repeat the argument of Huxley as to these rudimentary parts: "Either these rudiments are of no use, in which case they should have disappeared; or they are of use, in which case they are arguments for teleology." *(Darwinism and Design, p. 151.)*

Evidences of this nature are of that kind called circumstantial, and in law are least relied upon, for on such evidence some innocent men have been hung. Shall we condemn the whole race to a bestial origin on the same evidence? All arguments founded on such facts are weak, puerile and unworthy of scientists. No wonder that Prof.

The Other Side of Evolution

Paulsen said Haeckel's speculations are "a disgrace to the philosophy of Germany." Shall we suspend a philosophy of the universe upon a few long hairs? Shall we allow the guess as to the origin of the tip of the outer ear to revolutionize theology? Shall we risk our eternal destiny on the supposed uselessness of the so-called "gill-slits" in premature puppies? Yet this is the demand of Evolution reduced to plain English.

4. HUMAN CHARACTERISTICS IN ANIMALS.

The human characteristics found in animals form an argument for Evolution. We find the animals have memory, love, hatred, jealousy; that they can think and plan, use means and weapons, admire things of beauty, and some have sports. All of this, so Evolution claims, points to genetic connection with man. But all this only shows uniformity in the inner as in the outer being. There is as much reason for the one as for the other. Life is the same wherever we find it. The forces which operate in the rain drop are the same as in the universe of boundless space. The intellectual nature of man is the same as that of angels who have no genetic connection with us. Even devils are the same in the intellectual nature as God himself. Mind is the same thing wherever it ex-

70

The Other Side of Evolution

ists. To say therefore that because animals have certain characteristics like those of man, they are the ancestors of man, is a leap to a conclusion entirely unwarranted by either facts or logic. Yet it is on such conclusions that Evolution rests. Creation would proceed on the same comprehensive plan, and we have seen that man does also. He applies his forces as he does his materials to the most varied uses.

Nor has any instance of the development of a brute or his faculties to any approach to man's faculties ever been known. The highest animal is still immeasurably below the lowest and most bestial man, not only in the grade of the faculties that they have in common, but in others which the animal does not possess and cannot acquire. There is a great gulf fixed which they do not pass over—as our next section will show.

5. HISTORY FROM THE BRUTE TO THE MAN.

Many have essayed the relation of the story of the change from the brute to the man. In doing so, some have covered themselves with ridicule, yet the attempts continue to be made as do others to produce perpetual motion. To bridge this chasm is necessary in order to sustain Evolution, for this is the heart of the

The Other Side of Evolution

question. It is said that a famous professor of history abandoned his chair because of the uncertainty of the facts of history. One would expect that the attempt to relate what happened before man had any history, or even existed, would be even more hazardous. Yet we are given the account with such assurance as sometimes to deceive the very elect—who abandon their Bibles. Haeckel's attempt was the most impressive, and swept all before it, for a year or two. He presented a many-branched tree, whose roots were protoplasm, its trunk protozoa, its successive branches sponges, fish, reptiles, birds, marsupials, monkeys, apes, man-apes, and the topmost branches, man. Of the twenty-one stages, half have been proved to be "wrong" by evolutionists and the rest are "doubtful."

The home of the primeval man, or ascending-ape, whichever it or he was, is one of the difficult facts to settle. Haeckel locates it at the bottom of the Indian ocean. He can thus defy disproof. Another says it was in the tropics somewhere. This is also a safe assertion. The difficulty is that the remains of the pre-historic man are found in the northern regions, while the ancestor animal was a denizen of the tropics. So another declares that the original home was in the northern regions, to which a pair of wild animals of the an-

The Other Side of Evolution

cestor kind were driven by something or somebody, and their retreat cut off, and so they were forced to the life in caves and adopted the habits we find among cave dwellers.

But although our ancestor cannot be located we are told just who and what he was. Thus Prof. Edward Clodd, an authoritative evolutionist, tells us in his book, "The Making of a Man," as follows: "Whichever among the arboreal creatures possessed any favorable variation, however slight, of brain or sense organ, would secure an advantage over less favored rivals in the struggle for food and mates and elbow room. The qualities which gave them success would be transmitted to their offspring. The distance in one generation would be increased in the next; brain power conquering brute force and skill outwitting strength. While some for awhile remained arboreal in their habits, never moving easily on the ground, although making some approach to upright motion, as seen in the shambling gait of the manlike apes, others developed a way of walking on their hind legs, which entirely set free the fore limbs as organs of handling and throwing. Whatever were the conditions which permitted this, the advantage which it gives is obvious. It was the making of a man." (p. 126.)

It seems difficult, indeed unfair, to take this

The Other Side of Evolution

seriously. We must assure the reader that the author of this description shows no intention of humor either here or elsewhere in his work, or indeed any consciousness of it. All is given in perfect sobriety. We must therefore accept it as a profound scientific deliverance of the most authoritative kind and deal with it accordingly, and believe that walking on the hind legs and throwing things with the fore limbs was "the making of a man." How easily men are made!

1. This argument rests on the theory of Natural Selection now discarded by most evolutionists.

2. Apes have done all he here claims and far more. The chimpanzee has been taught to sit at a table, to drink out of cups, to eat with a knife and fork, to wipe his mouth with a napkin and use a toothpick, but has got no further in the ways of good society, and as to increase of cranial development, has obtained none save as the effects of undue potations have produced an enlarged feeling.

3. The whole account is purely imaginary as no professor of Evolution was there to observe the facts. It is in short an intrusion into the realm of fiction, which clearly belongs to Mr. Kipling in his wonderful jungle stories.

The Other Side of Evolution

Again in his book on "Man and His Ancestor," (p. 67,) Prof. Morris gives us a full description of this unseen and purely hypothetical ancestor as follows: "It was probably much smaller than existing man, little if any more than four feet in height, and not more than half the weight of man. Its body was covered, though not profusely, with hair; the hair of the head being woolly or frizzly in texture and the face provided with a beard. The face was not jet black, like a typical African, but of a dull brown color; the hair being somewhat similar in color. The arms were long and lank, the back being much curved, the chest flat and narrow, the abdomen protruding, the legs rather short and bowed, the walk a waddling motion somewhat like that of the gibbon. It had deep set eyes, greatly protruding mouth with gaping lips, huge ears and general "ape-like aspect." Prof. John Fiske thought it was much more than a million years since man diverged from the brute. During an active geologic age before the cave-man appeared on the scene, "a being erect upon two legs and having the outward resemblance of a man wandered hither and thither upon the face of the earth." *(Destiny of Man, p. 55.)*

We read all this with astonishment that any-one could penetrate the dim vista of millions of

The Other Side of Evolution

years ago and transcribe such a detailed and circumstantial account of what then existed. It reads like a picture from life. Yet not only was the writer not there, but no one else was present, for this was the father of us all, according to Evolution.

We are told that, given time enough, all this series of changes from the primeval cell to the modern philosopher or scientist is possible. But time for this is limited by the age of the earth. For Lord Kelvin has stated that only a few million years are possible on any calculation and this would all be needed for the change from ape to man to say nothing of the interminable ages necessary for the change from the protozoa to the fish and then to land animals and so on to mammals and up to the ape.

The after life of the ape-man is described with the same circumstantiality as the coming to manhood's estate. Dr. Robert Patterson combines the various features of Evolution's description and this creature's history in the following extract: "It is a fearful and wonderful picture they give us of the origin of marriage from the battles of baboons, of the rights of property established by terrible fights for groves of good chestnuts, of the beginning of morals from the instincts of brutes, and of the dawnings of religion, or rather

The Other Side of Evolution

of superstition, from the dreams of these animals; the result of the whole being that civilization and society and law and order and religion are all simply the evolution of the instincts of the brutes and that there is no necessity for the invoking any supernatural interference to produce them." (*Fables of Infidelity.*)

It is here we meet the "theistic" account of the origin of man. It was to this creature we are told God imparted a soul or spirit supernaturally. For this strange creature was the Adam of theistic Evolution. Eve they say nothing about. Nor are we told how or when the soul was imparted, whether in a single animal, a pair, or a herd; whether awake or asleep. Nor are we told what they did next, or how the soul-ape got along with the rest of the species. Nor are we told what particular state, or act, or habit, entitled him to the new nature he received. It seems as if the ability to "stand on the hind legs and throw things with the fore limbs," which Prof. Clodd tells us was the "making of a man," scarcely entitled him to such a divine inheritance as an immortal soul.

This also was the Adam who fell according to the theistic evolutionist, though how such a creature could "fall" seems difficult to conceive. It was this thing whose sin, Paul tells us, brought death on the whole race. It was this who is a type of Christ who is "the Second Adam." Out and out Evolution has but a fraction of the difficulties, either physical or spiritual, to face that this make-shift compromise "theistic" theory has before it. It is not surprising that the thorough-going evolutionist rejects this strange compound of fiction and theology.

We appeal to the common, every-day man of fair judgment: Which takes more faith, or if preferred, credulity, the accepting of that strange, complex, unauthenticated account of man's origin or the simple and, with an omnipotent God in mind, entirely possible account of the Bible? "The Lord God formed man of the dust of the ground and breathed into his nostrils the breath of life: and man became a living soul." Which is the more noble, the more satisfying to our desires for a high and divine origin as well as high and divine destiny?

6. THE MISSING LINK.

The Missing Link is the great desideratum of Evolution, for the evolutionist indignantly disclaims the present apes or monkey as ancestors. He tells us the connecting link was a creature superior to these. But of which he is unable to show any specimen. It is purely mythical. We have the remains of millions of animals reaching through all the ages and why is this particular specimen wanting?

Dr. Rudolph Virchow, the great discoverer of the germ theory, has for thirty years, according to Haeckel, "opposed the theory of man's descent from the brute." *(Last Link, p. 27.)* He himself says: "The intermediate form is unimaginable save in a dream. . . . We cannot teach or consent that it is an achievement that man has descended from the ape or other animal." *(Homiletic Review,* January, 1901.)

Dr. Friedrich Pfaff, professor of natural sciences in the University of Erlangen, writes on the question as follows: "Nowhere in the older deposits is an ape that approximates more closely to man, or man that approximates more closely to an ape, or perhaps a man at all. The same gulf which is found to-day between man and the ape goes back with undiminished breadth and depth to the tertiary period. This fact alone is sufficient to make its unintelligibleness clear to every one who is not penetrated by the conviction of the infallibility of the theory of the gradual transmutation of and progressive development of all organized creatures. If, however, we now find one of the most man-like apes (gibbon) in the tertiary period, and this species is still in the same low grade, and side by side with it, at the end of the ice period, man is found in the same high grade as to-day, the ape not having approximated more nearly to man, and modern man not having become further removed from the ape than the first man, every one who is in a position to draw a right conclusion can infer, that the facts contradict a theory of constant progression, development and ceaselessly increasing variation from generation to generation, as surely as it is possible to do." *(Age and Origin of Man,* Am. Tr. Soc., p. 52.)

From time to time the discovery of the "missing link" is announced and telegraphed through the civilized world, only to be remanded to its place among the remains of brutes or men. We will consider the instances of such as they have been presented:

1. The Calaveras Skull now in the California State Museum. This has been shown recently to be a hoax. It was placed in a mine shaft 150 feet deep, by Mr. R. C. Scribner, a storekeeper at the mine, as a practical joke. This he lately acknowledged to the Rev. W. H. Dyer, of Los Angeles, a clergyman of the Episcopal church.

2. The Neanderthal Skull. This was found in 1856 in Prussia. It had narrow receding forehead and thick ridges over the eyes. It was claimed by

The Other Side of Evolution

the evolutionists as from two to three hundred thousand years old. Dr. Meyer of Bonn examined the evidence, and found it to be the skull of a Cossack killed in 1814. Many other scientists agreed with him. *(Bible Science and Faith, p. 278.)*

3. The Colorado specimen. Prof. Stephen Bowers of the Mineralogical and Geological Survey of California, gives this account of another such discovery: "A few years ago the newspapers contained an account of the discovery of a skeleton in Colorado, by a Columbia College professor, which he was pleased to call the 'missing link' between man and the apes. He gave this remarkable creature an antiquity of a million and a half of years. The friable bones were carefully wrapped in cotton and shipped east. But scarcely had the learned professor gotten away with his prize when certain cowboys came forward and claimed the bones to be that of a pet monkey which they buried but a dozen years previously."

4. The late find of skeletons at Croatia, Austria, is heralded as the discovery of a connecting link. But these are skeletons of men and not of brutes. They are degraded men and nothing is better known than the possibility of degeneracy in man. We have degenerates now with all the peculiarities of these low specimens, retreating brows and jaws and flat faces. Degeneracy does not prove

evolution. While the shape of these skulls is low and long it has not been shown that their cubical capacity is much less than that of normal man.

5. The Pithecanthropus Erectus. This is the most popular relic with Evolution. It consists of a piece of a skull from the eyes upward, a leg bone and two teeth. These were found in Java by Dr. von Eugene Du Bois in 1891. The cubic measurement of the skull is 60 inches, the same as that of an idiot, that of a normal man being 90 inches, and of an ape 30. These specimens were found at separate places and times. The skull is too small for the thigh bone. The age of the strata in which they were found is uncertain. Authorities are divided as to the nature of these. Haeckel admits that the belief that this is the missing link is strongly combatted by some distinguished scientists. At the Leyden congress, it was attacked by the illustrious pathologist Rudolph Virchow.

The assumptions based upon this specimen and necessary for evidence are as follows: First, that it is as old as claimed, a hundred thousand years at least, or a million as stated by some. Second, that these bones belong to the same individual. Third, that they are the remains of a full-grown individual. Fourth, that they are the remains of a human or semi-human being. Fifth, that they are not the remains of an idiot whose capacity the brain represents.

With all these unproven assumptions, and against the opinion of many of the finest scientists in Europe, Haeckel and some evolutionists have declared this is the missing link. They place this piece of a skull of one creature upon this leg of another and insert these teeth belonging to a third, all so far separated in life that they probably did not even know each other, and rechristen the whole "Pithecanthropus Erectus," which may be freely translated "The ape that walked like a man," being thus the first that arrived at that point which Prof. Clodd tells us was "the making of a man." And this specimen is Haeckel's *Last Link,* and this he says demonstrates the truth of Evolution.

The evidence of bones and other remains is now generally suspected. It has been found that even in the case of recent remains, as in criminal trials, experts are often unable to decide whether they are human or brute, recent or remote, and what part of the frame they occupied. It is said that Wallace, the great cotemporary with Darwin in the promotion of the theory, now admits there is no evidence of an evolutionary link between man and the lower animals.

The Other Side of Evolution

7. THE ARGUMENT FROM THE BRAIN.

The brain forms the principal difference between man's body and the brute's. The brain is especially used as proof by the evolutionist. It is the organ of mind. Its size corresponds with the intellectual state of the creature. It is the theory of Evolution that there was an increase in the size of the brain in some of the man-apes of that day, although none such is seen now.

Prof. Edward Clodd thus describes these supposed brain changes after the Ice Age: "The changes by which he met these new conditions were in a very small degree physical. They were almost wholly mental. The principal physical change was in the growth of the brain and the expansion of the cranium, giving rise to a less bestial physiognomy and an advanced mental power." *(Man and His Ancestor, p. 181.)*

How could man adapt himself by increasing the size of his brain? Why should the passing away of the ice age increase the size of the brain? However, he disposes of the whole matter, after arguing through pages of supposition and assumption, by stating, "The absence of facts forces us to confine ourselves largely to suggestions and probabilities." *(Making of a Man, p. 188.)* But probabilities are not science and we have a right to ask from those claiming to be scientists actual

The Other Side of Evolution

facts and not guesses, for so great an assertion as the descent of man from the brute.

The capacity of the ape brain is 30, of the human 90 cubic inches. There is no evidence of change in either the ape or the man. The prehistoric man has as good a head on his shoulders as his modern descendants. Bruner says the most ancient skulls even exceed ours. Dr. Pfaff says the stone age men are equal to the present generation. So if education does not increase the size of man's brain, why should the new tricks of Prof. Clodd's ancient "arboreal creature" enlarge that individual's brain 200 per cent? On the other hand, the ape of to-day and the ape of 3,000 years ago as mummied and preserved in Egypt are the same. The big-brained ape of Evolution has unaccountably disappeared and even his skull is missing.

8. MAN'S MIND AND CONSCIOUSNESS.

Evolution claims that all man's faculties have been derived from the brute, as was his physical frame. It is fair to say that this is met at the door by the protest of some of the greatest scientists, themselves sympathetic with Evolution.

Prof. John Fiske wrote on the origin of mind: "We can say when mind came on the scene of evolution, but we can say neither whence nor why. . . . It is not only inconceivable how mind should have been produced from matter, but it is inconceivable that it should have been produced from matter." *(Darwinism,* pp. 63, 69.) Prof. Dana has said, "The present teaching of geology is that man is not of nature's making. . . . Independently of such evidences, man's high reason, his unsatisfied longings, aspirations, his free will, all afford the fullest assurance that he owes his existence to the special act of the Infinite Being whose image he bears." *(Geologic Story,* p. 290.)

Prof. George H. Howison writes on this theme: "To make evolution the ground of the existence of mind in man, is destructive to the reality of the human person and therefore, of the entire world of moral good and of unqualified truth." *(Limits of Evolution,* p. 6.) Lord Kelvin, the most eminent living scientist, wrote in a letter to the London Times, "Every action of human free will is a miracle to physical and chemical and mathematical science."

9. LANGUAGE.

Evolution has long tried to create an argument for the derivation of man's speech from the cries of animals. This is met however by the philologist with positive denial. Prof. Max Mueller says: "There is one barrier which no one has yet ventured to touch,—the barrier of language. Language is our Rubicon and no brute will dare to cross it. . . . No process of Natural Selection will ever distill significant words out of the notes of birds and animals." *(Lessons on the Science of Language, pp. 23, 340, 370.)*

False claims have been made for the languages of savage people and ancient races. Darwin said that the people of Terra del Fuego were the lowest in the scale, so far as discovered, and their language correspondingly crude. But further investigation shows that they have 32,430 words; over twice as many as Shakespeare used. The language of some of the tribes of the Congo is described by a missionary as more complex than Greek. The history of languages shows the same want of evidence for an evolutionary origin. The oldest forms are the most complex. Modern Greek and Latin are simpler than the ancient forms. English is an improvement in this respect on the old Anglo Saxon, whose grammatical forms it has largely cast off and reduced the language to greater simplicity.

A scientist is now endeavoring to ascertain the speech of monkeys. He has ascertained that these animals have different sounds for different wants,

The Other Side of Evolution

a fact as to other creatures that he could have ascertained by a visit to the nearest poultry yard. The hen has as many calls as the monkey, and as many meanings too. Her call for food is one sound. Her cry of alarm at a passing hawk is another, and her brood perfectly understands all, and without previous education. All animals and birds, and many insects too, have sounds with meaning in them, but language is another matter.

10. PREHISTORIC MAN.

The remains of early races form an argument used by Evolution. These remains are found in many places in caves and are accompanied by tools of stone and vessels of pottery and the remains of animals. These degraded peoples are pointed to by Evolution as man in a state of development.

If the preceding arguments were well founded this would appear reasonable enough. But in view of the fallacious character of the prior reasoning, we must halt at this claim. There are many and conclusive reasons for rejecting this unproven claim. For it is unproven. It is only inference and assumption.

1. These men of the cave do not necessarily represent man in a course of progress, for we find to-day the same classes of people with their

The Other Side of Evolution

stone tools and pottery and living as prehistoric man lived. There to-day exist men in every stage of the supposed progress from the cave man to the highest in civilization. Such remains could be had in any burial place of these savage peoples. Prehistoric man, so-called, is still with us and we can interview him as to his state and history.

2. We have seen that modern man has not developed in brain capacity above prehistoric man. It is also true that he has not developed physically. Dana tells us that the skeleton found at Mentone compares favorably with the best modern men. Indeed we have degenerated in many respects. We have almost lost the sense of smell as compared with savage peoples or even animals. Our teeth are certainly not improving. If we are to find perfect specimens we do not look at the most advanced classes but to the reverse. Those who live to extreme old age are generally in the lowly ranks. But why has physical development ceased at all? Why are there not some superior beings by this time? But alas, there are no marks or indications of wings or halos on either the great saints or scientists of the day.

We are told that while physical evolution has ceased among men, evolution now works along mental lines of progress. This is a radical shifting of the ground of evolution, for heretofore all this has been not only omitted but discarded. If evolution is anything, it is physical. Nor does Evolution give any account of the causes of the stoppage of physical development and the change to mental evolution. We will also show later that this supposed progress has not been such as claimed.

II. ANTIQUITY OF MAN.

Evolution asserts that a vast antiquity for man has been proven by remains that have been found. It is commonly said that these remains are hundreds of thousands of years old. But the claims for these vast periods are now being greatly reduced and generally discredited. Dr. Zahm says of these speculations: "We could not give a better illustration of the extremes to which the unguided human intellect is subject than the vacillating and extravagant notions of the antiquity of man." *(Bible Science and Faith,* p. 315.) The age of the peat beds of Abbeville, in France, in which human remains were found, was once estimated at 20,000 years. The estimate has been reduced to a fifth of that age. The remains of the animals found with man are supposed to prove his extreme antiquity. The remains of the mammoth were once cited as such proof. But the mammoth has been found in such a state of preservation that its flesh has been fed to the dogs.

The enormous ages which have been credited to these remains are well illustrated by the discovery of a skeleton at New Orleans while digging for the gas works. From the depth of the stratum in which it was found it was estimated by scientists at the age of 57,000 years. Soon after, the gunwale of the skeleton's Kentucky flat boat was found in the same stratum, and the age therefore of the remains was reduced from 57,000 to 50 years. The evidences from peat bogs, stalagmite formations, stone, iron and bronze tools are all now considered unreliable by scientists. So many exposures of mistakes in the estimate of age from these have been made, that the whole is looked upon with suspicion. Instance after instance might be given.

It has been claimed that we can arrange these past races in an ascending order as they worked in stone, bronze, or iron, in their successive history. This is a false theory. We have all these "ages" existing to-day. On the other hand, Dr. Livingstone found no stone age in Africa. Dr. Schliemann found in the ruins of Troy the bronze age below the stone age. The early Egyptians used bronze, the later ones stone tools. In the Chaldean tombs all these are found together.

The Other Side of Evolution

Europe had the metal age while America had the stone age. *(Creation and Evolution.* Prof. Townsend.*)*

These prehistoric races to which Evolution points us as representing man in his early state, do not represent that early world. They are found at the outer limits of the world and not at the acknowledged center whence man came. They are, in short, what we find to-day at the outlying regions of earth. They therefore, are exceptional peoples and not representative of the world at that time, or now.

The dynasties of Egypt were once cited against the Bible narrative, but these have been reduced to moderate figures. A thousand years was taken off by one discoverer recently from the age of the middle kingdom. There is a question whether the Egyptian dynasties were successive or in some cases contemporary. There is also the well-known fact that the Egyptians had years of varying length. They often counted dynasties by years of three months and also of a month! Dr. Flinders Petrie lately discovered in the tombs of the kings, preceding the first dynasty of Egypt at Abydos, Grecian pottery of Mycean clay, and this in a tomb estimated to date from 5,400 B. C.! *(Atlantic Monthly,* October, 1900.*)*

The same kind of estimating is now being done

The Other Side of Evolution

from the Assyrian tablets and their records. We must remember these old kings were great boasters and liars, too. We don't know the basis of their calculations. Perhaps Assyria also had three month years. If their method was like Egypt's, and they were connected as we know by much intercourse and literature, we may expect like inaccuracy. The ancient dates given in the inscriptions found in Nuffar recently, are already suspected by scholars. The date for the temple uncovered there was 3,200 B. C. This number is the product of forty multiplied by eighty; evidently a round number for eighty generations, and not at all a careful or exact chronological statement.

However, let us compare the two accounts, the Bible and the Assyrian. The one precise in statement, accurate in ten thousand points as demonstrated, with us for thousands of years, trusted and tried. The other inexact, mythical in its legends, having all the marks of inaccuracy, just discovered, made by people we know nothing of and having no character to speak of, and full of vain boastings and absurd claims. Which is the true and which the false? Let the jury decide. We will abide the verdict.

Prof. A. H. Sayce of Oxford, writes: "The light that has come from the remnants of the past has been fatal to the pretenses of critical skepticism. The discoveries of Abydos have discredited its methods and results. They have shown that where they can be tested they prove to be absolutely worthless. It is only reasonable to conclude that methods and results, that thus break down under the test of monumental discovery, must equally break down in other departments of history where no such test can be applied. It is not the discoveries of the higher critics, but the old traditions which have been confirmed by archaeological discovery." *(Homiletic Review,* March, 1901.) This statement is made by one of the most able archaeologists and semitic scholars in the world.

The age of man on earth has much testimony from science agreeing with the Bible account. From many the following are cited:

Dr. J. A. Zahm, the distinguished scholar, says, "I am disposed to attribute to man an antiquity of about ten thousand years. It seems likely that the general consensus of chronologists will ultimately fix on a date which shall be below rather than above ten thousand years as the nearest approximate to the age of our race." *(The Bible, Science and Faith,* p. 311.) He quotes many other authorities.

Prof. Winchell tells us, "The very beginnings

The Other Side of Evolution

of our race are still almost in sight." *(Sketches of Creation.)* Dawson thinks man has been on earth about seven thousand years. Geology agrees that man did not exist before the ice age. The stone age is fixed at about seven thousand years ago by others.

Professor George Frederick Wright tells us, "The glacial period did not close more than ten thousand years ago. This shortening of our conception of the ice age renders glacial man a comparatively modern creature. The last stage of the excessive unstability of the earth was not so very long ago and continued down to near the introduction of man." *(Bibliotheca Sacra,* April, 1902.)

S. R. Pattison, F. G. S., tells us, "Science shows to us a number of converging probabilities which point to man's first appearance along with great animals about 8,000 years ago." *(Age and Origin of Man Geologically Considered, Am. Tr. Soc.,* p. 29.)

Dr. Friedrich Pfaff, professor of natural science in Erlangen, thus sums up the evidence from geology as to man: "(1) The age of man is small, extending only to a few thousand years. (2) Man appeared suddenly: the most ancient man known to us is not essentially different from the now living man. (3) Transitions from the ape to the man, or the man to the ape, are nowhere found. The conclusion we are led to is that the Scripture account of man, which is one and self-consistent, is true. . . . This account of man we accept by faith, because it is revealed by God, is supported by adequate evidence, solves the otherwise insoluble problems, not only of science and history, but of inward experience, and meets our deepest need. . . . The more it is sifted and examined the more well founded and irrefragable does it prove to be." *(Age and Origin of Man,* Am. Tr. Soc., pp. 55-56.*)*

12. SAVAGE RACES.

Evolution delights to compare savage peoples alternately with present civilized races and with the brute. Prof. Conn says, "There is a greater difference between a Newton and a Hottentot, than between the Hottentot and the orang-outang." He fails to notice, or state, that the first is a difference of degree only, and the latter a difference of kind. It would be possible to develop a Hottentot into a philosopher, but no attempt is ever dreamed of, to change an orang-outang into a Hottentot. On the other hand, the lowest savages have under culture shown their human inheritance of faculties beyond the brute. Two

The Other Side of Evolution

pigmies taken to Italy learned to speak Italian in two years with fluency. They showed themselves superior to many European children, and one became proficient in music. The skill of this race with poisoned arrows, pits for game, and cultivation of various kinds, is well known.

The savage races show the opposite of evolution. They are races in ruins. Max Mueller says, "What do we know of savage tribes beyond the last chapter in their history? They may have passed through ever so many vicissitudes, and what we consider as primitive may be for all we know a relapse into savagery, or corruption of what was something more rational and intelligible in former ages." This estimate of this great scholar is attested by facts. Where to-day is the Hindu race that could build the Taj Mahal? What Greek race to-day could reproduce the architecture or statuary of their ancestors? The ruins of all eastern and many western lands point to fallen races as well as ruined structures. The world's history is that of the fall of great nations such as Egypt, Babylonia, Greece, Rome, in all of which are sad examples of architecture and peoples alike in decay.

The Other Side of Evolution

13. THE ARGUMENT FROM HISTORY.

History is appealed to to show the progress of man and his continuance in the evolutionary line since his origin in the brute. Our present civilization is pointed to and compared with the past and we are told that this is the result of evolution.

Some remarks of a preliminary kind are called for here. It is to be remembered that history does not cover a very long period, that the record is often broken, and that the facts are often very uncertain. Large sections of the world we know historically nothing or little of, such as Asia and Africa. We must remember that progress is confined mostly to Europe and America and these form but a third of the population of the world. Also that European progress is a comparatively recent matter. We are now considering the entire history of the race and must take in these vast outside regions to arrive at correct conclusions. To judge the entire progress of mankind from a short-sighted view of a limited portion is as unscientific as it is unscriptural.

We must also remember that Europe owes its progress to the influence of Christianity. For today it is the Christian nations only that have progress and the most Christian have the most prog-

The Other Side of Evolution

ress. No fact is better seen or proven. Lange states, "Among human tribes left to themselves, the higher man never comes out of the lower. Apparent exceptions do ever, on close examination, confirm the universality of the rule in regard to particular peoples, while the claim, as made for the world's general progress, can only be urged in opposition by ignoring the supernal aids of revelation that have ever shown themselves directly or collaterally on the human path." *(Commentary on Genesis,* p. 355.) We have seen that so far as present savage races are concerned they have made no progress, and semi-civilized races, such as the Egyptians, Chinese and Hindus have retrograded.

We need also to consider the vast and great civilizations which existed in remote antiquity as is now revealed by archaeology. The recent discoveries in Assyria and Babylonia and Egypt show vast empires of culture as well as national extension and power, and that their earlier culture was the greatest. So Prof. Hilprecht, of the University of Pennsylvania, testifies of Babylonia: "The flower of Babylonian art is found at the beginning of Babylonian history." *(Recent Researches in Bible Lands,* p. 88.) Horace Bushnell tells us, "All great ruins are but a name for greatness in ruins."

The Other Side of Evolution

It is to Egypt we must go for the earliest records of human civilization. Here the account of Prof. Sayce, of Oxford, gives us the facts: "The earliest culture and civilization to which the monuments bear witness was in fact already perfect. It was full-grown. The organization of the country was complete. The arts were known and practiced. Egyptian culture as far as we know at present has no beginning." *(Recent Researches in Bible Lands,* pp. 101, 102.) "The older the culture, the more perfect it is found to be. The fact is a very remarkable one, in view of modern theories of development and of the evolution of civilization out of barbarism. Whatever may be the reason, such theories are not borne out by the discoveries of archaeology. Instead of the progress one should expect, we find retrogression and decay. Is it possible the Biblical view is right after all and that civilized man has been civilized from the outset?" *(Homiletic Review,* June, 1902.) Prof. Flinders Petrie tells us that the Great Pyramid bears on its stones the marks of the solid and tubular drill, edged with stone as hard as diamond, and cutting one-tenth of an inch at a revolution, and showing no sign of wear. They had also straight and circular saws. The same building reveals scientific and astronomical

The Other Side of Evolution

knowledge equal in some respects to modern science.

Not only were the past civilizations great, but, in many respects, far above the present. So that the race has even fallen from higher levels. Lecky thus writes of the Greeks: "Within the narrow limits and scant populations of the Greek states, arose men, who in almost every conceivable form of genius, in philosophy, in epic, dramatic and lyric poetry, in written and spoken eloquence, in statesmanship, in sculpture, in painting, and probably in music, attained the highest levels of human perfection." *(History of European Morals*, p. 408.) Galton says of the same civilization: "The millions of Europe, breeding as they have for two thousand years, have never produced the equal of Socrates and Phidias. The average ability of the Athenian race is, on the lowest possible estimate, nearly two grades higher than our own; that is, about as much as our race is above the African negro." *(Hereditary Genius*, p. 320.)

It does seem as if such testimony of these great scholars should make us not only chary of the theory which claims ever upward and onward progress, but also more modest in our boasted modern progress and position. Prof. Frederick Starr of the Anthropological department of Chicago University, says that the American race is reverting to the Indian state. He bases this on measurements of faces of 5,000 children. This is a dismal outlook. It is not what Evolution has promised us. The followers of Evolution have reason to be indignant at such a turn in its course. However, we may comfort them and ourselves with the hope that if Evolution fails us we have other resources.

EVOLUTION AND RELIGION.

Consciousness of God and the hereafter is the great distinction between man and brute. This is the basis of all religion. Of this Evolution gives the origin in the dreams of animals.

According to that department of the evolutionary theory popularly called Higher Criticism, all religion, including Israel's and Christianity, was derived from fetishism and from that it developed to animism, and so to polytheism and finally monotheism. But the lowest savages have, according to anthropology, the belief in a Supreme Being. Andrew Lang says, "It is among the lowest savages that the Supreme Beings are regarded as eternal, moral, powerful." *(Making of Religion,* p. 206.) Fetishism and animism are processes of decay, says Dr. John Smith, quoting Hartmann, DeRouge, Renouf, Lang and others.

102

The Other Side of Evolution

(Integrity of Scripture, p. 68.*)* Traces of monotheism are found in China, India, Egypt and elsewhere. In all nations is this decay found save in one, Israel.

It is further found that mankind had an original theistic religion common to the race, which is just what the Bible teaches. All the evidence is to the effect that the further back we go, the purer the religions are found to be. The earliest Romans were more pure in religion than the later people. The early Greeks more so than the more recent. The early handwritings give a purer and more theistic religion than the later books. Dr. Jacob Chamberlain thus sums up the evidence for the Hindu Vedas: "They all teach the Godhead is one, that he is good, that man is in a state of sin, not at peace with the Holy One, that man is in need of holiness and purity, that there can be no harmony between sinful man and a holy God unless sin is in some way expiated and expurgated, and that this is the greatest and most worthy end of existence." *(Northfield Echoes,* August, 1900, p. 256.*)*

The ruins of Assyria and Egypt point to a religion resembling that of the Israelites. So far is this noticed that some have said that Moses copied much of what he taught Israel from them. This conclusion is not necessary. The fact is that man

103

had a deposit of truth at the beginning, and all men had the same. Both Moses and Egypt and Assyria therefore, had much of what survived from that early revelation. The fact here stated agrees with the Bible account and not with Evolution.

"The study of the mythology and philosophy of the heathen world does not show an evolutionary progress to a higher state, but the reverse." (Francis M. Bruner in *The Evolution Theory.*) Christianity has not been a development of these religions, for it is and was, antagonistic to them at every point. It was an opposing force introduced suddenly and utterly at variance in every particular with all about it.

Sir M. Monier said in an address in 1887: "There can be no greater mistake than to force these non-christian writings into conformity with some scientific theory of development, and then point to the Christian's Holy Bible as the crowning product of religious evolution. So far from this, these non-christian books are all developments in the wrong direction. They begin with some flashes of true light and end in utter darkness."

The Other Side of Evolution

EVOLUTION AND ETHICS.

Evolution has a system or systems of Ethics. It traces the beginning of the sense of right and wrong to the instincts of animals, such as the parental instinct, the recognition of marital rights, and the right to respective properties such as nests and burrows. So that the animal, or man, came to see that it was best on all accounts to be good to oneself and others. So Mr. Spencer's definition of right is the happiness of oneself, one's offspring and others. Acts are good or bad as they increase happiness or misery. He ignores the moral instinct and exalts expediency and utility. This is the level of the uncivilized or savage races.

Dr. James Thompson Bixby of Leipsic, makes humanity the goal of Evolution's ethics. "The test of what is morally good is the tendency of the given motive to help forward the progress of the race toward the ideal humanity." *(Ethics of Evolution,* p. 212.) Every Bible believer will see how far short these fall of the standard of holiness and happiness the Bible places before us. But when or where did any people ever aim to help forward the "ideal perfection of humanity" who did not have the mighty impulse which the Bible, and only the Bible, gives to that object?

The Other Side of Evolution

There is not even the sense of brotherhood necessary for the motive. To point natural man to that is to ask him to act outside his nature.

The law of the Struggle for Existence never taught Christian ethics. The self-sacrificing Christian has something which never came from Evolution. The Cross is the final test of Evolution. By it that theory and all other false theories are weighed in the balances and found wanting. The struggle for existence is the law of self and is the antithesis of the Cross, which is the very opposite of the struggle for existence. Nor is the struggle for existence the law of the lower creature. That law is to bring forth fruit, to propagate their species. That is the plant's goal; when it has so done it retires or dies. The little bird will struggle more fiercely for its young than for its food, or even for its life, which it imperils often to save its brood. Below the unfallen creation and regenerated humanity is the unregenerated selfish man. Not Evolution but Revolution can create Christian ethics. History does not present an instance of progress in ethics save as aided by the Bible.

The Other Side of Evolution

EVOLUTION AND CHRISTIAN EXPERIENCE.

In undertaking to account for man, Evolution must account for the fact of Christian experience. Conversion revolutionizes a man. It turns him against his natural likes and dislikes. He even turns against himself and the selfish becomes unselfish. This is not development, for that operates according to the nature of the thing. Develop a wolf and you may get a dog. Develop man from the savage state and you may have the condition of the Greek in the highest state of culture and yet in the lowest state of vice. Introduce Christian experience and you have Christianity with all the civilization which proceeds and flows from it.

There is no such consistent body of testimony for any fact, science or truth as there is for Christian experience. It is the same in all ages, in all lands and in all classes of society, and in all circumstances of life. This evidence is perfectly legitimate and must be considered by the student of human life and character. Let Evolution then account for Conversion which changes man's inner nature, and gives a life which lives contrary to natural human instincts and conduct; and Christian hopes which yearn for deliverance from sin and self and long for the highest spiritual state and hasten to meet the holy and all-seeing God.

The Other Side of Evolution

The missions of our great cities as well as those of the foreign field are full of witnesses for the transforming effect of Christian experience. The author of this book can vouch for the following from personal knowledge. A business man in Illinois became addicted partly from use in disease to alcohol and the use of morphine and also cocaine. He used all these and in excessive quantities; as much as forty grains of morphine in a day. He tried seven "cures." He visited Europe to consult specialists. He spent in all over $15,000 in seeking a cure and all in vain. By the persuasions of Christians he was led to seek relief in prayer and experienced what Christians call conversion and was immediately delivered from all his appetites. The author of this saw him three months after and found him a sober man and without any desire for drink or drugs. He saw him again a year after and he was still rejoicing in full deliverance. Since beginning this book, a correspondence was had to verify the case still further, and he is reported as follows: "In January, 1899, his weight was 113 pounds. In January, 1901, his weight was 183 pounds. He is an official member of a prominent church, a director of the Young Men's Christian Association and a great worker in both." No evolution can account for such a change. It is as great a miracle as cleansing the leper.

Prof. George Romanes of Oxford, was, it is said, brought back from infidelity to faith by the letters of a Japanese missionary friend, dealing with experimental and practical religion. Evolution asks for facts. Here are facts, and they tell not of Evolution but of Regeneration.

EVOLUTION AND CHRIST.

Evolution cannot account for Christ. Without entering here on an argument for His divinity, we simply present him and ask the evolutionist to account for such a character and life. Let us listen to what the enemies of Christianity say of Christ.

Renan said: "The incomparable man to whom the universal conscience has decreed the title of the Son of God, and that with justice. . . . Between thee and God there will be no longer any distinction."

Jean Paul Richter said: "The holiest among the mighty, the mightiest among the holy, He lifted with pierced hands empires off their hinges and turned the stream of centuries out of its channel and still governs the ages." (Dr. Liddon's *Bampton Lectures.*)

The Other Side of Evolution

Rousseau testified as follows: "What sweetness, what purity in his morals! What force, what persuasion in his instructions! His maxims how sublime! His discourses, how wise and profound! such presence of mind, such beauty and precision in his answers, such empire over his passions! It would be much harder to conceive that a number of men should have joined together to fabricate this book than that a single person should furnish out the subject to its authors. Jewish writers would never have fallen into that style, and the gospel has such strong and such inimitable marks of truth that the inventor would be more surprising than the hero." *(Emilius and Sophia,* or An Essay on Education, pp. 79, 80, 81.)

Thomas Paine: "The morality that he preached and practiced was of the most benevolent kind. It has never been excelled." *(Age of Reason,* p. 5.)

Robert Ingersoll, to M. D. Landon, in a letter giving permission to print his speeches: "In using my speeches do not use any assault I may have made on Christ which I foolishly made in my earlier life. I believe Christ was the perfect man 'Do unto others' is the perfection of religion and morality. It is the *summum bonum."* *(Homiletic Review,* November, 1899, p. 475.)

The Other Side of Evolution

Theodore Parker: "Shall we be told such a man never lived—the whole story is a lie? Suppose that Plato and Newton never lived, that their story is a lie? But who did their works and thought their thoughts? It takes a Newton to forge a Newton. What man could have fabricated Jesus? None but a Jesus." *(Discourses on Religion, pp. 362-3.)*

Napoleon Bonaparte: "Everything in Jesus Christ astonishes me. His spirit overawes me. Between him and whoever else in the world there is no possible line of comparison. I search in vain in history to find the similar to Jesus Christ, or anything which can approach the Gospel. In him we find a moral beauty before unknown, and an idea of the Supreme superior even to that which creation suggests."

To say that Jesus was an evolution of that age, as some evolutionists do say, and that we may look for even a greater in the future, is to be guilty not only of blasphemy but of gross ignorance as to the age in which Jesus came. There was nothing in that age to give rise to such a character. He came as a flash of lightning in a dark sky, or, according to the Bible figure, as the rising of the sun in the world's night.

III

CHAPTER V.

EVOLUTION UNSCIENTIFIC AND UNPHILOSOPHICAL.

Before making so serious a charge against a scientific theory as that it is both unscientific and unphilosophical, we will show that others have held a similar view and that among these are many scholars. We have already seen Prof. Paulsen's remark that Haeckel's reasonings are a "disgrace to the philosophy of Germany." Prof. George Frederick Wright calls Evolution a "fad," "the cast-off clothing of the evolutionary philosophy of fifty years ago." The Duke of Argyle says, "It is such a violation of and departure from all that we know of the existing order of things as to deprive it of all scientific base."

EVOLUTION FAILS IN ALL THE STEPS OF SCIENTIFIC PROOF.

There are four stages of proof necessary for a full demonstration.
1. Observation of facts.
2. Classification of these facts.
3. Inferences legitimately drawn therefrom.
4. Verification of these conclusions.

The Other Side of Evolution

1. It fails in its facts. That this is true is evident from the reticence of the exact scientists to commit themselves to the theory. If the facts were all that they say, these laborious and faithful laborers in the laboratory and field would acknowledge the case. In the presentation of facts, the theoretical evolutionist culls out and magnifies those looking his way and passes in silence or minifies those antagonistic to the theory. It makes much of the change of a low salt water animal into its fresh water form, and passes over the immutability of all the great species. Evolution dwells upon the splints in the leg of the horse and passes over lightly the vast unbridged gaps between organic and inorganic matter, the origin of the vertebrates, the countless missing links between the species. It rests its argument on the "gill-slits" in the necks of embryonic fish, puppies and infants, and passes airily over the origin of matter, of life, of consciousness and of Christian experience. It presents ex-parte evidence.

2. Evolution fails in classification. We have seen the testimony of Evolution itself on this point Nor is there any agreed definition of species. Not a single species has been traced to its origin. The species defy chronological classification. The most primitive species exist to-day and the most advanced were in existence almost

The Other Side of Evolution

at the first. Nor can the classifications which are attempted be advanced as proof of evolution. They are as evidential of manufacture or of creation or of any other process of intelligent mind.

3. Evolution rests on inferences. As its great philosopher, Spencer, has said, no inference is warranted unless it accounts for all the facts. Not only does no inference of Evolution do this, but it admits again and again that it is beset with countless difficulties. Nor are these inferences the only ones that might be drawn. It is not only necessary to draw an inference but to show that no other inference is possible. Some of these are the wildest possible deductions from the facts,—as for example, the theories as to the origins, already cited, as to whales and giraffes. Sir J. William Dawson, the eminent geologist, says of Evolution's deductions as follows: "It seems to indicate that the accumulated facts of our age have gone altogether beyond its capacity for generalization, and but for the vigor which one sees everywhere, it might be taken as an indication that the human mind has fallen into a state of senility and in its dotage mistakes for science the imaginations which are the dreams of its youth." *(Story of the Earth and Man*, p. 317.)

The works of writers on Evolution abound in such phrases as "seems to be—I infer—it is con-

The Other Side of Evolution

ceivable—it might have been—it is probable—I think—apparently—must have been—no one can say—not difficult to conceive,"—and other unscientific terms, and on such deductions they project other inferences, and so leap skilfully from one supposition to another across the quagmire of Evolution.

Evolution is undertaking a philosophical impossibility—the proving of a negative, that there could be no other method than derivation. This is the philosophical basis of the whole theory.

4. Finally Evolution fails in the fourth step. It admits again and again that it has not demonstrated its case. Not a single instance of evolution of species has been shown or produced, and no law of the change is given. The gaps it does not bridge are many. We specially need to notice that it gives no account of the origin of matter or force. It can give no account of the origin of life. It utterly fails to account for man's self-consciousness or intellectual, moral or spiritual nature. It takes no account whatever of the other world or life and entirely disregards the facts of Christian experience. In short, so far from being a great universal philosophy, it is simply a disjointed combination of unproven theories.

The evolutionist, Prof. Conn, admitting the missing factors, says candidly, "It is therefore impossible to make Evolution a complete theory." (*Evolution of To-day*, p. 6.)

Sir J. William Dawson thus sums up the evidence: "The simplicity and completeness of the evolutionary theory entirely disappear when we consider the unproved assumptions on which it is based and its failure to connect with each other some of the most important facts in nature; that in short, it is not in any true sense a philosophy, but a mere arbitrary arrangement of facts in accordance with a number of unproved hypotheses. Such philosophies, falsely so-called, have existed ever since man began to reason on nature, and this last of all is one of the weakest and most pernicious of all. Let the reader take up either Darwin's great book or Spencer's Biology and merely ask, as he reads each paragraph, What is here assumed and what is proved? and he will find the fabric melt away like a vision. Spencer often exaggerates or extenuates with reference to facts and uses the art of the dialectician where argument fails." (*Story of the Earth and Man*, p. 330.)

Prof. William Jones tells us Evolution is "a metaphysical creed and nothing else; an emotional attitude rather than a system of thought." (*Homiletic Review*, August, 1900.)

The Other Side of Evolution

EVOLUTION RESTS ON IMAGINATION.

The evolutionist not only uses his imagination but claims the right to do so. Tyndall has written an essay on the Scientific Use of the Imagination. Now when the pictures of an evolutionist's imagination are held up as facts, as in the description of man's development from the brute, he leaves the realm of science and enters that of fiction. Mr. Gladstone has said of this: "To the eyes of an onlooker their pace and method seem to be like a steeple-chase. They are armed with a weapon always sufficient if not always an arm of precision, 'the scientific imagination.' They are impatient of that most wholesome state a Suspended Judgment." (*Homiletic Review,* October, 1900, quoted by Dr. Jesse B. Thomas.*)*

EVOLUTION IS THE DOCTRINE OF CHANCE.

The language used by the evolutionist is peculiar for persons claiming to believe in law as the great agency of nature and to base their conclusions on the operation of fixed causes. The changes which together make up the birth of a new species are occasioned they say by "chance happenings," "undesigned variations," "accidental variations," "utterly undetermined antecedents,"

The Other Side of Evolution

"unintentional variations," and other like expressions. The synonyms of this idea are exhausted by them in describing the way in which the changes first occurred, by which one species began the journey up to another stage of existence. It is simply a revival and revamping of the old doctrine of chance.

Prof. Frank Ballard says of this: "Chance manufactured protoplasm out of nebulosity. . . To accept this after rejecting faith on the ground of its difficulty, is to quibble and cavil."

An illustration of the appeal to chance and its use is found in the following account as given by Prof. Ernst Haeckel, the greatest living teacher of Evolution, of how tree-frogs became green: "Once upon a time there were among the offspring of ancestral tree-frogs some which among other colors exhibited green, not much, perhaps not even perceptible to our eyes. The occurrence of this color was spontaneous, a freak. The descendants of these greenish creatures, provided they did not pair with frogs of the ordinary set, became still greener and so on, until the green was pronounced enough to be of advantage when competition set in." *(Last Link,* p. 176.) Here the origin of greenness in the tree-frog begins with a chance happening and is promoted by a chance union of the greenish frog with one not in

The Other Side of Evolution

"the ordinary set," but of the more select circle of the green, and the favoring chances continued in this same remarkable way until the color became of use in protecting them.

It was with similar chance happenings, Evolution tells us, that all the great kingdoms, classes, orders, families, genera and species originated. It was by chance happenings that the present beautiful and infinite variety of nature came. It was by unintended accidents that the wonderful adjustments in the universe came. It has been calculated that the possibility of the letters of the alphabet, if thrown promiscuously, coming together in the present order is once in five hundred million million million times. What would be the chances of the innumerable combinations of nature coming together in the order in which they are by the chance happenings to which Evolution attributes them?

CHAPTER VI.

EVOLUTION AND THE BIBLE.

The interest in the question of how things came to be centers for the believer in the Bible narrative and doctrine. We have been accustomed to bring all things to Bible testing and so far with assured results. The Bible has never failed and we believe will not fail now. We therefore ask, What does it teach as to Evolution? We are amazed to find Evolution makes no appeal to the Bible, and the Bible makes no allusion to Evolution. They are strangers to each other. The argument from Scripture for Evolution has not yet been written. The best the theistic evolutionist can say as to the Bible account of the origin of man is an apology for its narratives, or some explanation which vaporizes its facts into figures of speech.

We have heretofore given the Bible account and that of Evolution printed in parallel columns (p. 61). The reader is again referred to these, and asked to notice the differences in these two accounts. The Bible account is not the description of the slow transformation of an ape into a man-like ape, and that into an ape-like man, and

The Other Side of Evolution

that into a cave man, and he into a stone-tool man, and that again into a pottery-making savage, and he into a weapon-making barbarian, and he into a Chinese and after that into a Roman or Greek, and last into an Englishman and American and he into a spiritual being in the image and likeness of God. Common literary honesty demands that we give an author his own intended meaning. If the Bible meant Evolution why did it not give it? Two accounts more utterly dissimilar could scarcely be given than the Bible account of man's creation and the account of Evolution. We may take one or other and be consistent but the rules of literary exegesis and common sense and Scripture alike forbid taking both.

To call it "poetry" or an "allegory" is no explanation. Why did not the writer make poetry or allegory which had some agreement with facts? Why lead us into a perplexing situation when he might as well have given us some other account or omitted it altogether?

The differences between these two accounts are obvious. The Bible account describes a definite act, the Evolution account a long-continued process through millions of years. The Bible account is a production *de novo* of a new and original creature; the Evolution account gives one of a numerous line of ancestors; the Bible

The Other Side of Evolution

account presents us with a perfect creature "in the likeness of God;" the Evolution account with a brute slightly raised above the common herd. The Bible account gives a descriptive narrative with accompanying events; the Evolution account leaves all the events unknown save as guessed at by the imagination of the various writers. The Bible account gives a high and noble origin by a special and creative act of his Creator; Evolution tells of a degraded origin from a brute by the operation of blind forces. The Bible account is noble and satisfying and, to one who believes in an omnipotent God, credible, calling for belief in one creative act; the Evolution account is filled with difficulties and paradoxes calling for the wildest stretch of imagination and the utmost application of credulity.

The Bible account is frequently referred to as an actual history by other Scripture writers; the evolutionary account has not one Scripture reference or the slightest hint from Scripture of its having any place whatever in fact. The Bible account agrees with and is the basis of the spiritual teachings of the Bible; the evolutionary account has no such agreement and needs to be explained away to be allowed any place whatever in sacred writings. If the Bible is the book the common consent of the wisest of all mankind and of every age has affirmed it to be, it should have some intimation of this "greatest discovery of the human mind." For the Bible does touch on the greatest problems of the world and life.

Not only does the Bible give a very different account of the origin of man, but also of nature. Its definition of the beginning of things is as follows: "By faith we understand that the worlds have been framed by the word of God, so that what is seen hath not been made out of things which do appear." (Heb. 11:3.) The term it applies to this is Creation. It gives also a circumstantial account of the coming of the present order as we have it, closing with man's creation.

EVOLUTION'S INTERPRETATION OF THE BIBLE.

In order to bring the evolutionary theories within the possibility of Bible sanction, a theory of interpretation is adopted which calls the narratives of Creation and the Fall myths, legends, allegories, parables, "scenic representation," or "idealized history" according to the theological bias of the interpreter. These all amount to the same thing, for they do away with the historical value of the accounts. It is only a play upon words to say they are "parables" for parables are not unhistorical. Every one of Christ's parables is true to life and facts. It is claimed that the Bible narratives are poetry and therefore are not historical. The evolutionist for his purpose confounds poetry and fiction. They are not synonymous. A poetical form does not imply fictitiousness. The Psalms have much history under their poetical form. But the first chapter of Genesis is not poetry. Hebrew poetry has a well-defined form as seen in the poetical books. This chapter does not conform to that form, and accordingly it is printed not in poetical form but as prose in the Revised Version. The mere repetition of certain phrases is not the mark of poetry, but is characteristic of the oriental languages in which the Bible was written.

But who is to decide what in the Bible is historical and what is not? What is to hinder anyone from so discarding any fact whatever in the Bible? Why has not the enemy of Christianity the same right to apply this reasoning to the accounts of the death and resurrection of Christ? Where will this process end? The proclaimer of such theories is putting a weapon into the hands of the opponent of Christianity that he will use one day to the destruction of the faith of many. Once having permission to apply these terms, it is easy to make these narratives, or anything else in the Bible. mean anything or nothing as is desired.

The Other Side of Evolution

As an ancient writer said, "Twenty doctors can make a text read twenty different ways." We protest against this loose method of interpretation for many reasons:

1. We object to every new theory interpreting the Bible to suit itself.

2. There is not the slightest warrant in these narratives or elsewhere for such interpretation. They are given as facts and are always so treated. Creation and the Fall are everywhere spoken of as actual facts both by Christ and all other Scripture writers.

3. It is on this system of interpretation that every false system rests, such as Mormonism. All the modern vagaries support themselves from Scripture by accommodation of its language to their doctrines.

4. The Bible is not a book of puzzles, a delphic oracle, to be read in any way suited to the occasion or desires. It has a plain meaning and is for everyday people and everyday needs.

5. The acceptance of the Bible account as unquestioned fact and the literal interpretation of it by Christ and his apostles ought to be enough for anyone calling himself Christian or even for any other who will accept good human testimony. These writers were 1900 years nearer the date of the events in question than we. They had access

The Other Side of Evolution

to knowledge now lost to us. From any standpoint, we may rest our view of these narratives on the testimony of the New Testament Scriptures. The references of the New Testament to the Old are numbered by hundreds. Any Bible with references, or any text book or Bible with Helps will show these. It is enough here to give those Christ refers to.

Christ himself cites from twelve books and about twenty-four narratives as follows: Creation, Matt. 19:4; Law of Marriage, Matt. 19:5; Cain and Abel, Matt. 23:35; The Deluge, Matt. 24:37; Abraham, John 8:56; Sodom and Gomorrah and Lot's wife, Luke 17:28-32; Manna, John 6:49; Brazen Serpent, John 3:14; Shew Bread, Matt. 12:3, 4; Elijah and his Miracles, Luke 4:25, 26; Naaman, Luke 4:27; Tyre and Sidon, Matt. 11:22; Jonah and "The Whale," Matt. 12:39; The Books of Moses, John 5:46; The Psalms, Luke 20:42; Moses and The Prophets, Luke 24:27; Isaiah, Matt. 13:14; Daniel's Prophecies, Matt. 24:15; Malachi, Matt. 11:10; The entire Old Testament, Luke 24:44. Of not one of these does he convey the slightest hint of aught but trustworthiness and literal interpretation.

6. The still more serious issue is presented of asserting that both Paul and Christ either did not know that these were myths, or knowing so gave

The Other Side of Evolution

no intimation that they used them in any way other than as true narratives. This would not only shake all confidence in Christ as divine and his apostles as inspired, but would shake all confidence in any fact or teaching from Scripture whatever. For Scripture rests on facts and these facts on witnesses. To these, appeal is constantly made. On the truth of these all depends. Here then is a "mythical" Adam made the basis of marriage; a "mythical" Adam and his fall, the argument for man's need and Christ's work, and the same "mythical" Adam made the proof of the resurrection. In short the whole system of Bible truth is attacked by these theories, from credibility in Christ himself to the last hope of the believer in the world to come.

Whom shall we believe? Shall we credit Evolution which admits that its theory is unproven and full of difficulties, with not a single case of Evolution to support it, nor a power which could produce it, and with countless facts to antagonize it, or shall we believe Jesus Christ who was never mistaken, or false in his facts, or teachings, and who believed these chapters, cited them and accepted their narratives without question?

The Other Side of Evolution

EVOLUTION AND BIBLE DOCTRINES.

We have arrived at the vital point in this discussion. If Evolution were only a scientific question, it would interest a limited circle. As a deeply religious question it interests all. That Evolution affects vitally all evangelical belief is apparent to the most superficial inquirer. It is not only a matter of historic fact but of doctrinal teaching. Man's nature and need as a descendant from the brute is one thing, and as a spiritual being, fallen from the likeness of God, another. The responsibility in either case is very different and therefore has to do with eternal destiny for weal or woe, and also with the work of Christ.

The theology of the Higher Criticism which is also the theology of Evolution, of which it is the Biblical branch, is thus summed up by an evolutionary writer, in a recent article giving the articles of belief of the theology of Evolution: "The Bible can no longer speak with unquestioned authority. . . . Poor old Adam disappears. . . . Christ's divinity is only such as we may possess. . . . the atonement is only such as we see in all life and nature. . . As to the future life we find ourselves left very much in the dark. . . . We no longer regard going to heaven as the center of our interest." (Theodore D. Bacon quoted in *Homiletic Review*, Nov. 1902.)

Evolution teaches, as stated by Dr. George A. Gordon, of Boston: "Man's state and fate is on account of the irrationality he has brought up with him from the animal world." *(Immortality and the New Theodicy,"* p. 100.) The future of man according to Evolution is that as he has risen from the brute state he ought not to be punished for his defects but rather rewarded for having done so well. Evolution teaches that man has in himself the elements of his salvation. These if developed will produce the change he needs for this world and that to come. He will proceed on the same lines as he has traveled to reach his present state. Development is the Saviour of Evolution. The Bible says that to develop man is to develop sin and, "Sin when it is finished bringeth forth death." It requires the intervention of the Supernatural in Regeneration to save man. Evolution is self-saving.

The future is radically affected by the theory of Evolution. The development of mankind is its objective point. To bring man to a point of development will bring the Kingdom of Heaven. The fate of the individual is not made much of.

The Other Side of Evolution

He is sacrificed for the race or species. But while not much is made of the individual the general teaching is that somehow it will be well with all at last. It is a fact that all universalists are evolutionists. Evolution makes Heaven and Hell terms which mean little or nothing. The present social state of man is the great quest. Evolution is a bridge which reaches neither shore. It knows not whence man came nor where he goes.

1. The Bible rests its doctrines upon its facts. There is no character in Scripture aside from Christ upon whose historical character so much Scripture doctrine depends as upon Adam. The creation of man is made the basis for the sanctity of marriage by Christ, who quotes the words of the account in Genesis. (Matt. 19:4-6; Mark 10:6-9.) Paul makes this narrative the basis of his great argument for the state and need of man and the work of Christ. "Through one man sin entered into the world and death through sin. . . . Death reigned from Adam to Moses. . . . By the trespass of the one the many died . . . the judgment came of one unto condemnation . . . as through the one man's disobedience the many were made sinners, even so through the obedience of the one shall the many be made righteous." (Rom. 5:12-21, R. V.) Here the

The Other Side of Evolution

actuality of the narrative is the very basis of the declaration of man's state in sin and a type of the extent and nature of Christ's work. So also the use by Paul in the account of the resurrection doctrine: "As in Adam all die, so also in Christ shall all be made alive." (1 Cor. 15:22-45.)

2. The Bible teaches that man was made in the image of God. That image was Christ who is elsewhere declared to be "the effulgence of his glory and the very image of his substance." (Heb. 1:3.) In this image man was made. This is a very different picture presented to us from that given by the evolutionist of a brute "which could stand on its hind legs and throw things with its forelegs."

3. The Bible teaches that all are guilty and condemned and lost, and without excuse. It teaches that man fell from a high state as a race and as a race is responsible for his condition. It cites death as the proof of this. It teaches that man is inherently averse to God by nature and wilfully continues to do wrong and in short is condemned and lost. It teaches that he once had the truth and wilfully gave it up for sin. That he does so now in spite of the law of God written in his conscience and that out of Christ he is lost and without hope. (Rom. 1-5; Ep. 2:1-3, 11, 12.)

4. The Bible teaches that what man needs is a

pardon, a reconciliation with God, a ransom, a regeneration, a resurrection. He must be translated from death to life, from the kingdom of darkness to that of light. If he has not all this he is lost and doomed.

5. The Bible teaches that in order that man might enjoy this, Christ had to come and die, "the just for the unjust that he might bring us to God." He died as a sacrifice, as an offering, as a ransom, as a propitiation, as a reconciliation. His death made it possible in justice as well as in mercy to save man.

6. The Bible gives a description of man's means of salvation which is most opposite to the hope held out by Evolution. It is by a radical and supernatural change that he becomes right and only as all men so change or are changed will the world become right. Conversion is not Evolution but regeneration, the implanting of a new and opposite nature.

7. The Bible teaches a different outcome of human life and history. It points to an end by supernatural means to the world and a judgment for mankind and the establishment of the Kingdom of Heaven by supernatural means. It cites the destruction of Sodom and Gomorrah and the Deluge as examples of the world's end. It gives the most awful combination of earthly figures as

The Other Side of Evolution

the picture of the doom of the impenitent and the most beautiful figures earth and sky can furnish or the mind of man conceive as the home of the saved. Nothing could be more different than the theologies of Evolution and of the Bible.

Many well-meant volumes have been written to reconcile Evolution and evangelical belief. None are satisfying, although the eagerness with which some were at first received are witness to the desire to retain both beliefs.

The theistic evolutionist thinks that to find a place for the Creator somewhere along the line is enough. St. James rebukes this insufficient theology in these words: "Thou believest that there is one God; thou doest well: the devils also believe, and tremble." (Jas. 2:19.) So also Christ himself said: "Ye believe in God believe also in me. . . . I am the way, the truth and the life. . . . No man cometh unto the Father but by me. . . . He that honoreth not the Son honoreth not the Father which hath sent him. . . . For as the Father hath life in himself even so gave he to the Son also to have life in himself. . . . He hath committed all judgment unto the Son that all men may honor the Son even as they honor the Father. He that honoreth not the Son honoreth not the Father." Theism then is not enough in the opinion of Jesus Christ.

The Other Side of Evolution

The whole Christian system is in question in this theory. The whole aim of Evolution is to dispose of the supernatural as much as possible. The radical evolutionist gets rid of God entirely he thinks. The theistic evolutionist limits the interference of the supernatural to the creation of matter, of life, of man's spiritual nature, and the incarnation and work of Christ. The tendency of evolution is to make the miracles of Christ mythical and the phenomena of conversion natural. The theistic evolutionist is on a side hill. He must go up or down. He is not consistent, and, as the human mind asserts its right to consistency, he is forced, willingly or unwillingly, often unconsciously, to the one side or the other, and he finds himself led along lines which take him far from evangelical belief. In its consistent form, Evolution leaves no room for a Creator. Indeed Haeckel, the greatest of living evolutionists and the legitimate successor to Darwin's place and greatness, states, as already quoted, thus: "It entirely excludes supernatural process, every prearranged and conscious act of a personal character. Nothing will make the full meaning of the theory of descent clearer than calling it the non-miraculous theory of creation." *(History of Creation, pp. 397, 422.)* Another evolutionist,

The Other Side of Evolution

Carl Vogt, says: "Evolution turns the Creator out of doors." Infidels all accept of it gladly. Every atheist is an evolutionist.

EVOLUTION A RELIC OF HEATHENISM.

James Freeman Clark thus writes: "In the system of the Greek and Scandinavian mythology, spirit is evolved from matter; matter up to spirit works. They begin with the lowest form of being; night, chaos, a mundane egg, and evolve the higher gods therefrom." *(Ten Great Religions,* p. 231.)

Sir J. William Dawson, the late eminent geologist of Canada, writes of the theory as follows: "The evolutionist doctrine is one of the strangest phenomena of humanity. It existed most naturally in the oldest philosophy and poetry, in connection with the crudest and most uncritical attempts of the human mind to grasp the system of nature; but that in our day a system destitute of any shadow of proof, and supported merely by vague analogies and figures of speech and by arbitrary and artificial coherence of its own parts, should be accepted as a philosophy and should find able adherents to string upon its thread of hypothesis our vast and weighty stores of knowledge, is surpassingly strange." *(Story of the Earth and Man, p. 317.)*

Evolution is working towards a pantheistic atheism. This is expressed in the creed of the late Cecil Rhodes, the late magnate of South Africa, as follows: "I believe in Force Almighty, the ruler of the universe, working scientifically through natural selection to bring about the survival of the fittest and the elimination of the unfit."

CHAPTER VII.

THE SPIRITUAL EFFECT OF EVOLUTION.

It is apparent that the adoption of such a theory as Evolution must affect the spiritual state of the person receiving it. Man's mental and spiritual natures are intimately connected. While those in a settled previous spiritual experience may carry Evolution as " a working theory" only, those in an immature state will be vitally affected. Especially is this true of youthful minds. It is indeed a fact that many young men have started with high purposes to prepare for the ministry, and even for foreign missions, and have, after adopting these modern theories, abandoned their purpose, and thousands have abandoned all personal religion. Pastors can tell of many such instances.

Some have said that the adoption of Evolution has helped their faith. They fail to see that bringing the Bible down to their faith is not bringing their faith up to the Bible. It is a weakening of faith and not a strengthening of it. This apparent increase of faith simply prepares the way for its utter ruin. The first step leads to a wider divergence, as many have shown, that leads to wreck of all faith in a supernatural God or world or Bible. The mind will follow its natural workings. Loss of faith in the facts of the Bible leads to loss of faith in its truths. The acceptance of this theory still further leads to a lessening of the sense of our need of Christ that the Bible teaches and man should feel. And further the acceptance of this theory, while it may not affect materially the minds of experienced Christians, will through them affect others.

There is also a latent unconscious loss of faith that is realized only in some great emergency, when in "the storm and stress" of life the soul looks out for something to hold to. It is then that the rotting platform of unbelief goes down in wreck. The other extreme is also a cause of ruin. In the time of great prosperity when all the allurements of life and time and sense present themselves, it requires all the purpose one has to stem the tide of temptations. It is here that a false belief will work havoc. The mind conceives that after all sin is not so hateful or salvation so needed or doom so fearful.

The effect on experimental personal experience is evident. Instead of looking for a regeneration, a revolution of the inner state, the believer in Evolution necessarily looks for a change from education or other form of development. Such a thing as conversion or a baptism of the Holy Ghost he will cease to look for or desire. There will come declining feeling, lessening devotion, prayer will become perfunctory and there will come increasing occupation with and love for other things. Evolution as a belief makes right many things that were before held to be wrong. It is an easy religion to hold. It strikes the world at the angle of least resistance and enables the holder to accept almost anything that the natural man desires. The conflict of "the flesh and the spirit" ceases; the flesh, that is the natural man, has conquered.

These theories in many seem to be but evidences of a previous wrong state of heart. The wish is father to the thought. The theory is accepted because it allows the laying aside of views that restrain the desires. Such persons are willing to admit the existence of God and his contact with man at Creation if relieved from any nearer relationship. It is therefore worse than unbelief. It is antagonism. It is enmity. Christ said, "Men love darkness rather than light because their deeds are evil." The heart and life are the basis of their opinions. It is evident that argument here fails. "A man convinced against his will remains an unbeliever still."

The Other Side of Evolution

Evolution is a comfortable theory to the world. It elevates man. It hides the presence of God. It calls for no repentance or consecration. It boasts of human progress and claims merit therefor. In short it is the worship of man rather than the worship of God. It deifies man and it ignores Christ. Once committed to this theory, there is no extreme the person may not reach. Some have abandoned Christ and Christianity because of it. It is in fact in doctrine and experience and conduct, the antithesis of Christianity.

Such a theory as Evolution and its vaporizing method of Bible interpretation, prepares the way for "isms" of every kind. It is to this we are indebted for the swarm of these that afflicts the church to-day. Once allow that the Bible may be interpreted to suit such theories and any heresy or absurdity can prove its position from the Bible as all of them by this same process do.

It is already weakening the power of the pulpit, and this in turn is one great reason for the declining effect of the preached word. Once received into a minister's heart the edge of his sword is dulled if indeed the sword is not itself sheathed. He may not preach Evolution either as a method of creation or a method of salvation, but his own inner faith is weakened in the old truth which had such power to convert the souls of hearers. When

The Other Side of Evolution

openly advocated and taught, it is useless to seek revivals among those so taught. So it is the fact that conversions to-day are mainly confined to the young and others not affected by the error.

All the indications point to the further weakening of the hold upon men of the supernatural and the eternal. To eliminate the former and, while acknowledging the latter, to disparage all reference to the future life, seems to be the tendency of the day. As already cited, one of its chief advocates tells us, "Heaven is no longer the center of the Christian's hope." The consequence is the material and intellectual interests receive chief attention and other agencies take the chief place religion should have. Education received in the United States over $200,000,000 in gifts during the last few years, to say nothing of the many fold more received from incomes and public funds. Meanwhile the causes of Christ are languishing, missions are dwarfed, small churches in great masses of the population are struggling for existence against fearful odds, while the money of professed Christians pours in these mighty streams for all other purposes. No sensible person will disparage education, but "Religion is the chief concern of mortals here below."

Further it is the few who can take advantage of the higher education for which these millions

The Other Side of Evolution

are given. But five per cent of the common school scholars can attend college. The many must toil for existence. It is to the poor the gospel was preached by its Founder. It is to the poor it means most. To those who have little else it is the all in all. It is to these it should be preached in its freedom and fullness. The principles of natural selection of the fittest which sends millions to higher institutions and neglects the masses of the people is the opposite of the gospel.

Cardinal Newman wrote: "There is a special effort made almost all over the world, but most visibly and formidably in its most civilized and powerful part, to do without religion. . . . Truly there is at this time a confederacy of evil marshalling its hosts from all parts of the world, organizing itself and taking measures enclosing the church of Christ as in a net and preparing the way for a general apostasy." *(Quoted in "Christianity and Anti-Christianity."* S. J. Andrews, p. 4.) Whether this is the final form of unbelief is difficult to say. It bears the marks of antichristianity the apostle speaks of. The unbelief of the latter days will rest on belief in the unvarying stability of nature. (2 Peter 3:4.) The coming of this theory is aimed to dissipate any looking for supernatural changes such as the

142

The Other Side of Evolution

Scriptures teach are coming to earth, such as the last day, the coming of Christ, the resurrection and all the vast series of changes therein declared. Hence that wholesome fear of God so operative in deterring evil and stimulating good is removed. Based on this unbelief, the enemy of God and man can advance to the accomplishment of his purposes as never before. All satanic methods before this have been crude and coarse compared with this last invention. It is the most subtle and sweeping of all evil methods to ensnare the mind of man. Based on what is called science, promoted by the scholars of the day, taught in the fountains of learning and preached from pulpit and platform, it must have a widespread effect. Heretofore attacks on Christianity have been made from without. This is from within. It is the trusted leaders who are now undermining the fortress in which they live.

But revivals always begin at the bottom. It was a few poor fishermen who commenced the gospel age. It is their successors to whom we must look as we have in the past for return of apostolic power. "God chose the foolish things of the world that He might put to shame them that are wise; and God chose the weak things of the world that He might put to shame the things that are strong; and the base things of the world, and the things that are despised did God choose, yea and the things that are not, that he might bring to naught the things that are: that no flesh should glory before God." (1 Cor. 1:27, 28, R. V.) So we look hopefully to God for that only which will deliver the church from this and all other pestilent evils, theoretical and practical, a revival of true religion by the power of the Holy Spirit, and the preaching of the old gospel of the cross of Christ.

INDEX.

	Page
Abbeville, peat beds	90
Abbott, Dr. Lyman	xi, 3
Abydos tombs	92
Adam	77–127
Adjustments, complex	56
Adaptation of species	55
Agassiz	13, 50
Age of earth	15
Antiquity of man	90
Ape-man	75
Ape, relics of	68
Assyrian antiquity	93
Assyrian religion	103
Armadillo	43
Architecture of body	58
Askenazy	9
Aurora Borealis	16
Authors, list of	xiv
Babylonian civilization	99–103
Backbone, origin of	31
Baer, Carl Ernest von	9
Balfour, Prof. Francis M	59
Ballard, Prof. Frank	118
Barrande, Joachim	38
Barrows, Dr. John Henry	62

Index

	Page
Beaumont, M.	16
Bee, cell of	57
Bermuda lizards	44
Bible account	61
Bible interpretation	121, 123
Bible theology	131
Bonaparte, Napoleon	111
Bowers, Prof. Stephen	81
Brain, argument from	84
Brewster, Sir David	59
Brown, A.	4
Bruner, F. M.	104
Bunge	9
Calavaras skull	80
Carlyle, Thomas	9
Chamerlain, Dr. Jacob	103
Chance	115
Chimpanzee	74
Christ	109
Christ and the Old Testament	126
Christian experience	107
Classification	41
Clodd, Edward	17, 29, 73, 75, 83, 84, 85
Colorado skeleton	81
Conn, Prof. H. W.	5, 25, 27, 29, 30, 39, 42, 48, 50, 96, 115
Concensus of scholarship	10
Congo languages	87
Cook, Dr. Joseph	13
Cope, E. D.	53
Coral theory	13
Croatian skeleton	81
Cross, test of evolution	106

146

Index

	Page
Crystallization	57
Dana, Prof.	42, 64, 86, 89
Darwin, Chas.	5, 17, 29, 41, 55, 61, 87
Darwinism	29
Dawson, Sir J. W.	9, 36, 95, 114, 116, 135
Degeneration	53
De Rouge	102
Distribution	43
DuBois, Dr. Von Eugene	82
Earth, age temperature	15, 20, 23, 58
Egypt, mummied animals	53, 85
Egyptian dynasties	92
Egyptian civilization	100
Embryology	49
Eohippus	46
Etheridge, Dr.	9, 59
Ethics	105
Evolution—Meaning	1
Definitions	3
Unproven	5
Scientists reject	7
Cause of	30
No case of	26
Geology against	38
Phantom tree	42
Mental	89
Unverified	112
Chance	115
Bible	120
Conversion	107
Eyes, origin of	32

Index

	Page
Fiske, Prof. John	85
Force, origin of	18
Fossils	59
Foval	8
French Institute	12
Galileo	12
Galton	101
Geology, argument from	37
Geologist, testimony of	38
Germ, the	50
Giraffe, origin of	33
Gladstone	117
Green frogs	118
Great Pyramid	100
Greeks	101
Gregory, Dr. D. S.	8
Grote, Dr.	8
Haeckel, Ernst	xiv, 3, 5, 8, 9, 19, 23, 39, 41, 118
Haecke, Dr. W.	8
Harmann, Otto	9
Harnack, Prof.	13
Harrison, Frederick	14
Hartmann	102
Heathen origin	135
Heer, Oswald	8
Herschell	15
Hilyrecht, Prof.	19
Hindu Vedas	103
History	98
Higher Criticism	13, 94
Hoffmann	9

148

Index

	Page
Home of primeval man	72
Howison, Prof. Geo	xiv, 86
Human characteristics	70
Humphrey, Gen	16
Huxley	6, 13, 25, 29, 30, 44, 45, 48, 69, 72
Ingersoll, Robt.	110
Jones, Prof. Wm.	116
Kelvin, Lord	18, 24, 74 86
Kangaroo	43
Kent Cavern	16
Kipling	74
Koelliker	8
Land, animals, origin of	33
Lang, Andrew	102
Lange	99
Language	86
Lecky	101
Le Conte, Prof. Joseph	3, 23, 24, 40
Legs, origin of	32
Liebig	24
Life, origin of	23
Livingston, Dr.	91
Lyell	16
Making of a man	73
Mathematical adjustments	56
Matter, origin of	17
Mental changes	90
Mentone skeleton	89
Meyer, Dr.	81

149

Index

	Page
Mind and consciousness	85
Missing link	78
Mississippi Delta	16
Molecular creation	50
Monier, Sir M.	104
Monkey language	88
Moon, mountains of	15
Morphological argument	44
Muller, Prof. Max	86, 87, 97
Murchison, Sir Roderick	38
McLaughlin	57
Naegali	8
Natural selection	29, 34
Neanderthal Skull	80
Nebular Hypothesis	21
New Orleans skeleton	91
Newman Cardinal	142
Origin of life	23
Orion, Nebula	21
Paine, Thomas	viii, 110
Parker, Theodore	110
Patterson, Dr. Robert	40, 70
Pattison, S. R.	95
Patton, Prest. Francis L.	xiv
Paulsen, Prof.	8
Petrie, Prof. Flinders	110
Pfaff, Dr. Frederick	79, 85, 95
Pflieder, Prof.	62
Pithecanthropus-Erectus	82
Poetry	121
Post, Dr. Geo. E.	9

150

Index

	Page
Prehistoric man.	89
Protoplasm.	49
Quatrafoges	45
Religion.	102
Renan.	109
Renouf.	102
Reymond, DuBois.	9
Rhode , Cecil.	136
Richter, Jean Paul.	109
Ridpath, J. Clark.	41
Rocks, origin of.	37
Romans.	103
Rousseau.	110
Rudimentary organs.	67
Ruskin.	9, 67
Savage Races.	96
St. Pierre.	13
Sayce, Prof. A. H.	93, 100
Schliemann.	13, 91
Schmidt, Dr. Rudolph.	5
Schults, D. Kerfort.	41
Scientific theories.	15
Sedgwick, Adam.	40
See, Prof.	19
Simultaneousness.	42
Snell.	8
Solar System.	19
Species, evolution of.	26
Spencer, Herbert	xv, 2, 14, 17, 20, 31, 41, 105, 114
Spiritual effect.	137

151

Index

	Page
Star, Prof. F	101
Stone age	91
Stuckenburg, Dr. J. H. W	8
Succession	2, 37
Sully, Prof. James	62
Swim-Bladder	48
Taj, Mahal	97
Terra Del Fuego	87
Theistic Evolution	4, 77
"Theistic," Adam	77
Theology of Evolution	128
Thomas, Dr. Jessie B	28
Thomson, Sir. Wm	13, 34
Thomson, Dr. J. Arthur	30, 51
Thompson, Dr. James	105
Troy	13
Tyndall	2, 5, 20, 24, 50, 52
Universe, evolution of	17
order of	19
Varieties	28
Vedas, Hindu	103
Virchow, Dr. Rudolph	7, 9, 65, 82
Wagner, M	8
Wallace	66, 83
Whales origin	33
White, Andrew	12
Whitney, Prof	5
Wiseman, Cardinal	12
Wilson Woodrow	15
Wilson, on the cell	25

Index

	Page
Wilson, Andrew	55
Winchell	26, 94
Wright, Geo. Frederick	xv, 12, 21, 58, 95, 112
Zahm, Dr. J. A.	6, 12, 90, 94
Zoeckler	9

A COMMENDATION AND AN APPEAL FROM DR. GRAY

After the Bible, a concordance, a Bible dictionary and, perhaps, an all-round work like Angus' "Bible Hand-Book," the next book I would recommend as indispensable for the library of the pastor, missionary or Christian worker of to-day is, "Christianity and Anti-Christianity in Their Final Conflict," by Rev. Samuel J. Andrews, he who wrote "The Life of Our Lord," which is recognized as the best history of Christ from the chronological standpoint ever published.

Dr. Andrews was not only a Bible student of exceptional insight and breadth of vision, but a prophet for these times beyond any man I know.

In this work he is dealing with the conflict in which we are now engaged, treating, first, of the teachings of the Old and New Testaments respecting the Antichrist and the falling away of the Church, and then the tendencies which are preparing the way for the final climax of the age. These tendencies include modern philosophy, Biblical criticism, science, literature and Christian socialism, leading up to the deification of humanity. The book concludes with a foreview of the actual reign of the Antichrist on earth as the head of the nations, and a study of the Church of that period.

Pastors, missionaries, Sunday-school teachers and social workers, bear with me if I say, **YOU MUST READ THIS BOOK.** Here are no wild fancies, no foolish setting of times and seasons, no crude and sensational interpretations of prophecy, but a calm setting forth of **WHAT THE BIBLE SAYS ON THE MOST IMPORTANT SUBJECT FOR THESE TIMES.** The Christian leader who does not know these things is **NO** leader, but the blind leading the blind. And, oh, there are so many of such leaders! JAMES M. GRAY.

The Moody Bible Institute of Chicago

=== NOW READY IN REVISED EDITION ===

CHRISTIANITY AND ANTI-CHRISTIANITY
IN THEIR FINAL CONFLICT
By Rev. Samuel J. Andrews
Fine cloth covers, 392 pages, 6¼x9¼ inches

Price, $2.00 net; postage 15c.

The Bible Institute Colportage Association
826 North LaSalle Street, CHICAGO

AT THE DEATHBED of DARWINISM

A SERIES OF PAPERS

By E. DENNERT, Ph. D.

Authorized Translation

By E. V. O'HARRA and JOHN H. PESCHGES

1904
GERMAN LITERARY BOARD
Burlington, Iowa

Copyright 1904
By R. NEUMANN

CONTENTS

PREFACE 9

INTRODUCTION 27

CHAPTER I.—The Return to Wigand—The Botanist, Julius von Sachs—The Vienna Zoologist, Dr. Schneider 35

CHAPTER II.—Professor Goethe on "The Present Status of Darwinism"—Explains the Reluctance of certain men of Science to Discard Darwinism.. 41

CHAPTER III.—Professor Korchinsky Rejects Darwinism—His Theory of Heterogenesis—Professor Haberlandt of Graz—Demonstration of a "Vital Force"—Its Nature—The Sudden Origination of a New Organ—Importance of the Experiment. 49

CHAPTER IV.—Testimony of a Palaeontologist, Professor Steinmann—On Haeckel's Family Trees—The Principle of Multiple Origin—Extinction of the Saurians—"Darwinism Not the Alpha and Omega of the Doctrine of Descent"—Steinmann's Conclusions 60

CHAPTER V.—Eimer's Theory of Organic Growth—Definite Lines of Development—Rejects Darwin's Theory of Fluctuating Variations—Opposes Weismann—Repudiates Darwinian "Mimicry"—Discards the "Romantic" Hypothesis of Sexual Selection—"Transmutation is a Physiological Process, a Phyletic Growth"..................... 69

CHAPTER VI.—Admissions of a Darwinian—Professor von Wagner's Explanation of the Decay of Darwinism—Darwinism Rejects the Inductive Method, Hence Unscientific—Wagner's Contradictory Assertions........................... 90

CHAPTER VII.—Haeckel's Latest Production—His Extreme Modesty—Reception of the Welt-raetsel—Schmidt's Apologia—The Romanes Incident—Men of Science Who Convicted Haeckel of Deliberate Fraud.......................... 104

CHAPTER VIII.—Grottewitz Writes on "Darwinian Myths"—Darwinism Incapable of Scientific Proof—"The Principle of Gradual Development Certainly Untenable"—"Darwin's Theory of "Chance" a Myth" 118

CHAPTER IX.—Professor Fleischmann of Erlangen—Doctrine of Descent Not Substantiated—Missing Links—"Collapse of Haeckel's Theory"—Descent Hypothesis "Antiquated"—Fleischmann Formerly a Darwinian—Haeckel's Disreputable Methods of Defense................. 124

CHAPTER X.—Hertwig, the Berlin Anatomist, Protests Against the Materialistic View of Life"—No Empiric Proof of Darwinism—"The Impotence of Natural Selection"—Rejects Haeckel's "Biogenetic Law" 137

CONCLUSION.—Darwinism Abandoned by Men of Science—Supplanted by a Theory in Harmony With Theistic Principles...................... 146

PREFACE.

The general tendency of recent scientific literature dealing with the problem of organic evolution may fairly be characterized as distinctly and prevailingly unfavorable to the Darwinian theory of Natural Selection. In the series of chapters herewith offered for the first time to English readers, Dr. Dennert has brought together testimonies which leave no room for doubt about the decadence of the Darwinian theory in the highest scientific circles in Germany. And outside of Germany the same sentiment is shared generally by the leaders of scientific thought. That the popularizers of evolutionary conceptions have any anti-Darwinian tendencies cannot, of course, be for a moment maintained. For who would undertake to popularize what is not novel or striking? But a study of the best scientific literature reveals the fact that the attitude assumed by one of our foremost American zoologists, Professor Thomas Hunt Morgan, in his recent work on "Evolution and Adaptation," is far more general among the leading men of science than is popularly supposed. Professor Morgan's position may be stated thus: He adheres to the general theory of Descent, i.e., he believes the simplest explanation which has yet been offered of the structural *similarities* between species within the same group, is the hypothesis of a common descent from a parent species. But he emphatically rejects the notion—and this is the quintessence of Darwinism—that the *dissimilarities* between species have been brought about by the purely mechanical agency of natural selection.

To find out what, precisely, Darwin meant by the term "natural selection" let us turn for a moment, to his great work, *The Origin of Species by Means of Natural Selection*. In the second chapter of that work, Darwin observes that small "fortuitous" variations in individual organisms, though of small interest to the systematist, are of the "highest importance" for his theory, since these minute variations often confer on the possessor of them, some advantage over his fellows in the quest for the necessaries of life. Thus these chance individual variations become the "first steps" towards slight varieties, which, in turn, lead to sub-species, and, finally, to species. Varieties, in fact, are "incipient species." Hence, small "fortuitous" fluctuating, individual variations—i. e., those which chance to occur without predetermined direction—are the "first-steps" in the origin of species. This is the first element in the Darwinian theory.

In the third chapter of the same work we read: "It has been seen in the last chapter that amongst organic beings in a state of nature there is some individual variability. * * * But the mere existence of individual variability and of some few well-marked varieties, though necessary as a *foundation* of the work, helps us but little in understanding how species arise in nature. How have all those exquisite adaptations of one part of the organization to another part, and to the conditions of life, and of one organic being to another being, been perfected? * * * Again it may be asked, how is it that varieties, which I have called incipient species, become ultimately converted into good and distinct species, which in most cases obviously differ from each other far more than do the varieties of the same species? How do those groups of species which constitute what are called distinct genera arise? All of these results follow from the *struggle for life.* Owing to this struggle, variations, however slight and from whatever cause proceeding, if they be in any degree profitable to the individuals of a species, in their infinitely complex relations to other organic beings, and to their physical conditions of life, will tend to the preservation of such individuals and will generally be inherited by the offspring. The offspring also will thus have a better chance of surviving, for of the many individuals of any species which are periodically born, but a small number can survive. I have called this principle by which each slight variation, if useful, is preserved, by the term, "natural selection." Mr. Darwin adds that his meaning would be more accurately expressed by a phrase of Mr. Spencer's coinage, "Survival of the Fittest."

It may be observed that neither "natural selection" nor "survival of the fittest" gives very accurate expression to the idea which Darwin seems to wish to convey. Natural selection is at best a metaphorical description of a process, and "survival of the fittest" describes the result of that process. Nor shall we find the moving principle of evolution in individual variability unless we choose to regard chance as an efficient agency. Consequently, the only efficient principle conceivably connected with the process is the "struggle for existence;" and even this has only a purely negative function in the origination of species or of adaptations. For, the "surviving fittest" owe nothing more to the struggle for existence than our pensioned veterans owe to the death-dealing bullets which did *not* hit them. Mr. Darwin has, however, obviated all difficulty regarding precision of terms by the remark that he intended to use his most important term, "struggle for existence" in "a large and metaphorical sense."

We have now seen the second element of Darwinism, namely, the "struggle for life." The theory of natural selection, then, postulates the accumulation of minute "fortuitions" individual modifications, which are useful to the possessor of them, by means of a struggle for life of such a sanguinary nature and of such enormous proportions as to result in the destruction of the overwhelming majority of adult individuals. These are the correlative factors in the process of natural selection.

In view of the popular identification of Darwinism with the doctrine of evolution, on the one hand, and with the theory of struggle for life, on the other hand, it is necessary to insist on the Darwinian conception of small, fluctuating, useful variations as the "first-steps" in the evolutionary process. For, this conception distinguishes

Darwinism from the more recent evolutionary theory, e. g., of De Vries who rejects the notion that species have originated by the accumulation of fluctuating variations; and it is quite as essential to the Darwinian theory of natural selection as is the "struggle for life." It is, in fact, an integral element in the selection theory.

The attitude of science towards Darwinism may, therefore, be conveniently summarized in its answer to the following questions: 1. Is there any evidence that such a struggle for life among mature forms, as Darwin postulates, actually occurs?

2. Can the origin of adaptive structures be explained on the ground of their *utility* in this struggle, i. e., is it certain or even probable that the organism would have perished, had it lacked the particular adaptation in its present degree of perfection? On the contrary, is there not convincing proof that many, and presumably most, adaptations cannot be thus accounted for?

The above questions are concerned with "the struggle for life." Those which follow have to do with the problem of variations.

3. Is there any reason to believe that new species may originate by the accumulation of fluctuating individual variations?

4. Does the evidence of the geological record—which, as Huxley observed, is the only direct evidence that can be had in the question of evolution—does this evidence tell for or against the origin of existing species from earlier ones by means of minute gradual modifications?

We must be content here with the briefest outline of the reply of science to these inquiries.

1. Darwin invites his readers to "keep steadily in mind that each organic being is striving to increase in geometrical ratio." If this tendency were to continue unchecked, the progeny of living beings would soon be unable to find standing room. Indeed, the very bacteria would quickly convert every vestige of organic matter on earth into their own substance. For has not Cohn estimated that the offspring of a single bacterium, at its ordinary rate of increase under favorable conditions, would in three days amount to 4,772 billions of individuals with an aggregate weight of seven thousand five hundred tons? And the 19,000,000 elephants which, according to Darwin, should to-day perpetuate the lives of each pair that mated in the twelfth century—surely these would be a "magna pars" in the sanguinary contest. When the imagination views these and similar figures, and places in contrast to this multitude of living beings, the limited supply of nourishment, the comparison of nature with a huge slaughter-house seems tame enough. But reason, not imagination, as Darwin observes more than once, should be our guide in a scientific inquiry.

It is observed on careful reflection that Darwin's theory is endangered by an extremely large disturbing element, viz., accidental destruction. Under this term we include all the destruction of life which occurs in utter indifference to the presence or absence of any individual variations from the parent form. Indeed, the greatest destruction takes place among immature forms before any variation from the parent stock is discernible at all. In this connection we may instance the vast amount of eggs and seeds destroyed annually irrespective of any adaptive advantage that would be possessed by the matured form. And the countless forms in every stage of individual development which meet destruction through "accidental causes which would not be in the least degree mitigated by certain changes of structure or of constitution which would otherwise be beneficial to the species." This difficulty, Darwin himself recognized. But he was of opinion that if even "one-hundredth or one-thousandth part" of organic beings escaped this fortuitous destruction, there would supervene among the survivors a struggle for life sufficiently destructive to satisfy his theory. This suggestion, however, fails to meet the difficulty. For, as Professor Morgan points out, Darwin assumes "that a second competition takes place after the first destruction of individuals has occurred, and this presupposes that more individuals reach maturity than there is room for in the economy of nature." It presupposes that the vast majority of forms that survive accidental destruction, succumb in the second struggle for life in which the determining factor is some slight individual variation, e. g., a little longer neck in the case of the giraffe, or a wing shorter than usual in the case of an insect on an island. The whole theory of struggle, as formulated by Darwin, is, therefore, a violent assumption. Men of science now recognize that "egoism and struggle play a very subordinate part in organic development, in comparison with co-operation and social action." What, indeed, but a surrender of the paramountcy of struggle for life, is Huxley's celebrated Romanes lecture in which he supplants the cosmic process by the ethical? The French free-thinker, Charles Robin, gave expression to the verdict of exact science when he declared: "Darwinism is a fiction, a poetical accumulation of probabilities without proof, and of attractive explanations without demonstration."

2. The hopeless inadequacy of the struggle for life to account for adaptive structures has been dealt with at considerable length by Professor Morgan in the concluding chapters of the work already mentioned. We cannot here follow him in his study of the various kinds of adaptations, e. g., form and symmetry, mutual adaptation of colonial forms, protective coloration, organs of extreme perfection, tropisms and instincts, etc., in regard to the origin of each of which he is forced to abandon the Darwinian theory. It will suffice to call attention to his conclusions concerning the phenomena of regeneration of organs. By his research in this special field Professor Morgan has won international recognition among men of science. It was while prosecuting his studies in this field that he became impressed with the utter bankruptcy of the theory of natural selection which Darwinians put forward to explain the acquisition by organisms of this most useful power of regeneration. "It is not difficult to show that regeneration could not in many cases, and presumably in none, have been acquired through natural selection (p. 379). If an earth worm

(*allolobophora foetida*) be cut in two in the middle, the posterior piece regenerates at its anterior cut end, not a head but a tail. "Not by the widest stretch of the imagination can such a result be accounted for on the selection theory." Quite the reverse case presents itself in certain planarians. If the head of *planaria lugubris* is cut off just behind the eyes, there develops at the cut surface of the headpiece another head turned in the opposite direction. "These and other reasons," concludes Professor Morgan (p. 381), "indicate with certainty that regeneration cannot be explained by the theory of natural selection."

The ingenuity of the Darwinian imagination, however, will hardly fail to assign some reason why two heads are more useful than one in the above instance, and thus reconcile the phenomenon with Darwinism. For, according to Professor Morgan "to imagine that a particular organ is useful to its possessor and to account for its origin because of the imagined benefit conferred, is the general procedure of the followers of the Darwinian school." "Personal conviction, mere possibility," writes Quatrefages, "are offered as proofs, or at least as arguments in favor of the theory." "The realms of fancy are boundless," is Blanchard's significant comment on Darwin's explanation of the blindness of the mole. "On this class of speculation," says Bateson in his "Materials for the Study of Variation," referring to Darwinian speculation as to the beneficial or detrimental nature of variations, "on this class of speculation the only limitations are those of the ingenuity of the author." The general form of Darwin's argument, declared the writer of a celebrated article in the North British Review, is as follows: "All these things may have been, therefore my theory is possible; and since my theory is a possible one, all those hypotheses which it requires are rendered probable."

3. We pass now to the question of the possibility of building up a new species by the accumulation of chance individual variations. That species ever originate in this way is denied by the advocates of the evolutionary theory which is now superseding Darwinism. Typical of the new school is the botanist Hugo De Vries of Amsterdam. The "first-steps" in the origin of new species according to De Vries are not fluctuating individual variations, but mutations, i. e., definite and permanent modifications. According to the mutation theory a new species arises from the parent species, not gradually but suddenly. It appears suddenly "without visible preparation and without transitional steps." The wide acceptance with which this theory is meeting must be attributed to the fact that men of science no longer believe in the origin of species by the accumulation of slight fluctuating modifications. To quote the words of De Vries, "Fluctuating variation cannot overstep the limits of the species, even after the most prolonged selection—still less can it lead to the production of new, permanent characters." It has been the wont of Darwinians to base their speculations on the assumption that "an inconceivably long time" could effect almost anything in the matter of specific transformations. But the evidence which has been amassed during the past forty yeas leaves

no doubt that there is a limit to individual variability which neither time nor skill avail to remove. As M. Blanchard asserts in his work, *La vie des etres animes* (p. 102), "All investigation and observation make it clear that, while the variability of creatures in a state of nature displays itself in very different degrees, yet, in its most astonishing manifestations, it remains confined within a circle beyond which it cannot pass."

It is interesting to observe how writers of the Darwinian school attempt to explain the origin of articulate language as a gradual development of animal sounds. "It does not," observes Darwin, "appear altogether incredible that some unusually wise ape-like animal should have thought of imitating the growl of a beast of prey, so as to indicate to his fellow monkeys the nature of the expected danger. And this would have been a first step in the formation of a language." But what a tremendous step! An ape-like animal that "thought" of imitating a beast must certainly have been "unusually wise." In bridging the chasm which rational speech interposes between man and the brute creation, the Darwinian is forced to assume that the whole essential modification is included in the first step. Then he conceals the assumption by parcelling out the accidental modification in a supposed series of transitional stages. He endeavors to veil his inability to explain the first step, as Chevalier Bunsen remarked, by the easy but fruitless assumption of an infinite space of time, destined to explain the gradual development of animals into men; as if millions of years could supply the want of an agent necessary for the first movement, for the first step in the line of progress. "How can speech, the expression of thought, develop itself in a year or in millions of years, out of unarticulated sounds which express feelings of pleasure, pain, and appetite? The common-sense of mankind will always shrink from such theories."

4. The hopes and fears of Darwinians have rightly been centered on the history of organic development as outlined in the geological record. It has been pointed out repeatedly by the foremost men of science that if the theory of genetic descent with the accumulation of small variations be the true account of the origin of species, a complete record of the ancestry of any existing species would reveal no distinction of species and genera. Between any two well-defined species, if one be derived from the other, there must be countless transition forms. But palaeontology fails to support the theory of evolution by minute variations. Darwinism has been shattered on the geologic rocks. "The complete absence of intermediate forms," says Mr. Carruthers, "and the sudden and contemporaneous appearance of highly organized and widely separated groups, deprive the hypothesis of genetic evolution of any countenance from the plant record of these ancient rocks. The whole evidence is against evolution (i. e., by minute modification) and there is none for it." (cf. *History of Plant Life and its Bearing on Theory of Evolution*, 1898). Similar testimony regarding the animal kingdom is borne by Mr. Mivart in the following carefully worded statement: "The mass of palaeontological evi-

dence is indeed overwhelmingly against minute and gradual modification." "The Darwinian theory," declared Professor Fleischmann of Erlangen, recently, "has not a single fact to confirm it in the realm of nature. It is not the result of scientific research, but purely the product of the imagination."

On one occasion Huxley expressed his conviction that the pedigree of the horse as revealed in the geological record furnished demonstrative evidence for the theory of evolution. The question has been entered into in detail by Professor Fleischmann in his work, *Die Descendenztheorie*. In this book the Erlangen professor makes great capital out of the "trot-horse" (Paradepferd) of Huxley and Haeckel; and as regards the evolutionary theory, easily claims a verdict of "not proven." In this connection the moderate statement of Professor Morgan is noteworthy: "When he (Fleischmann) says there is no absolute proof that the common plan of structure must be the result of blood relationship, he is not bringing a fatal argument against the theory of descent, for no one but an enthusiast sees anything more in the explanation than a very probable theory that appears to account for the facts. To demand an absolute proof is to ask for more than any reasonable advocate of the descent theory claims for it." (Professor Morgan, as we have already seen, rejects Darwinism, and inclines to the mutation theory of De Vries.) The vast majority of Darwinians must, therefore, be classed as enthusiasts" who are not "reasonable advocates of the descent theory." For has not Professor Marsh told his readers that "to doubt evolution is to doubt science?" And similar assertions have been so frequently made and reiterated by Darwinians that the claim that Darwinism has become a dogma contains, as Professor Morgan notes, more truth than the adherents of that school find pleasant to hear.

More interesting, however, than Huxley's geological pedigree of the horse is Haeckel's geological pedigree of man. One who reads Haeckel's *Natural History of Creation* can hardly escape the impression that the author had actually seen specimens of each of the twenty-one ancestral forms of which his pedigree of man is composed. Such, however, was not the case. Quatrefages, speaking of this wonderful genealogical tree which Haeckel has drawn up with such scientific accuracy of description, observes: "The first thing to remark is that *not one* of the creatures exhibited in this pedigree has ever been seen, either living or in fossil. Their existence is based entirely upon theory." (*Les Emules de Darwin*, ii. *p.* 76). "Man's pedigree as drawn up by Haeckel," says the distinguished savant, Du Bois-Reymond," is worth about as much as is that of Homer's heroes for critical historians."

In constructing his genealogies Haeckel has frequent recourse to his celebrated "Law of Biogenesis." The "Law of Biogenesis" which is the dignified title Haeckel has given to the discredited recapitulation theory, asserts that the embryological development of the individual (ontogeny), is a brief recapitulation, a summing up, of the stages through which the species passed in the course of its evolution in the geologic past, (phylogeny). Ontogeny is a brief recapitulation of phylogeny. This, says Haeckel, is what the "fundamental Law of Biogenesis" teaches us. (The reader of Haeckel and other Darwinians will frequently find laws put forward to establish facts: whereas other men of science prefer to have facts establish laws). When, therefore, as Quatrefages remarks, the transition between the types which Haeckel has incorporated into his genealogical tree, appears too abrupt, he often betakes himself to ontogeny and describes the embryo in the corresponding interval of development. This description he inserts in his genealogical mosaic, by virtue of the "Law of Biogenesis."

Many theories have been constructed to explain the phenomena of embryological development. Of these the simplest and least mystical is that of His in the great classic work on embryology, "Unsere Koerperform." His tells us: "In the entire series of forms which a developing organism runs through, each form is the necessary antecedent step of the following. If the embryo is to reach the complicated end-form, it must pass, step by step, through the simpler ones. Each step of the series is the physiological consequence of the preceding stage, and the necessary condition for the following." But whatever theory be accepted by men of science, it is certainly not that proposed by Haeckel. Carl Vogt after giving Haeckel's statement of the "Law of Biogenesis" wrote: "This law which I long held as well-founded, is absolutely and radically false." Even Oskar Hertwig, perhaps the best known of Haeckel's former pupils, finds it necessary to change Haeckel's expression of the biogenetic law so that "a contradiction contained in it may be removed." Professor Morgan, finally, rejects Haeckel's boasted "Law of Biogenesis" as "*in principle, false.*" And he furthermore seems to imply that Fleischmann merits the reproach of men of science, for wasting his time in confuting "the antiquated and generally exaggerated views of writers like Haeckel."

"Antiquated and generally exaggerated views." Such is the comment of science on Haeckel's boast that Darwin's pre-eminent service to science consisted in pointing out how purposive adaptations may be produced by natural selection without the direction of mind just as easily as they may be produced by artificial selection and human design. And yet the latest and least worthy production from the pen of this Darwinian philosopher, *The Riddle of the Universe*, is being scattered broad-cast by the anti-Christian press, in the name and guise of *popular* science. It is therein that the evil consists. For the discerning reader sees in the book itself, its own best refutation. The pretensions of Haeckel's "consistent and monistic theory of the eternal cosmogenetic process" are best met by pointing to the fact that its most highly accredited and notorious representative has given to the world in exposition and defense of pure Darwinian philosophy, a work, which, for boldness of assertion, meagerness of proof, inconsequence of argument, inconsistency in fundamental principles and disregard for facts which tell against the author's theory, has certainly no equal in contemporary literature. In the apt and expressive phrase of Professor Paulsen, the book "fairly drips with superficiality" (von Seichtigkeit triefen). If the man of science is to be justified, as Huxley suggested, not by faith but by verification, Haeckel and his docile Darwinian disciples have good reason to tremble for their scientific salvation.

EDWIN V. O'HARA.

St. Paul, Minn.

INTRODUCTION.

During the last few years I have published under this title short articles dealing with the present status of Darwinism. In view of the kind reception which has been accorded to these articles by the reading public I have thought it well to bring them together in pamphlet form. Indeed, the Darwinian movement and its present status are eminently deserving of consideration, especially on the part of those before whom Darwinism has hitherto always been held up triumphantly as a scientific disproof of the very foundations of the Christian faith.

By way of introduction and explanation some general preliminary remarks may not be amiss here. Previous to twenty or thirty years ago, it was justifiable to identify Darwinism with the doctrine of Descent, for at that time Darwinism was the only doctrine of Descent which could claim any general recognition. Consequently, one who was an adherent of the doctrine of Descent was also a Darwinian. Those to whom this did not apply were so few as to be easily counted. The dispute then hinged primarily on Darwinism; hence, for those who did not admit the truth of that theory, the doctrine of Descent was for the most part also a myth.

I say, for the most part; for there were already even at that time a few clear-sighted naturalists (Wigand, Naegeli, Koelliker and others) who saw plainly the residue of truth that would result from the discussion. But to the overwhelming majority, the alternatives seemed to be: Either Darwinism or no evolution at all. Today, however, the state of things is considerably altered. The doctrine of Descent is clearly and definitely distinguished from Darwinism at least by the majority of naturalists. It is therefore of the utmost importance that this luminous distinction should likewise become recognized in lay circles.

My object in these pages is to show that Darwinism will soon be a thing of the past, a matter of history; that we even now stand at its death-bed, while its friends are solicitous only to secure for it a decent burial.

Out of the chaos of controversy which has obtained during the last four decades there has emerged an element of truth—for there lurks a germ of truth in most errors—which has gained almost universal recognition among contemporary men of science, namely, the doctrine of Descent. The fact that living organisms form an ascending series from the less perfect to the more perfect; the further fact that they also form a series according as they display more or less homology of structure and are formed according to similar types; and, lastly, that the fossil remains of organisms found in the various strata of the earth's surface likewise represent an ascending series from the simple to the more complex—these three facts suggested to naturalists the thought that living organisms were not always as we find them today, but that the more perfect had developed from simpler forms through a series of modifications. These thoughts were at first advanced with some hesitation, and were confined to narrow circles. They received, however, material support when, during the fourth decade of the 19th century the splendid discovery was made (by K. E. von Baer) that every organism is slowly developed from a germ, and in the process of development passes through temporary lower stages to a permanent higher one. Even at that time many naturalists believed in a corresponding development of the whole series of organisms, without of course being able to form a clear conception of the process. Such was the state of affairs when Darwin in the year 1859 published his principal work, *The Origin of Species by Means of Natural Selection.* In this work for the first time an exhaustive attempt was made to sketch a clear and completely detailed picture of the process of development.

Darwin started with the fact that breeders of animals and growers of plants, having at their disposal a large number of varieties, always diverging somewhat from each other, choose individuals possessing characteristics which they desired to strengthen, and use only these for procreation. In this manner the desired characteristic is gradually made more prominent, and the breeder appears to have obtained a new species. Similar conditions are supposed to prevail in Nature, only that there is lacking the selecting hand of the breeder. Here the so-called principle of Natural Selection holds automatic sway by means of the

Struggle for Existence. All the various forms of life are warring for the means of subsistence, each striving to obtain for itself the best nourishment, etc. In this struggle those organisms will be victorious which possess the most favorable characteristics; all others must succumb. Hence those only will survive which are best adapted to their environment. But between those which survive, the struggle begins anew, and when the favoring peculiarities become more pronounced in some, (by chance, of course) these in turn win out. Thus Nature gradually improves her various breeds through the continued action of a self-regulating mechanism. Such are the main features of Darwinism, its real kernel, about which of course,—and this is a proof of its insufficiency,—from the very beginning a number of auxiliary hypotheses attached themselves.

Darwin's theory sounds so clear and simple, and seems at first blush so luminous that it is no wonder if many careful naturalists regarded it as an incontrovertible truth. The warning voice of the more prudent men of science was silenced by the loud enthusiasm of the younger generation over the solution of the greatest of the world-problems: the genesis of living beings had been brought to light, and—a thing which admitted of no doubt—man as well as the brute creation was a product of purely natural evolution. The doctrine which materialism had already proclaimed with prophetic insight, had at length been irrefragably established on a scientific basis: God, Soul and Immortality were contemptuously relegated to the domain of nursery tales. What further use was there for a God when, in addition to the Kant-Laplacian theory of the origin of the planetary system, it had been discovered that living organisms had likewise evolved spontaneously? How could man who had sprung from the irrational brute possess a soul? And thus, finally, disappeared the third delusion, the hope of immortality. For with death the functions of the body simply cease, as also do those of the brain, which people had foolishly believed to be something more than an aggregation of atoms. The body dissolves into its constituent elements and serves in its turn to build up other organisms: but as a human body it all turns to dust nor 'leaves a wrack behind'. Thus Darwinism was made the basis first for a materialistic, and then for a monistic, view of the world, and hence came to be rigorously opposed to every form of Theism. But since, at that time, Darwinism was the only theory of evolution recognized by the world of science, the opposition of the Christian world was directed not specifically against Darwinism, but against the theory of evolution as such. The wheat was rooted up with the tares.

I will not discuss here which of the two views concerning creation; the origin of the world in one moment of time, or a gradual evolution of the world and its potentialities, is the more worthy of the creative power of God. Manifestly the greatness and magnificence of creation will in no way be compromised by the concept of evolution. This, of course, is simply my opinion. Any further statement would be out of place here.

But what is the Darwinian position?

It is merely a special form of the evolutionary theory, one of the various attempts to explain how the process of development actually took place. Darwinism as understood in the following chapters possesses the following characteristic traits:

(1) Evolution began and continues without the aid or intervention of a Creator.

(2) In the production of Variations there is no definite law; Chance reigns supreme.

(3) There is no indication of purpose or finality to be detected anywhere in the evolutionary process.

(4) The working factor in evolution is Egoism, a war of each against his fellows: this is the predominating principle which manifests itself in Nature.

(5) In this struggle the strongest, fleetest and most cunning will always prevail, (the Darwinian term "fittest" has been the innocent source of a great deal of error).

(6) Man, whether you regard his body or his mind, is nothing but a highly developed animal.

A careful examination of Darwinism shows that these are the necessary presuppositions, or, if you will, the inevitable consequences of that theory. To accept that theory is to repudiate the Christian view of the world. The truth of the above propositions is utterly incompatible, not only with any religious views, but with our civil and social principles as well.

The most patent facts of man's moral life, however, cannot be explained on any such hypothesis, and the logic of events has already shown that Darwinism could never have won general acceptance but for the incautious enthusiasm of youth which intoxicated the minds of the rising generation of naturalists and incapacitated them for the exercise of sober judgment. To show that there is among contemporary men of science a healthy reaction against Darwinism is the object of this treatise.

The reader may now ask, What, then, is your idea of evolution? It certainly is easier to criticise than to do constructive work. An honest study of nature, however, inevitably leads us to the conclusion that the final solution of the problem is still far distant. Many a stone has already been quarried for the future edifice of evolution by unwearied research during the last four decades. But in opposition to Darwinism it may, at the present time, be confidently asserted that any future doctrine of evolution will have to be constructed on the following basic principles:

(1) All evolution is characterized by finality; it proceeds according to a definite plan, and tends to a definite end.

(2) Chance and disorder find no place in Nature; every stage of the evolutionary process is the result of law-controlled factors.

(3) Egoism and struggle among living organisms are of very subordinate importance in comparison with co-operation and social action.

(4) The soul of man is an independent substance, and entirely unintelligible as a mere higher stage of development of animal instinct.

A theory of evolution, however, resting on these principles cannot dispense with a Creator and Conserver of the world and of life.

CHAPTER I.

"It was a happy day that people threw off the straight-jacket of logic and the burdensome fetters of strict method, and mounting the light-caparisoned steed of philosophic science, soared into the empyrean, high above the laborious path of ordinary mortals. One may not take offense if even the most sedate citizen, for the sake of a change, occasionally kicks over the traces, provided only that he returns in due time to his wonted course. And now in the domain of Biology, one is led to think that the time has at length arrived for putting an end to mad masquerade pranks and for returning without reserve to serious and sober work, to find satisfaction therein." With these words did the illustrious Wigand, twenty-five years ago, conclude the preface to the third volume of his large classical work against Darwinism. True, he did not at that time believe that the mad campaign of Darwinism had already ended to its own detriment, but he always predicted with the greatest confidence that the struggle would soon terminate in victory for the anti-Darwinian camp. When Wigand closed his eyes in death in 1896, he was able to bear with him the consciousness that the era of Darwinism was approaching its end, and that he had been in the right.

Today, at the dawn of the new century, nothing is more certain than that Darwinism has lost its prestige among men of science. It has seen its day and will soon be reckoned a thing of the past. A few decades hence when people will look back upon the history of the doctrine of Descent, they will confess that the years between 1860 and 1880 were in many respects a time of carnival; and the enthusiasm which at that time took possession of the devotees of natural science will appear to them as the excitement attending some mad revel.

A justification of our hope that Wigand's warning prediction will finally be fulfilled is to be found in the fact that today the younger generation of naturalists is departing more and more from Darwinism. It is a fact worthy of special mention that the opposition to Darwinism today comes chiefly from the ranks of the zoologists, whereas thirty years ago large numbers of zoologists from Jena associated themselves with the Darwinian school, hoping to find there a full and satisfactory solution for the profoundest enigmas of natural science.

The cause of this reaction is not far to seek. There was at the time a whole group of enthusiastic Darwinians among the university professors, Haeckel leading the van, who clung to that theory so tenaciously and were so zealous in propagating it, that for a while it seemed impossible for a young naturalist to be anything but a Darwinian. Then the inevitable reaction gradually set in. Darwin himself died, the Darwinians of the sixties and seventies lost their pristine ardor, and many even went beyond Darwin.

Above all, calm reflection took the place of excited enthusiasm. As a result it has become more and more apparent that the past forty years have brought to light nothing new that is of any value to the cause of Darwinism. This significant fact has aroused doubts as to whether after all Darwinism can really give a satisfactory explanation of the genesis of organic forms.

The rising generation is now discovering what discerning scholars had already recognized and stated a quarter of a century ago. They are also returning to a study of the older opponents of Darwinism, especially of Wigand. It is only now, many years after his death, that a tribute has been paid to this distinguished savant which unfortunately was grudgingly withheld during his life. One day recently there was laid before his monument in the Botanical Garden of Marburg a laurel-wreath with the inscription: "To the great naturalist, philosopher and man." It came from a young zoologist at Vienna who had thoroughly mastered Wigand's great anti-Darwinian work, an intelligent investigator who had set to work in the spirit of Wigand. Another talented zoologist, Hans Driesch, dedicates to the memory of Wigand two books in rapid succession and reprehends the contemporaries of that master of science for ignoring him. O. Hammann abandons Darwinism for an internal principle of development. W. Haacke openly disavows Darwinism; and even at the convention of naturalists in 1897, L. Wilser was allowed to assert without contradiction that, "anyone who has committed himself to Darwinism can no longer be ranked as a naturalist."

These are all signs which clearly indicate a radical revolution, and they are all the more significant since it is the younger generation, which will soon take the lead, that thinks and speaks in this manner. But it is none the less noteworthy that the younger naturalists are not alone in this movement. Many of the older men of science are swelling the current. We shall recall here only the greatest of those whom we might mention in this connection.

Julius von Sachs, the most gifted and brilliant botanist of the last century, who unfortunately is no longer among us, was in the sixties an outspoken Darwinian, as is evident especially from his History of Botany and from the first edition of his Handbook of Botany. Soon, however, Sachs began to incline toward the position assumed by Naegeli; and as early as 1877, Wigand, in the third volume of his great work, expressed the hope that Sachs would withdraw still further from Darwinism. As years went by, Sachs drifted more and more from his earlier position, and Wigand was of opinion that to himself should be ascribed the credit of bringing about the change. During his last years Sachs had become bitterly opposed to Darwinism, and in his masterly "Physiological Notes" he took a firm stand on the "internal factors of evolution."

During recent years I had the pleasure of occasional correspondence with Sachs. On the 16th of September, 1896, he wrote me: For more than twenty years I have recognized that if we are to build up a strictly scientific theory of organic structural processes, we must separate the doctrine of Descent from Darwinism. It was with this intention that he worked during the last years of his life and it is to be hoped that his school will continue his researches with this aim in view.

The tendency among naturalists to return to Wigand is well exemplified in an article contributed to the "Preussischen Jahrbuecher" for January, 1897, by Dr. Karl Camillo Schneider, assistant at the zoological Institute of the University of Vienna. This article which is entitled The Origin of Species, pursues Wigand's train of thought throughout, and whole sentences and even paragraphs are taken verbatim from his main work. This, at all events, is a very instructive indication of the present tendency which deserves prominence: and its significance becomes more evident when we recall how the work of Wigand was received by the non-christian press a quarter of a century ago. It was either ridiculed or ignored. The two methods of treatment were applied to his writings which are always readily employed when the critic has nothing pertinent to say. It is interesting to note that Darwin himself employed this method. Wigand once told me that he had sent Darwin a copy of his work and had addressed a letter to him at the same time merely stating that he had sent the book, making no reference to the line of thought contained in it. Darwin answered immediately in the kindest manner that he had not as yet received the book, but when it arrived he would at once make a careful study of its contents. Darwin did not write to him again, and when a new edition of his works appeared, the work of Wigand, the most comprehensive answer to Darwin ever written, was passed over without even a passing mention. Thus Darwin completely ignored his keenest antagonist.

As has been said, the majority of those who wrote about Wigand ridiculed him: very few regarded him seriously, and even these indulged chiefly in personal recriminations. Thus matters stood twenty-five years ago. Wigand's prediction passed unheeded. That a periodical not having a specifically Christian circle of readers should now publish a condemnation of Darwinism entirely in accordance with the views of Wigand, is a fact which indicates a notable change of sentiment during the intervening years. I should not be at all astonished if many who sneered at Wigand twenty years ago, now read the article in the Freussischen Jahrbuecher with entire approval. Ill-will towards Wigand has not altogether disappeared even to-day. This is evident from the fact that as yet Dr. Schneider does not venture to defend Wigand publicly, nor to acknowledge him as his principal authority. We must be content, however, if only, the truth will finally prevail.

CHAPTER II.

Striking testimony relative to the present position of Darwinism is borne by the Strasburg zoologist, Dr. Goette, who has won fame by his invaluable labors as an historian of evolutionary theory. In the "Umschau," No. 5, 1898, he discusses the "Present Status of Darwinism," and the conclusions he arrives at, are identical with mine. At the outset Goette indicates the distinction between Darwinism and the doctrine of Descent, and then points out that the distinguishing features of the former consist not so much in the three facts of Heredity, Variation, and Overproduction, but rather in Selection, Survival of the Fittest, and also in that mystical theory of heredity—the doctrine of Pangenesis—which is peculiarly Darwinian. Since this theory of Pangenesis has found no adherents, the question may henceforth be restricted to the doctrine of natural selection. This Goette very well observes.

He points, moreover, to the fact that the misgivings that were entertained concerning the doctrine of natural selection on its first appearance, were, on the whole, precisely the same as they are to-day; only with this difference, that formerly they were disregarded by naturalists whose clearness of vision was obscured by excessive enthusiasm; whereas, today men have again returned to their sober senses and lend their attention more readily to objections.

Goette recalls the fact that M. Wagner tried to supplement natural selection with his "Law of Migration," and that later on, Romanes and Gulick endeavored to supply the evident deficiencies in Darwin's theory, by invoking other principles; and that even at that time, Askenasy, Braun, and Naegeli—and more recently, the lately deceased Eimer—insisted on the fact of definitely ordered variations, in opposition to the theory of Selection.

Many naturalists recognize the difficulties but do not abandon the theory of Selection, thinking that some supplementary principle would suffice to make it acceptable: many others refuse to decide either for or against Darwinism and maintain towards it an attitude of indifference. The younger investigators, however, are utterly opposed to it. "There can be no doubt that since its first appearance the influence of Darwinism on men's minds has notably diminished, although the theory has not been entirely discarded."—But the very fact that the younger naturalists are hostile to it, makes it evident that Darwinism has a still darker future in store for it: that sooner or later it will come to possess a merely historical interest.

"The present position of Darwinism," says Goette, "is characterized especially by the uncertainty of criticism which is unable to declare definitely in favor of either side." Goette finds the chief cause of this uncertainty in the fact "that men of science (even Darwin himself) have widened the concept of selection as a means of originating new species through the interaction of individuals in the same species, so as to express the mutually antagonistic relations existing between several such species." The latter alone is subject to experimental verification, but it can only cause the isolation of existing forms and is not a species-originating selection—with which alone we are here concerned. This kind of selection can enfeeble the existing flora and fauna, but cannot produce a new species. Selection productive of new species "is not actually demonstrable; it is a purely theoretical invention."

Goette next points out that the investigator is everywhere confronted by definitely-directed variation: a fact which does not harmonize with the theory of selection, nor, consequently with Darwinism. If some scientists have not as yet accepted Eimer's presentation of this doctrine, their action is most probably to be attributed to the fear lest "they should have to accept not merely, variation according to definite laws, but likewise a principle of finality and other causes lying beyond the range of scientific investigation." The rejection of the theory of selection often promotes, as Goette rightly observes, a reactionary tendency towards *a priori* explanations of phenomena with which we are but slightly acquainted. "There are naturalists who do not discard the theory of selection simply because it seems to furnish a much-desired mechanical explanation of purposive adaptions" (a momentous admission to which we shall have occasion to revert).

Others have broken entirely with selection and the principle of utility and extend the idea of finality to the general capacity of organisms to persist. Thus adaptation becomes a principle which transcends the limits of natural science and pervades the whole domain of life. Goette observes that Darwin spoke of useful, less useful and indifferent organisms, by which he meant those adaptations destined for particular vital functions which tend to make the organs more and more specialized. Since the ability to live is threatened by this specialization it cannot be purposive. This is not wholly true, because the more specialized the individual organ becomes, the more perfect is the whole organism which is composed of these specialized organs. The functions of the individual organ may be restricted, but the power of the entire organism is notably increased, according to the law of the division of labor. Goette therefore has not sufficient grounds for rejecting this expression. He considers that a real and permanent purpose for the individual living forms is out of the question, but that this purpose may be sought for in the development and history of the collective life of nature. Definitely ordered variation, he thinks, a scientific explanation of which is indeed yet forthcoming, will explain adaptation equally as well as does selection. After what has been said this statement of Goette must come as a surprise, for one would think that according to his view definite variation explains adaptations better than selection. Goette sums up his main conclusion in the following words: "The doctrine of Heredity or of Descent, which comes from Lamarck though it was first made widely known by Darwin, has since continually gained a broader and surer foundation. But Darwin's own doctrine regarding the causes and process of Descent which alone can be called Darwinism, has on the other hand doubtlessly waned in influence and prestige."

This is exactly what we also maintain: The establishment of the theory of Descent in general, and the continual retrogression of Darwinism in particular. Wigand was entirely right when he said that Darwinism would not live beyond the century.

We may, however, derive from the discussions of Goette something else that is of the highest importance, namely, an admission in which is to be found the real and fundamental explanation of the conduct of the majority of naturalists who still cling to Darwinism. It does not consist in the fact that they are convinced of the truth of Darwinism but in their "reluctance to give up the mechanical explanation of finality proposed by Darwin," or rather in the fear of being driven to the recognition of theistic principles. With commendable candor Goette attacks this method of keeping up a system notwithstanding its recognized deficiencies. Goette furthermore points out especially that this recognition is more widespread than one might be able to gather from occasional discussions on the subject.

From the account which Goette gives of the present status of Darwinism we may safely conclude that Darwinism had entered upon a period of decay; it is in the third stage of a development through which many a scientific doctrine has already passed.

The four stages of this development are the following:

1. The incipient stage: A new doctrine arises, the older representatives of the science oppose it partly because of keener insight and greater experience, partly also from indolence, not wishing to allow themselves to be drawn out of their accustomed equilibrium; among the younger generation there arises a growing sentiment in favor of the new doctrine.

2. The stage of growth: the new doctrine continually gains greater favor among the young generation, finding vent in bursts of enthusiasm; some of the cautious seniors have passed away, others are carried along by the stream of youthful enthusiasm in spite of better knowledge, and the voices of the thoughtful are no longer heard in the general uproar, exultingly proclaiming that to live is bliss.

3. The period of decay: the joyous enthusiasm has vanished; depression succeeds intoxication. Now that the young men have themselves grown older and become more sober, many things appear in a different light. The doubts already expressed by the old and prudent during the stage of growth are now better appreciated and gradually increase in weight. Many become indifferent, the present younger generation becomes perplexed and discards the theory entirely.

4. The final stage: the last adherents of the "new doctrine" are dead or at least old and have ceased to be influential, they sit upon the ruins of a grandeur that even now belongs to the "good old time." The influential and directing spirits have abandoned this doctrine, once so important and seemingly invincible, for the consideration of

living issues and the younger generation regards it as an interesting episode in the history of science.

With reference to Darwinism we are in the third stage which is characterized especially by the indifference of the present middle-aged generation and by growing opposition on the part of the younger coming generation. This very characteristic feature is brought into prominence by the discussion of Goette. If all signs, however, are not deceptive, this third stage, that of decay, is drawing to an end; soon we shall enter the final stage and with that the tragic-comedy of Darwinism will be brought to a close.

If some one were to ask me how according to the count of years, I should determine the extent of the individual stages of Darwinism, this would be my answer:

1. The incipient stage extends from 1859 (the year during which Darwin's principal work, *The Origin of Species*, appeared) to the end of the sixties.

2. The stage of growth: from that time, for about 20 years, to the end of the eighties.

3. The stage of decay: from that time on to about the year 1900.

4. The final stage: the first decade of the new century.

I am not by choice a prophet, least of all regarding the weather. But I think it may not be doubted that the fine weather, at least, has passed for Darwinism. So having carefully scanned the firmament of science for signs of the weather, I shall for once make a forecast for Darwinism, namely: Increasing cloudiness with heavy precipitations, indications of a violent storm, which threatens to cause the props of the structure to totter, and to sweep it from the scene.

CHAPTER III.

As further witnesses to the passing of Darwinism, two botanists may be cited; the first is Professor Korschinsky who in No. 24, 1899, of the *Naturwissenschaftliche Wochenschrift* published an article on "Heterogenesis and Evolution," which was to be followed later by a large work on this subject. With precision and emphasis he points to the numerous instances in which there occurs on or in a plant, suddenly and without intervention, a variation which may become hereditary under certain circumstances; thus during the last century a number of varieties of garden plants have been evolved. On the basis of such experiments Korschinsky developed the theory which had been proposed by Koelliker in Wuerzburg thirty years earlier, namely, the theory of "heterogeneous production" or heterogenesis," as Korschinsky calls it. When one understands that a plant gives rise suddenly and without any intervention to a grain of seed, which produces a different plant, it becomes evident that all Darwinistic speculations about selection and struggle for existence are forthwith absolutely excluded. The effect can proceed only from the internal vital powers inherent in the specified organism acting in connection, perhaps, with the internal conditions of life, which suddenly exert an influence in a new direction.

49

Korschinsky distinguishes clearly and definitely between the principles of Heterogenesis and Transmutation (gradual transformation through natural selection in the struggle for existence), and in so doing comes to a complete denial of Darwinism.

The other naturalist who has dealt Darwinism a telling blow is the botanist of Graz, Professor Haberlandt.

He published some very interesting observations and experiments in the "Festschrift fuer Schwendener" (Berlin 1899, Borntraeger). They are concerned with a Liane javas of the family of mulberry plants (Conocephalus ovatus.) The free leaves possess under the outer layer, a tissue composed of large, thin-walled, water-storing cells; flat cavities on the upper side, having, furthermore, organs that secrete water, which the botanist calls hydathodes. These are delicate, small, glandular cells over which are the bundles of vascular fibres (leaf-veins) that convey the water to them; over these in the top layer are so-called water-crevices through which the water can force itself to the outside. It is unnecessary to enter upon a closer explanation of the anatomical structure of these peculiar organs. The water which is forced upward by the root-pressure of the plant is naturally conveyed through the vascular fibres into the leaves and at every hydathode the superfluous water oozes out in drops, a phenomenon which one can also very nicely observe e.g. on the "Lady's cloak" (Alchemilla vulgaris) of the German flora. A portion of the night-dew must be attributed to this secretion of water On the Liane, then, Haberlandt observed a very considerable secretion of water: a full-grown leaf secreted during one night 2.76 g. of water (that is 26 per cent. of its own weight.) Through this peculiarity the water supply within the plant is regulated and the danger avoided that any water should penetrate the surrounding tissue in consequence of strong root-pressure,—which would naturally obstruct the vital function of the entire leaf. Besides it is to be noticed that in this way an abundant flow of water is produced: the plant takes up large quantities of water from the earth, laden with nutritive salts, and the distilled water is almost pure (it contains only 0.045 g. salts), so that the nutritive salts are absorbed by the plant.

From these considerations it necessarily appears that the hydathodes are of great biological importance to the plant.

Haberlandt then "poisoned" the plant, by sprinkling it with a 0.1 per cent sublimate solution of alcohol. The purpose of this experiment was to ascertain whether in the secretion of water there was question of a merely physical process or of a vital process. In the first case the action of the hydathode should continue even after the treatment with the sublimate solution, while in the latter case it should not. As the secretion ceased the obvious conclusion to be deduced from this experiment is that the hydathodes do not act as purely mechanical filtration-apparatuses, as one might have thought, but that there is here evidence of an active vital process in the plant; the unusual term "poisoning" is therefore really justified under present circumstances.

Let me dwell for a moment on this result, for, although it may be somewhat foreign to our present purpose and to the further observations of Haberlandt, it is very significant in itself. The water moves in the plant in closed cells, as the cells of the aqueous gland are entirely closed, but the organic membrane, as every one knows, has the peculiar physical property of allowing water to pass through, the pressure, of course, being applied on the side of least resistance; when therefore the water is forced into the cells by root-pressure, it is easily intelligible that according to purely physical laws it should come to the surface of the leaf on the side of the least resistance, that is, by way of the water-crevices. Even the defenders of "vital force" would not find any reason in this for not considering the phenomenon of distillation in this case a purely physical phenomenon. And still according to Haberlandt's experiments it is not. The sublimate could at most only impede the process of filtration, but should under no circumstances have destroyed it. But it does destroy it, and the hydathode dies. The conclusion certainly follows from this that this process is connected with some vital function. Even if the hydathode is treated with sublimate solution, all the conditions for mechanical filtration still remain: the earth has moisture which can be taken up by the roots so that root-pressure still exists. The water is in all cases conveyed to the hydathodes through the vascular fibres, the cell walls of the hydathodes are still adapted for filtration, and yet they do not filter. Hence some other factor must join itself to the physico-mechanical process of filtration and affect or destroy it, and this factor can be found only in the protoplasm, the vital element of the cells; for we know that the sublimate acts with pernicious effect on it and in such a manner that it destroys its entire power of reaction; it kills it, as we say.

The experiment under discussion has, therefore, great significance for our view of the vital processes in the plant; it proves beyond doubt that these processes are in no way of a purely mechanical nature, but that there is something underlying all this, a hitherto inexplicable something, which we call "life." In all vital activities, physical and chemical processes certainly do occur; they do not, however, take place spontaneously but are made use of by the vital element of the plant to produce an effect that is desirable or necessary for the vital activity of the plant. If the vital element is dead, no matter how favorable the conditions may be for chemical and physical processes, these do not take place and the effect necessary for life is not obtained. It is very remarkable after all that according to the experiment of Haberlandt this peculiar relation should become apparent in a process that is so open to our investigation as the filtration of water through the cell-wall of a plant.

After what has been said I consider this simple experiment of Haberlandt of great significance; for it is a direct proof of the existence of a vital force. One may resist to his heart's content, but without avail; vital force is again finding its way into science. More and more cognizance is being taken of the fact that 60 and 70 years ago people jumped at conclusions very imprudently when they believed that the first artificial preparation of organic matter (urea, by Woehler) had proven the non-existence of a vital force. Since then there has been great rejoicing in the camp of materialists who scoffed at the "ignorant" who would not as yet forsake vital force. "Behold," they said, "in the chemist's retort the same matter is produced chemically that is produced in the body of the animal, without the direction of a hidden vital force, which, if it is not necessary in the one case, neither is it necessary in the other." Any one who had given the matter careful consideration could even at that time have known where the "ignorant" really were. That in both cases chemical processes take place is clear and undisputed, but the materialists forgot entirely that even in the laboratory it was not the mere contact of the elements that produced the urea; a chemist was needed and in this case not any one arbitrarily chosen, but a man of the genius and knowledge of a Woehler to watch over the process, and utilize and partly direct the laws of chemistry in order to obtain the desired result. Hence it was even then absurd to deny vital force as a consequence of that experiment. Since, however, it was well-adapted for materialistic purposes, this denial was proclaimed with the sound of trumpet throughout the land, and repeated again and again with surprising tenacity, with the result that even thoughtful investigators rejected vital force almost universally in the seventies and eighties.

54

It has always been a problem to me how this could have happened. It can, indeed, be explained only on the supposition that naturalists were adverse to the introduction of anything into nature, that appeared to them mystical and mysterious. Nor is such a procedure at all necessary: vital force is by no means a mysterious, ghostly power that soars above nature, but a force of nature like its other forces, as mysterious and as definite as they are, only that it dominates a specified group of beings, namely, living organisms. It may readily be compared with any other natural phenomenon. For instance, the phenomenon of crystalization has its well determined sphere of activity, viz., the mineral world. It employs definite mathematico-physical laws to obtain a specified result, and even acts differently in different mineral substances in so far as it produces in the one case this, in the other case that form; but still it should be a similarly directed force which has the effect of producing these peculiar forms. Precisely similar is it with vital force. It has its determined sphere of activity, the kingdom of living organisms; it acts according to definite physico-chemical laws in producing a specified result; it acts differently in different living organisms; it is therefore a force of nature as clear yet as mysterious as the force of crystallization or as any other force of nature. Hence one has no cause to complain of its mysteriousness, for all other forces of nature are just as much, or if you will, just as little mysterious as vital force. The only thing to be maintained is this, that living organisms are dominated by a special force with special phenomena and special activities, even as in mineral substances there is a special dominant force which produces special phenomena and exercises special activities.

It is possible to produce crystals in the laboratory, but no one will be so foolish as to maintain that in nature crystals are not formed in consequence of a very definite force inherent in the mineral-substances; nor will any one deny the existence of the force of crystallization because it does not appear in living organisms.

Nor have I ever despaired of a return of the theory of vital force. A change of opinion has really taken place during this decade; at present the voices for a vital force are constantly growing stronger and it will most probably not be very long before it will be again universally recognized, not as something preternatural, of course, but as a force of nature on an equal footing with the other forces of nature, with activities, just as mysterious and just as well-attested as the activities of the other forces of nature.

Haberlandt's experiment, however, had also an indirect consequence that is of far-reaching importance. He observed that within a few days new water-secreting organs of an entirely different structure and of different origin were formed on the leaves that had been sprinkled with sublimate. Over the bundles of vascular fibres, little knots as large as a pin head arose in larger numbers out of a tissue underlying the top layer; out of these the water now oozed every morning. Closer investigation disclosed the fact that these organs develop only on young immature leaves where groups of peculiar, perishable gland-hairs are found; beneath these dead mucous glands the substitute secretive organs originate in the inner tissue. It is of no importance to state in what particular cells they originate.

Suffice it to say that they are colorless capillary tubes originating in various cells; projecting like the hairs of a brush, containing living protoplasm and evanescent chlorophyl. It is also important to note that this new organ is immediately connected with the water-conducting system consisting of bundles of vascular fibres. Haberlandt furthermore indicates especially that these organs when viewed in connection with the process of secretion give evidence of an active vital principle as well as of simple mechanical filtration.

These substitute organs are all indeed well adapted to their purpose and adequately replace the old secretive organs, but they so easily dry out and are so little protected that after a week they become parched and die because wound-cork forms under them. The leaf no longer produces new hydathodes, but on its lower side it produces growths that function as vesicles, by means of which it continues to sustain itself.

Haberlandt furthermore records a phenomenon perhaps analogous to this on the grape-vine, but with this exception the case described by him is unique. In order to pass any further judgment regarding it, we should have to ascertain whether the whole phenomenon is not a case of so-called adaptation; if so, processes should be found in nature, analogous to the poisoning of the hydathodes in this experiment, which result in the destruction of the hydathodes so that in consequence the plant would have gained the power of making good the loss, by means of the substitute organs. Such processes, however, (even through poisoning or through parasites) would be very highly improbable. Equally incredible is the alternative possibility that the new organs would be produced by the plant not as a substitute but as a supplementary apparatus when the old ones would not suffice for secretion in case of very large absorption of water. This also must doubtlessly be rejected, as Haberlandt has observed.

Powers of adaptation should, of course, according to Darwinism, be gradually acquired in the struggle for existence, as in that case they should also have stability; but since this is not possessed by the new organs, the presumption is that they do not possess the character of adaptation. They are therefore new organs that originated after an entirely unnatural and unforseen interference with the normal vital functions and in consequence of a self-regulating activity of the organism.

What then is there in the whole phenomenon worthy of notice with regard to the theory of Descent?

1. An immediately well adapted new organ has here originated very suddenly without any previous incipient formation, without gradual perfection and without stages of transition.

2. In its formation struggle for existence and natural selection are entirely excluded, neither can find any application whatever even according to the newer exposition of Weismann. Haberlandt himself draws this conclusion.

3. If this phenomenon of a suddenly appearing change can take place in the course of the development of the individual, there can be no obvious reason why it should not take place in the same manner (without natural selection or struggle for existence) in the course of the phylogenetic development.

It is manifestly of the greatest importance that in this case a direct, experimental proof has been given that an organ has originated suddenly and without the aid of Darwinian principles. Haberlandt's article is nothing less than a complete renunciation of Darwinism on the part of Haberlandt, a renunciation which we greet with great satisfaction.

In fact one such observation would really suffice to set aside Darwinism and prove the utter insufficiency of its principles to give explanation of the origin of natural species. On the other hand, this observation plainly proves two things: first, that the above mentioned doctrine of Koelliker, now held by Korschinsky is a move in the right direction for the discovery of the causes of descent; and secondly, that the principal cause of the evolution is not to be sought in environment and blind forces but in the systematically working, internal vital principle in plants and animals. With that, however, an important part of the foundation of the mechanical-materialistic view of the world is demolished.

CHAPTER IV.

Since we have heard the verdict of zoologists and botanists concerning Darwinism, it is but right that we should now listen to a palaeontologist, a representative of the science, which investigates the petrified records of the earth's surface, and strives to collect information regarding the world of life during remote, by-gone ages of the earth. It is evident to every one that the verdict of this science must be of very specal importance in passing on the question of the development of living organisms. Darwin himself recognized this at the outset. He and his followers, however, soon perceived that, while the revelations of palaeontology were on the whole favorable to the doctrine of Descent, in so far as they proved the gradual change of organization, in consecutive strata, from the simple to more complex forms, palaeontology revealed nothing that would sustain the Darwinian theory as to the method of that development. As soon as the Darwinians, and first of all Darwin himself, perceived this, they at once brought forward a very cheap subterfuge. Since Darwinism postulates a very gradual, uninterrupted development of living organisms, there must have been an immense number of transition-forms between any two animal or plant species which to-day, although otherwise related, are separated by characteristic features. Consequently, on the Darwinian hypothesis, all of these transition-forms must have perished for the singular reason that other better organized forms overcame them in the struggle for existence. If therefore the millions of transition-forms were still missing, and the known petrified forms of older strata of the earth did not reveal them, the Darwinians were able to console themselves until from 20 to 40 years ago, with the assertion that our knowledge was still too deficient, that a more thorough investigation of the earth's surface and especially of out-of-the-way parts would eventually bring to light the supposed transition forms. Such assertion affords very poor consolation, and is anything but scientific. The method of natural science consists in establishing general principles on the basis of the materials actually furnished by experiments and observation and not in excogitating general laws and then consoling oneself with the thought that while our knowledge of nature is as yet extremely imperfect, time will furnish the actual material necessary to substantiate our guesses. But since then many a year has come and gone and Darwinism has caused, and for that alone it deserves credit, a diligent research in every field of natural science, and has promoted among palaeontologists a search for the missing transition-forms. The materials of investigation from the field of palaeontology have also wonderfully increased during these decades. Hence it is worth while now at the dawn of the new century to examine this material with a view to its availableness for the theory of Descent and especially for Darwinism.

Professor Steinmann has recently done so in Freiburg in Breisgau, on the occasion of an address as Rector of the University. What conclusions did he reach?

Steinmann declares it to be the primary task of post-Darwinian palaeontology "to arrange the fossil animal and plant-remains in the order of descent and thus to build up a truly natural, because historically demonstrable, classification of the animal and plant-world." At the outset it is to be noted that for various reasons palaeontology is unable to execute this momentous task in its full extent. The evidence of palaeontology is deficient, if for no other reason than that many animal organisms could not be preserved at all on account of their soft bodies; many animal groups have, nevertheless, received an unusual increase (mollusks, radiata, fish, saurians, vertebrates, and dendroid plants).

As regards the attempt made in the sixties to draw up lines of descent, Steinmann repudiates, without, of course, mentioning names, the family tree constructed by Haeckel and his associates as wholly hypothetical and hence unjustified; he rightly remarks that their method smacks of the closet. He finds fault with them chiefly because they predicated actuality of this imaginary family-tree and fancied that the historical research of the future would have but isolated facts to establish.

In speaking of the palaeontological research of the last few decades, Steinmann says: "In the light of recent research, fossil discoveries have frequently appeared less intelligible and more ambiguous than before, and in those cases in which an attempt has been made to bring the descent-system into agreement with the actual facts, the incongruity between the two has become obvious." Thus, for instance, the well-known archaeopteryx is not, as was maintained, a connecting link between reptile and bird, but a member of a blindly ending side branch. In fact palaeontological research has proven incapable of finding the transitions between different species, clearly determined by the theory. But the overwhelming abundance of matter called for new endeavors to master it. It was then further discovered—Steinmann finds an illustration of this fact in the echinodermata—that the well-known "fundamental law of biogenesis" of Haeckel can be accepted only in a very restricted sense and may even lead to conclusions absolutely false. We desire to remark here that a "fundamental principle" should never mislead; if it does so, it is not a fundamental principle.

It is of importance to know that according to palaeontological investigation, empiric systematizing and phylogenetic classification do not always coincide, as, for instance, in the case of the ammonites. Acording to palaeontological investigation the great systematic categories are only grades of organization. Hence present day systematizing is being more and more discarded, and the said categories —as indeed also the lesser groups of forms—must be of polyphyletic origin, that is, they must have descended from different primitive stocks. It may be asked: What bearing has this principle of multiple origins? For a long time reptiles were the predominating vertebrates; when mammals and birds appeared, numerous, varied and strange saurians inhabited land and sea; but "with the end of the chalk-period most saurians seem to have vanished suddenly from the scene, and soon we behold the mainlands and oceans inhabited by mammals of most diverse kinds." The saurians have become almost extinct and the mammal-tribe suddenly shows a most extraordinary variability and power of development. How is either phenomenon to be explained?

"The disappearance of a group of organisms has been preferably explained since the time of Darwin, by defeat in the struggle with superior competitors. If ever an explanation lacked pertinency, it does so in this case, in which the succumbing group is represented by gigantic and well preserved animal forms, widely distributed and accustomed to the most varied methods of nutrition, whereas the competitor appears in the form of small, harmless marsupials. It would be equivalent to a struggle between the elephant and the mouse."

We acknowledge with pleasure this clear rejection of Darwinism on the part of Steinmann.

Steinmann also rejects the natural extinction of those forms, perhaps from the weakness of old age; whether he is wholly warranted in doing so, seems somewhat doubtful. He tries to explain the phenomenon on the basis of the multiple origin of the mammals; and in fact there is already speculation regarding triple origin, viz: tambreets, marsupials, and the other mammals. Now if the latter also possessed a multiple origin, the problem of the extinction of the saurians would, according to Steinmann solve itself. One would not need to consider the number of extinct forms as large as is now done. However, he does not enter upon any closer consideration of this question. But he points out, for instance, that to-day the shells of mollusks (snails and conchylia) are regarded as structures that were acquired only in the course of time for the sake of protection, the disappearance of which, therefore, implied a disadvantage for the respective organisms. This transition would be something extraordinary—"but if on the contrary, one regards the shells as the necessary products of a special kind of assimilation and of the immoveableness of certain parts of the body, the gradual disappearance might well be considered a process which may take place in various animal-groups with a certain regularity in the course of the phyletic development." The snails devoid of shells, for instance, may be derived with certainty from those possessed of shells; this process has very probably also taken place in different genetic lines.

This view is well worth consideration; it stands in sharp opposition, in fundamental principles, to the Darwinian explanation. This calls for special emphasis here. How should one explain the origin of uncrusted mollusks from crusted ones through the struggle for existence, since in such a contest the latter must have had far greater prospect of survival than the former?

This view together with the principle of multiple origin opens up, according to Steinmann, "the prospect of

65

an altered conception of the process of formation of the organic world." According to the new conception, the many extinct forms of antiquity are not, as Darwin supposed, "unsuccessful attempts and continued aberrations of nature"—how this reminds one of that old, naive, much-ridiculed idea that fossils were models that God had discarded as unserviceable—but would gain new life and assume hitherto unsuspected relationship to the present organic creation.

"Science, which seeks after operative causes, at the beginning of the century regarded creation as a multiplicity of phenomena without any causal connection as to their origin. Darwin taught as a fundamental principle the unity and the causal inter-relation of creation, but was not entirely able to save this hypothesis from a violent and sudden death. In the future sketch creation will appear as wholly restricted in itself and lasting, the causes of its limitation lie, up to the time of the intervention of men, solely in the balanced motion of the planet which it peoples."

At the close of his address Steinmann points out that behind the problem of the manner of development, there stands "the unsolved question regarding its operative causes." "Regarding this point," he continues, "opinions have perhaps never been so divergent as they are to-day. The times have passed when the Darwinian explanations were regarded with naive confidence as the alpha and omega of the doctrine of Descent. Not only are the adherents of Darwinian ideas divided among themselves, but the theory of Lamarck, somewhat altered, favored by the results of historical investigation, appears more striking and now seems more in harmony with facts than formerly. What is considered by one as the ruling factor in the evolution of organisms is regarded by another as a "quantite negligeable" or even as the greatest mistake of the century. In this discord of opinions the principle of Descent alone forms the stable pole."

Thus Steinmann, and we can but applaud his conclusions with undisguised pleasure, for they tend throughout in the direction of our anti-Darwinian view, and deal Darwinism another fatal blow. It is also worthy of special note that this time the blow is dealt from the side of palaeontology; for, even if now and again we dissent from Steinmann, in this we fully agree with him that the historical method of considering the evidences of bygone periods of creation is at the very least quite as important for passing correct judgment regarding descent, as is the investigation of contemporary living organisms. Indeed, family-trees were constructed without regard for palaeontology, almost exclusively from an examination of present conditions, and sometimes the author did not even shrink from falsification. This procedure has been bitterly revenged and will take further revenge unless at length a definite end be put to the family-tree nuisance and the respective books instead of being published anew, be relegated to the lumber-room of science, there to turn yellow amid dust and cobwebs— the curious evidence of gross folly. But only have patience, even that time will come.

The conclusions of Steinmann, that are most important for us, may be summarized as follows:

1. The family and transition forms demanded from palaeontology by Darwinism for its family-trees, constructed not empirically but *a priori*, are nowhere to be found among the abundant materials which palaeontological investigation has already produced.

2. The results of the investigation do not correspond with the family groups drawn up according to the so-called "biogenetic principle," which principle has in fact led men of science into false paths.

3. At best, the biogenetic principle has a limited validity, (we add that later it will undoubtedly follow Darwinism and its family trees into the lumber-room).

4. The results of palaeontology, in so far, for instance, as they testify to the sudden disappearance of the saurians and the advent of mammals, everywhere contradict the Darwinian principle of the survival of the fittest in the struggle for existence.

5. "The time has long passed when the Darwinian explanations were regarded with naive confidence as the alpha and omega of the doctrine of Descent."

6. Only the principle of Descent is universally recognized; the "how" of it, its causes, are to-day entirely a matter of dispute.

CHAPTER V.

The strongest evidence of the decay of Darwinism is to be found in the fact that, since Darwin first enunciated his theory, many and diverse attempts have been made to explain the origin of species on other principles. Names of men, like M. Wagner, Naegeli, Wigand, Koelliker, and Kerner mark these attempts; but of these investigators Naegeli alone proposed a well-developed hypothesis. Finally, however, Eimer, professor of zoology in Tuebingen came forward with a detailed theory of Descent. As early as 1888 he published a comprehensive work dealing with it, under the title: "The Origin of Species by Means of the Transmission of Acquired Characters According to the Laws of Organic Growth." As the title itself indicates, a very marked divergence was even at that time manifesting itself between Eimer and his former teacher and friend, the great defender of Darwinism in Germany, Aug. Weismann, professor of zoology in Freiburg in Breisgau. For, while the latter vigorously attacks the transmission of acquired characters, Eimer's whole theory is founded on this very transmission. Observations regarding the coloring of animals, in fact, form the basis of Eimer's theory.

Eimer attributes the origin of species to "organic growth" by which he means not merely increase in size, but also change of form, etc. This growth does not proceed blindly or aimlessly, but proceeds on rigidly determined lines, which depend upon the structure and constitution of the particular organism. External influences, however, also affect it. Eimer specially emphasizes four points in this connection: 1. This rigidly determined development of a character exhibits well defined, regular stages, and the evolution of each individual repeats the whole series of transformations (the Mueller-Haeckel "biogenetic-law." 2. New characters are first acquired by strong adult males (the law of male dominance). 3. New characters appear on definite parts of the body, spreading especially from the rear to the front, (the law of undulation). 4. Varieties are stages in the process of development, through which all the individuals of the respective species must pass.

These points indicate how important for Eimer is the transmission of those characters which the parents themselves have acquired in the course of their own development. He conceives that this transmission takes place when the causative influences exert themselves permanently on many succeeding generations. Eimer thinks that in this way the constitution of the respective species is gradually transformed. Besides the effect of external influences (which may vary according to the climate, etc.: Geoffroy St. Hilaire), Eimer mentions as important and active factors in this development, (1). The use and disuse of organs (Lamarck); (2). The struggle for existence (Darwin); (3). The correlation of organs, that is, the inner relation of organs in consequence of which a change in one organ may occasion a sudden change in another organ; (4). Cross fertilization and hybridism.

It is clear that with reference to the factors of evolution Eimer is, and perhaps not unreasonably, an eclectic, whose aim is to do justice to the predecessors of Darwin as well as to Darwin himself. His antagonism to Darwin and Weismann in this work is still quite moderate, although even here it appears with sufficient clearness that selection and the struggle for existence, the two principles peculiarly characteristic of Darwinism, do not give rise to new species, but can at best only separate and differentiate species already existing.

The second part of Eimer's work dealing with the origin of species, which appeared after an interval of ten years, bears the title: "Orthogenesis of Butterflies." The Origin of Species, II. Part (2 tables and 235 illustrations in the text). Leipzig, 1897. In this book substantially the same thoughts occupy the mind of the author as in the former volume, but in many respects they are more mature, and conspicuously more definite and precise. The most salient features are the following:

1. Eimer establishes his theory by means of very minute observations on a definite species of animals, viz., butterflies.

2. He attributes evolution almost exclusively to development along definitely determined lines.

3. He proves the utter untenableness of Darwinian principles and repudiates them unqualifiedly.

4. In a very distinct and severe manner he gives expression to his opposition to his former friend Weismann.

5. He attacks with telling effect the fantastic Darwinian "Mimicry."

In his "General Introduction" Eimer first treats of Orthogenesis in opposition to the Darwinian theory of selection. The very first sentence gives evidence of this antagonism: "According to my investigation, organic growth (Organophysis), which is rendered dependent on the plasm by permanent external influences, climate and nourishment, and the expression of which is found in development along definitely determined lines, (Orthogenesis), is the principal cause of transformation, its occasional interruption and its temporary cessation and is likewise the principal cause of the division of the series of organisms into species."

Lamarck's theory of the use and disuse of organs and Darwin's hypothesis of natural selection are consequently pushed into the background. Here also Eimer at once places himself at variance with Naegeli who had enunciated a similar theory. Naegeli took as a starting point an inherent tendency in every being to perfect itself, thus presupposing an "inner principle of development," and making light of external influences as transforming causes. Eimer flatly contradicts this view. We shall revert to this point in our criticism of his theory. In opposition to the theory of selection, Eimer lays special stress on the fact that its underlying assumption, viz., fortuitous, indefinite variation in many different directions, is entirely devoid of foundation in fact, and that selection, in order to be effective, postulates the previous existence of the required useful characters, whereas the very point at issue is to explain how these characters have originated. Since, therefore, according to Eimer's investigations, there are everywhere to be found only a few, definitely determined lines of variation, selection is incapable of exercising any choice. The development, furthermore, proceeds without regard for utility, since, for instance, the features that characterize a species of plants are out of all reference to utility. "Even if nothing exists that is essentially detrimental, nevertheless very much does exist that bears no reference whatever to immediate good, and was therefore never affected by selection."

Further on, Eimer expresses still more clearly the opposition of his theory to that of Darwin, and in so doing he attacks vigorously the omnipotence of selection, so unreasonably proclaimed by the followers of Darwin. Eimer's theory, consequently, asserts that: "The essential cause of transmutation is organic growth, a definite variation, which, during long periods of time proceeds unswervingly and without reference to utility, in but few directions and is conditioned by the action of external influences, of climate and nourishment." In consequence of an interruption of orthogenesis a stoppage ensues in certain stages of the development, and this stoppage is the great cause of the arrangement of forms in different species. Of vital importance also "is development through different stages (Hetero-epistase), which results in the arrested development of certain characters in an organism, while others progress and still others become retrogressive. As a rule use and disuse are of great efficacy in this regard, and conjointly with these compensation and correlation." Occasionally also irregular development sets in, which proceeds by leaps.

Of course, Eimer could not but in his turn burn incense before Darwin by declaring that he would not dare to cross swords with such a man, while in reality he repudiates all of Darwin's fundamental tenets.

It may be well to state here in addition a few important supplementary considerations: "Development can everywhere proceed in only a limited number of directions because the constitution, the material composition of the body, conditions these directions and prevents variation in all directions." This is an important statement because Eimer clearly expresses therein the difference between his own theory and that of Naegeli. He makes the direction of development dependent on the material composition of the body, whereas Naegeli considers it dependent upon an internal tendency of every being to perfect itself, hence upon a power inherent in the body. Eimer's view therefore tends towards a mechanical explanation, while Naegeli postulates a vital energy. The "internal causes" according to Eimer find their explanation in the material composition of the body. Since the growth of the individual organism depends on this composition and on the external influences, Eimer compares family-development with it and designates the latter as "organic growth." In opposition to Naegeli he maintains that this "organic growth" does not always aim at perfection but often tends to simplification and retrogression.

The following, then, according to Eimer, are the directive principles of variation: (1). The general law of coloration (stripes running lengthwise change into spots, stripes running crosswise change to a uniform color). (2). The law of definitely directed local change (new colors spread from the rear to the front and from above downward or vice versa, old colors disappear in the same directions. (3). The law of male predominance (males are as a rule one step in advance of the females in development). Female predominance is an exception. (4). The law of age-predominance (new characters appear at a well-advanced age, and at the time of greatest strength). (5. The law of wave-like development (during the course of the formation of the individual organism a series of changes proceed in a definite direction over the body of the animals). (6). The law of independent uniformity of development (the same course of development is pursued in non-related forms and results in similar forms). (7). The law of development through different stages (different characteristics of the same being may develop to a different degree and in different directions). (8). The law of unilateral development (the progeny does not present a complete combination of the characters of the parents but manifests a preponderance of the characteristics of either parent). (9). The law of the reversal of development (the direction of develpoment may reverse and tend towards the

75

starting point). (10). The law of the cessation of development (a protracted cessation of development frequently ensues in one or the other stage).

The origin (perhaps rather the distinction) of species is accounted for principally by the last named law, by means of which Eimer also explains the so-called atavism or reversion. To this law are joined other factors, e. g., development proceeding in leaps, as demonstrated by Koelliker and Heer; local separation (through migration; prevention of fertilization, e. g., the impossibility of cross-fertilization between certain individual organisms (which Romanes had already opposed to natural selection), and crossing.

The second main division of the book is taken up with a very searching and detailed criticism of Weismann. This criticism seems to me entirely warranted; because not only the latter's unintelligible position with regard to natural selection (the repudiation of which he seems to regard as synonymous "with cessation of all investigation into the causal nexus of phenomena in the domain of life") but likewise his fanciful theory of heredity, utterly devoid as it is of any support from actual observation, bespeak an utter lack of qualities essential to a naturalist; and the manner in which he ignores his former pupil and his labors, because they proved embarrassing to him, is entirely unworthy of a man of science.

Eimer devotes special attention to "mimicry"; and indeed he was forced to be very solicitous to dispel this fanciful conception of Darwinism which radically contradicted his own views. Moreover, the untenableness of the mimicry hypothesis must have revealed itself very clearly to him in the course of his investigations regarding the coloring of butterflies. Mimicry, as our readers are well aware, consists in this, that living beings imitate other organisms or even inanimate objects; Darwinism maintains that this is done for the sake of protection against enemies. This phenomenon is said to have been produced by selection Those animals that possessed, for instance, some similarity to a leaf, in consequence escaped their enemies more easily than others and survived, while those that had no leaf-like appearance succumbed; when this process had been repeated a few times, many animals (butterflies) gradually developed that marvelous leaf-like appearance, which frequently deceives the most practiced eye.

It appears so simple and natural that one need not wonder that this peculiar phenomenon gained many an adherent for Darwinism. But, of course, it is directly opposed to the views of Eimer; and it is for this reason that he endeavors so assiduously to disprove the error of Darwinism in this regard. As the underlying color design of the butterfly Eimer designates eleven longitudinal designs; and the examination of the leaf-like forms leads him to the conclusion, that their appearance always depends on "the unaltered condition or the greater prominence of certain parts of this fundamental design." There is to be observed a shifting of the third band, so that in conjunction with the fourth, which is curved, it forms the mid-rib of the leaf. Eimer finds the cause of this phenomenon in the alteration of the form. The leaf-like form results from an acumination and elongation of the wings, which in turn results from a marked elongation of the rim of the fore-wing. And this again is produced by the proportionately greater growth of one part of the wing-section than of the others.

With reference to the reason of this growth it is of importance to note that experiments, consisting in the application of artificial heat to the chrysales of the swallow-tail and sailor-butterfly, demonstrated that by this means "the fore-wing is drawn out more toward the outer wing-vein, and the rim of the fore-wing becomes more elongated and curved." It is observed, however, that the natural heat-forms of the same genera and species, namely, the summer-forms and those which live in the warm southern climate, exhibit, for instance, in the case of butterflies akin to the sailor, the same features, the elongation and more marked curvature of the fore-rim of the fore-wings and the consequent more extended form, that are produced by the action of artificial heat. Manifestly this is a matter of vital importance for the solution of the question: heat, whether artificial or natural, produces a difference in growth, which results in a change of form and coloring. There is consequently no room for natural selection or the struggle for existence.

The leaf-like form is generally associated with the dark, faded colors of dry leaves, and when this similarity disappears even bright colors appear on the fore-wings. In many cases the resemblance to leaves is very imperfect;

different forms of the same species live side by side and among them are to be found those, the resemblance of which to leaves is extremely slight. All these facts, and especially the frequently recurring retrogression of the leaf-like appearance, justify serious doubt regarding the Darwinian assumption, that adaptation was a necessity for the forest-butterflies on account of the protection which it provided.

An eye witness furthermore declares that the butterflies that resemble leaves most closely do not always alight on withered leaves, on which they would be almost invisible, but frequently rest on a green background, against which they show off very clearly, and therefore could not long escape the keen eye of birds. Besides, these butterflies are but seldom pursued by the birds, of which there is question here, and hence are in no need of protection.

The longer Eimer devoted his attention to the origin of this resemblance the more "the poetic picture of the imitated leaf" vanished out of sight, and he became convinced that it involved the necessary expression of the lines of development, which the respective beings were bound to follow, and that there was no question of imitation.

Apart from the resemblance to leaves, by reason of regular changes of color, design, and wing-structure, numerous non-related butterflies often develop such wonderful similarities—which are not, as hitherto supposed, imitations or disguises produced by selection, but are either the outcome of an entirely independent uniformity of development or, at least, of its consequence—that it must be admitted that external similarity may arise by different means and in various ways. These relations of similarity are of such frequent recurrence because of the limited number of directions of development in which changes or color and design in butterflies may tend. Eimer finds the reason of this small number of directions, in which development may proceed, in the fact "that the elementary external influences of climate and nourishment on the constitution of the organism are everywhere the cause of the transformations."

Another important point is the difference of sex. If the butterflies are of different sex, the males as a rule exhibit a more developed stage of design and color than the females. These frequently present on the upper side the stage of coloration, which the males present on the lower side, while the upper side of the males is one stage in advance. It is of special significance that the characters of the more advanced sex frequently correspond to those of a related, superior species, and occasionally to those of widely separated species. Eimer endeavors to explain male predominance "by a more delicate and more developed, i. e., more complex, chemico-physical organization of the male organism." Even this development tends toward simplification, the origin of dull-black colors.

This most interesting question brings Eimer into conflict with another Darwinian principle, the so-called principle of "sexual election," according to which the more striking characteristics of the male sex become strengthened for the reason that females invariably give the preference to the males endowed with them, over those that are less "attractive." These exceedingly romantic ideas have been often and deservedly repudiated, e. g., even by Wallace only a short time after their first appearance. Eimer really does them too much honor when he again undertakes, even with a certain amount of respect, a thorough refutation of them, "as in every regard unfounded." It is of primary importance to note here, that in the case of dimorphism of the sexes abrupt modifications occur in connection with unilateral heredity. "It is impossible for sexual selection to produce a change of design and color, which results in the sudden kaleidoscopic formation of wholly different designs, as we find actually taking place through the action of artificial heat and cold and other factors in nature."

This brings us to a brief consideration of the answer, which Eimer proposes to give to the question of the real causes of the formation of species among butterflies. A precise and clear statement of this important part of Eimer's theory of Descent, is contained in the following extracts: "The transformation of organisms is primarily conditioned by the action of immediate external influences on the organisms. The same causes, which produce individual growth, especially climate and nourishment, also produce the organic growth of organisms, that is, transmutation, which is but a continuation in the progeny of individual growth, through the transmission of the characteristics acquired during the lifetime of the individual.

Hence, transmutation is simply a physiological process, a phyletic growth.

The changes, which the individual organism experiences during its life in its material, physiological and morphological organization, are in part transmitted to its progeny. The changes thus acquired become more marked from generation to generation, until finally they result in a perceptible new structure."

"In this process, new or changing external influences undoubtedly exercise great activity, but the same influences, constantly repeated, must in the course of time also produce a change in the organisms through the physiological activity, which is conditioned by them, so that after a long time elapses, a species will have changed even in an unvarying environment and will react on new influences in a manner quite different from their progenitors; their "constitution" has undergone a change."

"This organic growth of living beings takes place regardless of the active use of the organs and in many cases remains independent of this (Lamarckian) factor of transformation. But use may exercise considerable influence on the formation resulting from the primitive organic growth, by modifying the growth, by restricting it to those parts most frequently called into use, or even by depriving other parts of the necessary matter (compensation)."

"The Lamarckian principle, therefore, offers but a possible and to transformation, the principal cause is to be found in organic growth."

"* * * The organic growth of butterflies is primarily conditioned by climatic influences. * * * The proof is to be found in the facts revealed by the geographical distribution of butterflies, by the variations corresponding to the seasons, and by experiments regarding the influence of artificial heat and cold on development."

Experimental proof is naturally of vital importance for Eimer's theory. He cites in this regard especially the experiments of Merrifield, Handfuss, Fischer, Fickert, and Countess Maria von Linden. In Eimer's own laboratory the latter performed experiments on Papilionides, "which prove in the most striking manner the recapitulation of the family-history in the individual." "The fact that it is possible by raising or lowering the temperature during the time of development to breed butterflies, possessed of the characteristics of related varieties and species living in southern and northern regions respectively, characteristics not merely of color and design, but also of structure, is complete irrefragable proof of my views."

Eimer therefore belongs to the class of naturalists, like Wigand, Askenasy, Naegeli, and many others, who reject the purely mechanical trend of Darwinism and recognize an "immanent principle of development." He seeks the essential cause of evolution in the constitution of the plasm of organisms. This very analogy between the development of the family and that of the individual should, in fact, convince any one of this. If Eimer chooses to refer the analogy to "growth" and to designate the evolution of the whole animated kingdom as also a process of growth, there is, strictly speaking, no room for objection. However, there is here a danger, which he does not seem to have guarded against. To designate the whole process as a growth, as Eimer does, really explains nothing, but merely defines more clearly the status of the problem. For, what do we know of the so-called process of growth? In truth, nothing, so that very little is gained by referring evolution to organic growth; the problem remains unsolved.

The most important and correct part of Eimer's conclusion seems to be the establishment of definite lines of development. He has, in fact, permanently disposed of the Darwinian assumption of universal chaos in evolution, upon which good mother Nature could at will exercise her choice. Fortuitously initiated development is a conditio sine qua non of Darwinism and Weismannism. For any one, who has studied the work of Eimer and still adheres to this fundamental error of Darwinism, there is no possible escape from the labyrinth into which he has allowed the hand of Darwinism to lead him.

If, on the one hand, Eimer recognizes the immanent principles of development, he, nevertheless, on the other hand, also accords due consideration and ascribes great efficacy to external influences; in fact, he represents them as perhaps the more essential factor. Climate, nourishment, etc., affect the inner structure, the plasm, transform it and thus produce variation which is transmitted to the progeny. But, however great may be the influence of environment, Eimer seems to overestimate it. Indeed, the analogy of "growth" should have led Eimer to a conception of the true relation between "internal" and "external" causes. Warmth, air, light, moisture and nourishment, are undoubtedly necessary factors in the process of growth, but they are only the conditions which render it possible, and not the causes which produce it. The latter are to be found in the individual organism itself. The conditions may be ever so favorable and well-adapted for growth, still the organism will not develop unless it bear within itself the power to do so. On the other hand, although it is hampered and may become abnormal, it will readily grow even in an unfavorable environment, as long as it retains its inherent vital force. The same is very likely true of the genealogical growth. Evolution took place in virtue of the power inherent in the developing organisms. But only when the environment was favorable and normal, did the evolution proceed favorably and normally, that is, toward the perfection of the animate kingdom.

It appears as if the internal principle of development were losing influence and significance with Eimer; but the ulterior reason for this is not far to seek. Whoever recognizes the validity of the internal principle of development, eliminates chance, that stop-gap of materialism, from evolution, and is lead at once to a supreme Intelligence which directs evolution. As soon as it comes in sight, however, certain persons take fright and turn aside or even turn back in order to avoid it. This was the case with Eimer, although perhaps in a lesser degree. This is sincerely to be deplored, since his theory would have gained in depth if he had but done full justice to the internal principle of development. For the same reason he seems to have attacked Naegeli's principle of perfection, another fact which is very much to be regretted. True, it is as anti-mechanical as it can be and hence has gained but few adherents; but it is based on truth nevertheless, and will some day prevail in the doctrine of Descent.

It is perfectly intelligible that the thought of "perfection" should not have occurred to Eimer or should have slipped his memory during his observations on butterflies. The fact however, reveals a one-sidedness which he could have avoided. When the notion of utility is rejected—and Eimer rejects it very emphatically in his discussions on mimicry—it is undoubtedly difficult to arrive at the concept of a perfecting tendency. This, however, can in no way mean that this concept should be entirely banished from nature, even as the notion of utility cannot be banished. Even if the coloration and design of the wings of the butterfly do not reveal utility, other characteristics certainly do reveal it. It is one of the fatal mistakes of Darwinism, that it fails to recognize the possibility of dividing the characters and qualities of organisms into two large groups, as I attempted to do with more detail, for instance, in my "Catechism of Botany." There I called them (p. 89) "Autochthon-morphological" and "adaptive-morphological characters." The former reveal no relation to utility, they are innate and distinguish the organism from other organisms; the latter can be explained by means of certain vital functions, hence they possess a certain utility and adapt themselves more or less to environment. The former are permanent, the latter changeable. Darwinians regard all the characters of organisms as useful, physiological, and adaptive. If they have been hitherto unable to make good this assumption, they appeal to our lack of knowledge and console themselves with the thought that the future may yet reveal the missing relations. The presence on plants and animals of any autochthon-morphological characters means death to Darwinism, because these can never be explained by means of selection and struggle for existence.

Eimer is too much inclined towards the other extreme; he does not admit the existence of adaptive-morphological characteristics. Viewed in this aspect, his repudiation of mimicry may perhaps also seem somewhat harsh and one-sided. In this narrowness of view must also be sought the reason for his complete repudiation of Naegeli's principle of perfection.

It is an incontrovertible fact that in the organic world there exists an ascending scale from the imperfect to the perfect. Every organism is indeed perfect in its own sphere and from its own point of view. But perfection with reference to things of earth is a very relative concept; many an organism which is perfect in itself, appears very imperfect when compared with others. If, then, there is a gradation of animals and plants from the lower to the higher, it is the task of the theory of Descent to explain this gradual perfection. The crude and aimless activity of Darwinian selection, which necessarily operates through "chance," can never explain this perfection, which remains, as far as selection is concerned, one of the greatest enigmas of nature. Far from solving the enigma, selection but makes it obscurer.

If, then, one refuses to recognize a directing creative Intelligence, whose direction produces this perfection, nothing remains but Naegeli's principle of perfection. The outer world with its influences can certainly not produce perfection, hence this power must lie within the organism itself. But when one has once brought himself to accept an immanent principle of development, it surely cannot be difficult to take the next step and ascribe to it the tendency towards perfection.

That Eimer does not take this step, is, to my mind, a mistake, which must be attributed to his one-sidedness, which, in turn, results from the fact that he generalizes too arbitrarily his observations on butterflies and the conclusions which he draws from them. Animals and plants certainly possess many characteristics which cannot be explained by means of his theory alone. The conclusion will probably be finally arrived at, that nature is inexhaustible and many-sided, even in the lines on which it proceeds to attain this or that end.

One thing, however, of primary importance is evident from the investigations of Eimer, namely the proof that the same lines of development may be entered upon from entirely different starting-points, and that the number of these lines is limited. This fact is of importance because it enjoins more caution in arguing from uniformity of development to family-relation, than has been usually employed since the days of Darwin. The method commonly employed is undoubtedly very convenient, but is somewhat liable to be misleading. Hence, if one wishes to establish the genealogical relationship of forms, nothing remains but to set out on the laborious path of studying the development of both; and even then it remains questionable whether the truth will be arrived at. However, he who concludes to relationship from a comparison of developed forms, is much less likely to arrive at the truth.

In one point Eimer concedes too much to Darwinism, in the matter of the famous fundamental principle of biogenesis, according to which an organism is said to repeat in its individual development the whole series of its progenitors. Although he does not enter upon a discussion of the principle, it is evident from one passage that he accepts it. One is inclined to think that his careful observations and experiments should have convinced him of the contrary. It appears to me, at least, that the abundant materials of his observations bear evidence radically opposed to the principle. During late years, the antagonism to it has been on the increase, and the day is not very distant when it shall have passed into history. It would certainly be a laudable undertaking to enter upon a thorough investigation of the actual basis of the principle.

CHAPTER VI.

In every disease, especially in a lingering one, there are times when life's flickering embers glow with an unnatural brightness. Hence, it would not be at all surprising if a similar phenomenon were to be observed in the case of dying Darwinism; for it cannot be doubted that its disease is chronic. It has, in fact, been dying this long time. Certain indications render it very probable that we are at present witnessing such a phenomenon, for to-day we behold once more a few naturalists stepping before the public in defense of Darwinism. We are desirous of presenting the present status of the Darwinian theory as objectively as possible, hence, since we have hitherto heard exclusively anti-Darwinian testimonies—as the nature of the case demanded—we shall now lend our attention to a Darwinian. The reader may then decide for himself whether this treatise should not still bear the title, "At the Death-bed of Darwinism."

The naturalist in question is the zoologist, Professor F. von Wagner. In the "Umschau" (No. 2, 1900) he published an article, "Regarding the Present Status of Darwinism," which is highly instructive and important in more respects than one.

We wish, in the first place, to call special attention to the following statements embodied in the article: "It is not to be denied that in serious professional circles the former enthusiasm has considerably decreased and a scepticism is gaining ground more and more, which betrays a widespread tendency towards revolutionizing current theories. The *fin de siecle* therefore, finds Darwinism not with the proud mien of a conqueror, but on the defensive against new antagonists." And again: "It seems, in fact, as if Darwinism were about to enter a crisis, the outcome of which can scarcely be any longer a matter of doubt."

To what outcome reference is made, appears from two sentences in the Introduction: "Thus it happens that a theory which was once accorded enthusiastic approval, is treated with cold disdain or vice versa. Examples of this are to be found in the history of all sciences and circumstances seem to indicate that Darwinism is to add another to the number of these theories."

Is not this exactly what we have repeatedly asserted? It is most significant that these words are not written by an opponent of Darwinism, but by one who seems to be thoroughly convinced of the truth of Darwinism. I am of opinion that it can be no longer a matter of doubt to any one, that the position of Darwinism is hopeless. If this were not true, a Darwinian would be very careful about making such an open and unreserved statement.

We therefore accept Professor von Wagner's words as a very welcome endorsement of what we have constantly maintained. Professor von Wagner, however, proposes to himself the further question: Whence comes the unfavorable attitude of present-day natural science towards Darwinism? A discussion of this question by a Darwinian cannot but be of interest to us, and indeed is an important contribution to the problem. With Goette, Professor von Wagner admits that the objections, which are raised against Darwinism to-day, are the very same which were raised from thirty to forty years ago. But when he then proceeds to assert that this is not to be explained on the assumption that the pristine enthusiasm for selection was due to a serious over-estimation of that theory, he fails to furnish even a shred of evidence in support of his assertion.

Anyone can readily point out that Darwinism explains the totality of the world of organisms by interlinking them, but has generally failed to account for the individual case, Wagner admits this as far as the "actual" is concerned, for it is quite impossible to trace with any certainty the action, in any particular case, of natural selection in the process which results in the production of a new species. At the outset it was reasonable to hope, that with the progress of science this difficulty would be solved or at least lessened; but this expectation has not been realized. * * *" It is wholly unintelligible how a naturalist can make this statement five hundred years after Bacon of Verulam, without drawing therefrom the proper conclusion. This lack of logic reminds me strongly of the assertion recently made by an eminent authority, that the principal cause of the difficulties of many naturalists in matters of religion is their deficient philosophical training.

Wagner's statement implies that, in the case of Darwinism one may in defiance of all established law, actually reverse the methods of natural science. How justifiable and how necessary was it not, then, that even three decades ago Wigand should have written his comprehensive work: "Darwinism and the Scientific Researches of Newton and Cuvier."

Ordinarily the scientific (inductive) method proceeds from the "actual" and attempts to deduce from the "individual case" an explanation, which applies to the whole. Here, however, we are face to face with a theory, which, according to the candid confession of an advocate, fails in the individual case, but furnishes a unifying explanation of the whole. This means nothing less than a complete subversion of all scientific methods. Usually a theory is deduced from separate observations regarding the "actual," but here—and this is what Wigand constantly asserted— the theory was enunciated first, and then followed the attempt to establish it in fact. One could then rest content and trust to the future to establish the theory by producing evidences of the "actual" in the individual case. But forty years have elapsed since the Darwinian hypothesis first became known, naturalists by the thousands have spent themselves in the endeavor to corroborate it by proofs based on actual facts, and to-day one of its own advocates has to confess that the endeavor has been a total failure. Instead of drawing the conclusion, however, that the theory is unwarranted and that the decrease of enthusiasm for it is therefore a natural consequence, he gratuitously enters a flat denial of this inference.

Every intelligent observer must conclude with absolute certainty from this confession of a Darwinian, that Darwinism is, in fact, not a scientific but a philosophic theory of nature.

But let us proceed to a consideration of the other reasons which Wagner suggests as an explanation of the retrogression of Darwinism. He states as a first reason, that scientific research since Darwin "has amassed such an abundance of empiric materials for the truth of the principle of Descent, that this doctrine has been able, even for some time past, to maintain an independent position and to draw proofs of its truth immediately from nature itself, without the intervention of Darwinism." * * * "From which it follows as a matter of course, that the question, whether the manner indicated by Darwin for the origin of species is the correct one, has decreased by no means inconsiderably in significance, inasmuch as Darwin's theory could now, if it were necessary, be abandoned with less concern than formerly because it could be relinquished without detriment to the doctrine of Descent."

It is unintelligible how one can attempt to explain a fact of such importance so superficially. With naive unconcern there appears on the face of it the acknowledgemen that Darwinism has really not been based on actual observation but has been enunciated for the sake of the doctrine of Descent. Come what may, this must be vindicated. Other means are now said to substantiate it, hence the Darwinian crutches may safely be discarded. The principle of action twenty or thirty years ago was therefore: a poor explanation is better than no explanation. I cannot understand, how Wagner dares to credit present-day naturalists with such motives.

When he then proceeds to say "that with the advance of the principle of development, new lines were entered upon, which led primarily to the corroboration and empiric demonstration of the doctrine of Descent, and not of Darwinism"—that the theory of Darwin was consequently neglected and, in fact, forced into the background—"that the labors specifically attributable to Darwinism as compared with the theory of Descent, put the former more and more into a false position to the detriment of its prestige"—when, I say, Wagner has marshalled all these considerations to explain the present aversion to Darwinism, he is guilty of a total subversion of facts. The true state of the case is the very contrary.

The credit given by Wagner to the Darwinian theory for stimulating research, is the very same as I also accorded it. The purpose of this research undoubtedly was to substantiate not only the doctrine of evolution in general, but also the Darwinian hypothesis in particular. To verify this, one need only glance over the various numbers of the "Kosmos," the periodical, which Haeckel and his associates established for that very purpose and which continued to publish good and bad indiscriminately until

95

some time in the eighties when lack of interest compelled its discontinuance. Wagner therefore misconstrues facts when he asserts that there have been no specifically Darwinian researches. Since the thoughts of Darwin first found expression these researches have been most abundant and their results have been consigned to the printer's ink. No doubt—and this is the salient point, which Wagner passes over in complete silence—they have been of service only to the doctrine of Descent in general, and in spite of the energetic efforts of the Darwinians, they have never led to the ardently desired proof from facts of the hypothesis of selection. This and no other is the state of the case.

In view of these vain endeavors, however, intelligent investigators have gradually become perplexed and have turned away from Darwinism, not because they have lost interest in it nor even because they no longer feel the need of it to assist the doctrine of Descent, but for the one sole reason that its insufficiency has become more and more apparent and that all experiments undertaken on its behalf have made the fact clearer and clearer that the first criticism of the great naturalists of the sixties and seventies was perfectly justified.

In forming a judgment concerning the whole question it cannot but be a matter of the utmost significance, that men have turned away from Darwinism to entirely different theories of Descent. It is a mistake to suppose, as Wagner would have us suppose, that the last decades have produced nothing but generalities regarding the doctrine of

Descent. For they have also witnessed the publication of a number of significant works, which aimed at giving a better individual explanation than was found in Darwinism. I need but recall Naegeli, Eimer, Haacke and a host of others. The most noteworthy feature of these new views regarding theories of Descent, is the constantly spreading conviction that the real determining causes of evolution are to be sought for in the constitution of the organisms themselves, hence in internal principles. This view, however, is not only absolutely and diametrically opposed to Darwinism but completely destructive of it as well.

The actual circumstances, therefore, are the very reverse of those pictured by Wagner. Darwinism has been rejected not on account of a lack of research but on account of an abundance of research, which proved its absolute insufficiency.

Besides these "general points of view," as he calls them, Wagner finds two other "considerations of no less importance" for explaining the decay of Darwinism. It is an incontrovertible fact, that the hereditary transmission of acquired characters has in no way been proved. On the contrary after it had at first received a general tacit recognition and was postulated by Lamarck, Darwin and Haeckel, it was denied by Weismann. Wagner asserts "that the number of those who have allied themselves with Weismann in this matter is obviously on the increase as is naturally the case, since, to the present day not a single incontestable case of hereditary transmission of acquired characters has been demonstrated, where as actual facts are at hand to prove the contrary."

It is perfectly evident that the doctrine that acquired characters are not inherted is fatal to Darwinism. Hence Wagner rightly considers its ascendancy a notable factor in bringing about the decay of Darwinism.

Finally, Wagner briefly indicates that certain new theories necessarily exercised an influence on Darwinism. Haeckel and the palaeontologists of North America supplemented it with a number of Lamarckian elements without alteration of its essential principles (the Neo-Lamarckians); Eimer regards the transmission of acquired characters as an established fact, but rejects natural selection as wholly worthless; Weismann, on the contrary, denies the transmission of acquired characters, but nevertheless regards natural selection as the main factor in the formation of species (the theory of the Neo-Darwinians). Eimer speaks of the impotence of natural selection, Weismann of its omnipotence. All this has shaken men's confidence in the trustworthiness of the Darwinian principles. This fact we are in no way inclined to doubt, but we must again differ from Wagner with regard to its significance. We maintain that matters had to take this turn, since the reason why Darwinism is now meeting with such serious opposition, is to be found in its very nature. This indeed should have been recognized forty years ago instead of just beginning to dawn on men of science at the present day. For if acquired characters are not transmitted by heredity, Darwinism is an impossibility. Forty years ago Darwinism should have recognized that its first and supreme task was to prove the hereditary transmission of acquired characters, so as to establish itself, first of all, on a sound footing.

One of the most peculiar incidents in this scientific tragi-comedy is the fact that Weismann, the mainstay of contemporary decadent Darwinism, attacks with might and main its fundamental assumption, the transmission of acquired characters, whereas Eimer, who is thoroughly convinced that he has proved that doctrine, in his turn attacks Darwinism and proves with telling effect the impotence of its principles. The amused observer can really demand nothing more. He can but rub his hands for joy and cheer on the heated combatants: Well done! On with the struggle! and the last vestige of Darwinism will soon have disappeared.

If, then, we were to summarize our strictures on the reasons which Wagner adduces to account for the decay of Darwinism, we would say this: Some of them are unwarranted, others are falsely interpreted.

There is, however, a third point which is of special interest to us, in the article under consideration; we refer to the view, which there finds expression, regarding the nature and outcome of the present crisis—a crisis, which, as a candid naturalist, Wagner is not in a position to deny.

This view rests on the entirely gratuitous assertion, "that the decline, in the esteem enjoyed by Darwinism, is not due to a better insight arising from widened experience, but is primarily the expression of a tendency—a tendency which resulted almost as a psychological necessity from the precarious position into which Darwinism was forced under the sway of the theory of Descent." This assertion rests, as stated above, on wholly erroneous assumptions. It is a serious mistake, to speak in this connection of tendencies and even to brand them as a "psychological necessity." The decline in esteem is essentially due to experience, and indeed to experience which has made it certain that Darwinism has everywhere failed.

The importance of the present crisis in Darwinism is to be restricted even further, according to Wagner, by the fact, "that the real objections, urged against the theory of Darwin, are almost in every instance based on theoretic considerations, the validity of which can be put to the test only in fictitious cases. This manner of proceeding manifestly leads to the inevitable consequence, that the results thus obtained can claim no decisive weight against Darwinism. A decisive critique can be constructed only on the basis of experience, and in this connection it cannot be emphasized sufficiently, that, as yet, the path to it has been scarcely indicated, to say nothing of its having been actually pursued." The reason for this fact according to Wagner, is to be found "in the numerous and most extraordinary difficulties that arise in the way of the empiric investigation of the theory of selection."

After we have read all this, we instinctively ask our-

100

selves: do we actually live at the beginning of the 20th century? Is it possible, that even at this late day the whole structure of scientific method is to be subverted in this fashion?

Just consider for a moment, what according to these words is the actual import of the whole article: Darwinism is a unifying explanation of the origin of the totality of the world of organisms, but fails in the individual case; in any specfied case it is "almost impossible" to trace with any certainty the action of natural selection in the process which results in the production of a new species; that is, Darwinism was enunciated with a complete disregard for inductive method, as an hypothesis to explain the whole, and without actual proof in the concrete—a most unscientific procedure. Immediately after, however, the adversaries of Darwinism are asked in all seriousness to produce individual facts in disproof of the theory.

In the same strain Wagner goes on to say that "from no point of view is our vision so penetrating as to be able to grasp the coherence which according to Darwin pervades the complex course of natural selection. When men of science take occasion to repudiate Darwinism because of our inability to explain satisfactorily any particular case by means of the theory of selection, this inability arises not from the theory of Darwin but from the inadequacy of our experience. For as yet the empiric prerequisites for an objective judgment regarding the validity or futility of the theory of selection are entirely lacking."

Every naturalist who believes in the inductive method must needs draw the conclusion from these naive admissions, that, as Darwinism lacks the empiric prerequisites, it should be discarded. Moreover, the demand is made in all seriousness, that, in order to refute Darwinism which has not as yet been established empirically, empiric proofs should be forthcoming.

To my mind, the scientific and logical bankruptcy of Darwinism was never announced more bluntly and ingenuously. Furthermore it must be remarked that Wagner's statement, regarding "fictitious cases," is not even pertinent. He seems to have no idea of the observations and experiments of Sachs, Haberlandt, Eimer, and a host of other investigators. The disproof of Darwinism on the basis of scientific research is an accomplished fact.

A word about the conclusion of Wagner's article, which in view of what has been already said, cannot be a matter of surprise. He maintains that the considerations which he adduces, "clearly" prove that there is no "reasonable ground for despairing of the theory of Darwin —; for a theory, which neither proceeds from questionable assumptions, nor loses itself in airy hypotheses, but rests throughout and exclusively on facts, need never fear the advance of science."

But a moment ago it was asserted that the theory of selection is lacking "entirely as yet the empiric prerequisites" and now only twenty-three lines further on, it rests "throughout and exclusively on facts." It is difficult to know what conclusion to come to regarding a naturalist and University professor who can commit himself to such a contradiction. I shall abstain from any comment and let the reader form his own judgment.

Does this article betoken the death-bed of Darwinism? For my own part I repeat what I said above, that I consider it the most valuable contribution to the characterization of decadent Darwinism that has appeared up to the present time. The sooner a theory, which is thus treated and characterized by one of its own advocates, is stored away in the lumber-room of science, the better. In view of the sound judgment, which is to-day becoming more and more apparent in scientific circles, there is reason to hope that this article of Professor von Wagner will be additional incentive for many naturalists to break completely with Darwinism.

CHAPTER VII.

In the year 1899 Haeckel published a new work, which he intended as a kind of testament; for with the close of the nineteenth century the author desired to put a finishing touch to his life-work.

In the Preface Haeckel states with very remarkable modesty that his book cannot reasonably claim to present a complete solution of the riddles of existence; that his answer to the great questions can naturally be only subjective and only partly correct; that his attainments in the different branches is very unequal and imperfect; and that his book is really only a sketch book of studies of very unequal value. In this way the author naturally gains at once the confidence of his reader who is thus prepared to yield assent when the author makes pretense to sincerity of conviction and an honest search after truth. The reader's surprise at the contents of the book and at the manner of its presentation is, however, only increased by this ruse. All modesty has vanished, monistic doctrines are presented as absolute truth, every divergent opinion is contemptuously branded as heretical; in short, the book reveals a Darwinian orthodoxy of the purest type, with all the signs of blind bigotry and odious intolerance which the author imagines he discovers in his Christian adversaries. It is difficult to see where, in view of such a contradiction between the work and its Preface, there is room for an honest striving after truth. Personally I do not wish to deny Haeckel all honesty of purpose, for it is my endeavor to understand the *whole* man. The one prominent feature of the "Weltraetsel" is the fact that, owing to a very marked deficiency in philosophical training, Haeckel has become so completely absorbed in his system that he has lost all interest in everything else and takes cognizance only of what suits his purpose. What he lacks above all, is the ability to appreciate even the "honest" opinion of others; hence, from the very outset he brings into the discussion that bitterness of which he complains in others (in the Weltraetsel he once makes this accusation against me). Notwithstanding all this, honest conviction may be present, but if so, it is joined with total blindness. But what is to be thought of his search after truth since he completely ignores his adversaries? For instance, in spite of Loofs' attacks, he continues to have his book reprinted without alteration, without submitting it to revision. The "Reichsbote" is perfectly in the right when it says: Haeckel, in fact, takes account only of what suits his purpose.

As regards the contents of the "Weltraetsel," it is not my intention to enter here upon a criticism of it but merely to discuss it as illustrating the general status of the theory of Descent. It is to be noted, in the first place, that it is really not a scientific book at all; for of its 472 pages, the first or "Anthropological Part," with which alone we are here concerned, occupies only 74 (from pages 27 to 100), even less than one-sixth of the whole, whereas the "Theological Part" is almost twice as long. The book is, in fact, rather a theologico-natural-philosophical treatise than a work of natural science. The scientific part is, however, the foundation on which Haeckel builds up his natural philosophy, and which he uses as the starting point of his criticism of theology. Hence it is worth our while to discuss it.

How then fares it with the anthropological basis of Haeckel's whole system? As an attentive student of his age the naturalist-philosopher of Jena must have perceived the true position of Darwinism, namely, that the foremost naturalists of to-day have no more than an historical interest in it. Since, in accordance with the well known tendency of old men to persevere in the position they have once assumed and not easily to accept innovations, Haeckel is still an incorrigibly orthodox Darwinian, we should naturally expect him to embody in this testament some new cogent evidence of the truth of Darwinism. But nothing of that nature is to be found in the book.

The first chapter of the "Anthropological part" is taken up with a "general history of nineteenth century culture," in itself a sign of peculiar logical acumen, that he should include this and the "struggle regarding world-views" in the "anthropological part'" instead of embodying it in a general introduction. The remaining chapters treat: "Our Bodily Structure," "Our Life," "Our Embryonic-history," "Our Family-history." It is not to be supposed, however, that any arguments are here adduced, nothing but assertions; a large part of the chapter is taken up with historical sketches, in which Haeckel again proves himself utterly devoid of all appreciation of history and all sense of justice. He attributes the decay of the natural sciences to the "flourishing condition of Christianity" and dares to speak of the unfavorable influence of Christianity on civilization. Apart from the historical sketch, each chapter presents only the quintessence of Darwinism, fairly bristling with assertions, which are boldly put forth as incontrovertible truths. In view of the author's demand to have at least his sincere love of truth recognized, we can but throw up our hands out of sheer astonishment. To illustrate Haeckel's "love of truth" let it suffice to observe that in the second chapter he asserts that man is not only a true vertebrate, a true mammal, etc.—which indeed is passable—but even a true ape (having "all the anatomical characteristics of true apes"). With a wonderful elasticity he passes over the differences. What, indeed, is to be said, when he states as a "fact" that "physiologically compared (!), the sound-speech of apes is the preparatory stage to articulate human speech." It is so simply monstrous, that even Garner's famous book of ape-speech, cannot surpass it. As a third illustration of Haeckel's method of argumentation, if we are still justified in speaking of such a thing, we may mention his assertion (p. 97) as a "certain historical fact," "That man is descended directly from the ape, and indirectly from a long line of lower vertebrates." If, in view of the results of research during the last forty years any one can assert this as a "certain historical fact" and can still wish to be credited with honest conviction and love of truth, there remains, to adopt Haeckel's own expression, but one explanation for this psychological enigma, namely, intellectual *marasmus senilis*, which may very easily have set in with a man of sixty-six, who himself complains (p. 7) of "divers warnings of approaching age."

Thus, the anthropological part of the "Weltraetsel" contains nothing new; always the same old story, the same threadbare assertions without a shred of evidence to corroborate them.

The remaining parts also contain various scientific assertions, which are proposed as facts without being such, but these parts do not immediately pertain to our theme. Suffice it to say that, after reading Haeckel's "Weltraetsel," one would be led to think that there is no question of a "deathbed of Darwinism," but that on the contrary Darwinism, as remodeled by Haeckel, is more in the ascendant to-day than ever. Let us judge of its prestige by the reception accorded the "Weltraetsel."

One unaltered edition after the other, thousand after thousand, the book is given to the public. Hence it must meet with approval. It does indeed meet with approval, but the question is, from whom? Immature college and university students will doubtless receive it with reverential awe, just as they received the "Natural History of Creation" twenty-five years ago. Bebel accepts the book as an infallible source of truth, and after him the social democrats and free-church members will add it to the list of their "body and stomach books," which alone will afford it a respectable clientele, at least in number. In no one of my "deathbed articles," however, have I as yet ever maintained that Darwinism was decadent in *these* circles. I know full well, that Darwinism has filtered down into that sphere and there satisfies the anti-Christian and anti-religious demands of thousands.

Nothing, however, really depends on these senseless blind adherents of Haeckel's unproved assertions. We are now intent upon investigating how the world of eminent thinkers and natural science regards the latest product of Haeckel's fancy. That alone is of importance in ascertaining the real status of Darwinism.

As regards, in the first place, the other parts of the book, it is well known that all of them were vigorously attacked. Loofs in particular exposed Haeckel's theology, according to its deserts, in the clear light of truth, and convicted Haeckel of "ignorance" and "dishonesty;" while the philosopher Paulsen made short work of the "Weltraetsel" from his own standpoint, ("if a book could drip with superficiality, I should predicate that of the 19th chapter"). Harnack also condemned the theological section in the "Christliche Welt," and Troeltsch, Hoenigswald, and Hohlfeld took Haeckel severely to task on philosophic grounds. The naturalists have thus far maintained silence.

Scientific journals, and, I believe, only the more popular ones, pass a varying judgment on the book according to the intellectual bent of their book reviewers; but no one of the eminent and leading naturalists has publicly expressed his opinion regarding it. They all maintain a very significant silence, which speaks for itself. Now, however, just at the proper time a book, *Die Descendenz-theorie* has appeared from the pen of the zoologist, Professor Fleischmann of Erlangen, in which Haeckel is severely condemned. (See Chapter IX.)

The press-notices of the Weltraetsel, which are quoted in the book will be considered presently. It appears that with reference to natural science, only "laymen" discuss the book and approve of Haeckel's views. This is a point of great importance since it proves satisfactorily that men of science will have nothing to do with the "Weltraetsel." The large number of replies would, however, not allow Haeckel's friends to remain silent. The most extensive defense forthcoming was a pamphlet published by a certain Heinrich Schmidt of Jena. It cannot be gathered from his book (Der Kampf um die Weltraetsel, Bonn, E. Strauss 1900) to what profession the author belongs, hence I am unable to judge whence he derives the right to treat Haeckel's opponents in summary a manner. It is significant to note what class of men, according to Schmidt, received the "Weltraetsel" with enthusiasm and joy. They are August Specht, the free-church editor of "Menschentum" and of the "Freien Glocken," Julius Hart, Professor Keller-Zuerich, the philosopher and "Neokantian" Professor Spitzer of Graz, the popular literateur W. Boelsche,

W. Ule, and a few unknown great men, Dr. Zimmer, Th. Pappstein, R. Steiner, A. Haese; but stay, I came very near forgetting the great pillar, Dodel of Zuerich. But where is there mention of the professional colleagues of Haeckel whose testimonies could be taken seriously? Under the heading "Literary Humbug," which evidently has reference to the contents of his own work, Schmidt then meets numerous objections. Here vigorous epithets are bandied about, as, for instance, "absolute nonsense," "muddler," "foolish and senseless prattle," "idle talk," etc.; and from Dodel he copies the words with which the latter once sought to annihilate me: Job, verse 10, "Thou hast spoken like one of the foolish women." And he ventures to express indignation at Loofs' "invectives." As a compliment to Lasson he declares that he could easily conceive of the possibility of an ape ascending the professor's chair and speaking as intelligently as he (Lasson); which remark he probably intended as a witticism. He informs his readers that the criticism of Haeckel by men like Virchow, His, Semper, Haacke, Baer, and Wigand have been examined by professional specialists and proved practically worthless. This statement alone so clearly reveals Schmidt's lack of critical facultly and judgment that by it he at once forfeits his right to be taken seriously.

The whole book is nothing more than a collection of cuotations from the reviews of the "Weltraetsel," interspersed with characteristic expressions like "idle talk," "nonsense," etc., as exemplified above. A really pertinent reply and refutation of objections is entirely beyond

Schmidt's range; he waives the demand for a direct reply, for instance, in the following amusing way (p. 28): "Two reasons, however, prevent me from being more explicit: In the first place I do not like to dispute with people who adduce variant readings and church-fathers as proofs and can still remain serious. In the second place I would not like to fall into the hands of a Loofs." In this manner it is indeed easy to evade an argument, which for good reasons one is not able to pursue. Loofs' criticism is so serious and destructive that it should be of the utmost concern to Haeckel's friends to refute it. Since they are unable to do so, they content themselves with references to Loofs' caustic style, which he should indeed have avoided. There are, nevertheless, cases in which one must employ trenchant phraseology, and Haeckel himself has given an occasion for it; a dignified style is simply out of the question in his case. Haeckel extricated himself with even greater ease, by declaring that he had "neither time nor inclination" for reply, and that a mutual understanding with Loofs was impossible because their scientific views were entirely different. Could anything be more suggestive of the words of Mephistopheles:

> "But in each word must be a thought—
> There is,— or we may so assume,—
> Not always found, nor always sought,
> While words—mere words supply its room.
> Words answer well, when men enlist 'em,
> In building up a favorite system."

There are two other points in Schmidt's book that are of interest to us. The first of these is the manner in which the author treats the Romanes incident. Romanes ranks, as is well known, among the first of Haeckel's authorities. Hence it is a very painful fact that, but a short time before the publication of the first edition of the "Weltraetsel," my translation into German of Romanes' "Thoughts on Religion" should have appeared. From this book it was evident that Haeckel and his associates could no longer count this man among their number since he—a life-long seeker after truth—had abandoned atheism for theism, and died a believing Christian. Troeltsch and the "Reichsbote" asked whether Haeckel had purposely concealed this fact, and Schmidt now explains that Haeckel first became acquainted with the "Thoughts on Religion" through him towards the end of January, 1900. Unfortunately he does not add that since then a number of new editions of the "Weltraetsel" have appeared, in which Haeckel could have explained himself in an honorable manner. Schmidt has therefore not been successful in his attempt to clear up this matter.

But how does he settle with Romanes? He says: *"We are assured* that the thoughts were written down by the English naturalist George John Romanes"; and again: "The thoughts are published by a Canon of Westminster, Charles Gore, to whom *they are said* to have been handed over after the death of Romanes in the year 1894." Then he has the audacity to place Romanes in quotation marks. And finally he asserts that they would abide by Romanes' former works as their authority, the more so, because these were not, like the "Thoughts," "published and glossed by a Canon only after his (Romanes') death." By means of all this and of a comparison with the "Letters of the Obscurantists" he wishes to create the suspicion that there might be question here of forgery. Such an insinuation, (I employ Schmidt's own words) "cannot be characterized otherwise than as contemptible." "Here it is even worse than contemptible." I must beg my reader's pardon for overstepping the bounds of reserve with these caustic words, although they originated with Schmidt; but really the flush of anger rightfully mounts to one's cheeks when a man, from the mere fact that he is a disciple of the "great" Haeckel assumes the right to charge Canon Gore and indirectly myself with forgery. It is really very significant that these men should have to resort to such base and despicable expedients to extricate themselves from their unpleasant predicament. Apart from this, it was very amusing to me personally to think that for the sake of my unworthy self, Schmidt should have borrowed from his lord and master the epithet "pious," which Haeckel in his turn has drawn from his cherished friend Dodel. In all probability they will continue to hawk it about in order to bring me into disrepute with the rest of their kind. The few remarks Schmidt still finds it proper to make regarding the "Thoughts," betray his inability to understand the book. But as I stated in the preface it was a difficult book to read and understand. It is obviously not reading matter for shallow minds. I refer Schmidt to the biography of Romanes, published by his wife, (The Life and Letters of G. J. Romanes, London, Longmans, Green & Co., 1898), where he will find Romanes' religious development described by a well-informed hand. This development began as early as 1878, hence during the time of his intimate friendship with Darwin. In this book on pages 372 and 378 Schmidt will also find the words in which, *before* his death, Romanes begged that, if he were personally unable to publish the "Thoughts," they should be given to his friend Canon Gore after his own death. But why waste so many words on Mr. Schmidt, for since all these things must be doubly disagreeable and painful to him and Haeckel, he will very probably resort without delay to personal insinuation and accuse Mrs. Romanes of forgery.

To us, however, who thoroughly appreciate the situation, it is a matter of great moment that of one of the few really eminent naturalists, to whom Haeckel thought to be able to lay full and exclusive claim, for the last twenty years of his life should have been moving towards the Christian faith in his eager search for truth and should die not a monist, but a convinced Christian. Neither did he die an old man, to whom the adherents of monism would certainly have the effrontery to impute feeble-mindedness, but at the early age of forty-six years. Nor was his a sudden deathbed conversion—an impression which Schmidt attempts to create (p. 62) in order to be able with H. Heine to relegate the conversion to the domain of pathology—but followed after many years of diligent and honest study and research. The other point of which we must treat here, is the manner in which, after the example of Dr. Reh, Schmidt attempts in the "Umschau" to exonerate Haeckel in the matter of the "History of the three cliches." To begin with, it is at the very least dishonest on the part of Schmidt to say that, "in default of scientific arguments, theological adversaries have for the last thirty years been using it as the basis of their attacks." That is untrue, the "theological adversaries" have not had knowledge of it for that length of time. On the contrary Haeckel's own scientific colleagues were the first to discover and publish the matter some time in the seventies, and in consequence excluded Haeckel from their circle. Why does Schmidt not mention here the names of Ruetimeyer, His, and Semper? Furthermore Schmidt writes as if Haeckel had satisfied his colleagues in the matter of his forgery by declaring soon after (1870) that he had been "guilty of a very ill-considered act of folly." Why does Schmidt not mention the fact that the weighty attacks of His (Our Bodily Form and the Physiological Problem of its Origin, Leipzig, 1875) dates from the year 1875, five years after Haeckel's forced, palliative explanation? Besides, this incident of the three cliches is only one instance; the other examples of Haeckel's sense of truthfulness are for the most part entirely unknown to his "theological adversaries," who have nowhere to my knowledge made use of them; but *all* of them have been brought to light and held up before Haeckel by naturalists, namely, by Bastian (1874), Semper and Kossmann (1876 and 1877), Hensen and Brandt (1891), and Hamann (1893). Does this in any way tend to establish Schmidt's honesty? (Dr. Dennert has entered into a more searching criticism of Haeckel in his book, *Die Wahrheit ueber Haeckel.* 2 Aufl Halle a. S., 1902.)

In a word, the manner in which the "Weltraetsel" was received and in which Haeckel has been defended by Schmidt, are valuable indications of the decay of Darwinism. I repeat that I am speaking of course of the leading scientific circles. Those who hold back are never lacking, and one cannot be surprised that, in the case of Darwinism, their number is considerable: for on the one hand, to understand it an extraordinarily slight demand is made on one's mental capacity; and on the other hand it is a very convenient and even a seemingly scientific means of obviating the necessity of belief in God. These facts appeal very strongly to the multitude.

In concluding this section, we shall quote a positive testimony to the decay of Darwinism. On page 3 of his "Outlines of the History of the Development of Man and of the Mammals" (Leipzig, W. Engelmann, 1897) Prof. O. Schultze, Anatomist in Wuerzburg, says: "The idea entertained by Darwin, that the development of species may be explained by a natural choice—Selection—which operates through the struggle of individuals for existence, cannot permanently satisfy the spirit of inquiry. Even the factors of variability, heredity, and adaptation, which are essential to the transformation of species, do not offer an exact explanation."

CHAPTER VIII.

I have already called attention several times to the fact that Darwinism is indeed on the wane among men of science, but that it has gradually penetrated into lay circles where it is now posing as irrefragable truth. Especially the circles dominated by the social democrats swear by nothing higher than Darwin and Haeckel. In fact, only a short time ago Bebel publicly professed himself a convert to Haeckel's wisdom.

It is inevitable, however, that light should gradually dawn even in these circles, for it would be indeed strange, if no honest man could be found to tell them the truth regarding Darwinism. This has occurred sooner than I dared to hope. This chapter can announce the glad tidings that even in "social-democratic science" Darwinism is doomed to decay. Much printer's ink will, of course, be yet wasted before it will be so entirely dead as to be no longer available as a weapon against Christianity; but a beginning at least has been made.

In the December number of the ninth year of the *Sozialistische Monatshefte*, a social-democratic writer, Curt Grottewitz, undertakes to bring out an article on "Darwinian Myths." It is stated there that Darwin had a few eminent followers, but that the educated world took no notice of their work; that now, however, they seemed to be attracting more attention. "There is no doubt, that a number of Darwinian views, which are still prevalent to-day, have sunk to the level of untenable myths. True, the main doctrine of Darwin—the origin of new species from existing ones—is incontestably established, but apart from this even some very fundamental principles, which the master thought he discerned in the development of organisms, can scarcely be any longer maintained."

It may be well to remark here, that this was not really Darwin's main doctrine, for it already existed before his time (Lamarck, Geoffroy St. Hilaire). Darwin's main doctrine is the explanation of the origin of species by natural selection operating through the struggle for existence. It is therefore the old error repeated: Darwinism is confounded with the doctrine of Descent, of which it is merely one form. It is not our intention to derogate in the least from Darwin's merit, which consists in the fact that he gained general recognition for the doctrine of Descent; but that was not his main work. He wished above all to explain the *How* of Descent; this is his doctrine, and this doctrine we attack and declare to be on the point of expiring.

Grottewitz very frankly continues: "The difficulty with the Darwinian doctrines consists in the fact that they are incapable of being strictly and irrefutably demonstrated. The origin of one species from another, the conservation of useful forms, the existence of countless intermediary links, are all assumptions, which could never be supported by concrete cases found in actual experience." Some are said to be well established indirectly by proofs drawn from probabilities, while others are proved to be absolutely untenable. Among the latter Grottewitz includes "sexual selection," which is indeed a monstrous figment of the imagination. There was moreover really no reason for adhering to it so long. It is eminently untrue, that the biological research of the last few years proved for the *first* time the untenableness of this doctrine, as Grottewitz seems to think. Clear thinkers recognized its untenableness long ago, and surely Grottewitz and the whole band of Darwinian devotees as well, could have known that as early as twenty-five years ago this doctrine had been subjected to a reductio ad absurdum with classic clearness in Wigand's great work.

It is certainly a very peculiar phenomenon; for decades we behold a doctrine reverently re-echoed; thoughtful investigators expose its folly, but still the worship continues, the Zeitgeist must have its idol. It appears, however, as if the Zeitgeist were gradually tiring of its golden calf and were on the point of casting it into the rubbish-heap. Misgivings arise on all sides; here one class of objections are considered, there another. A closer examination reveals that these are by no means new reasons, based on new researches, but the very oldest, urged long ago and perhaps much more clearly and forcibly. At that time, however, the Zeitgeist was under the spell of the suggestion of individual men: it heard and saw nothing but the captivating, obvious simplicity of the doctrine; but now when the subject begins to be tedious and the discussion lags, the interest consequently abates and the Zeitgeist suddenly grasps the old objections, presented in a new garb, and what was hitherto truth, clear and irrefutable, now sinks into the dreary, gray mists of myth. Sic transit gloria mundi!

This has been the history of Darwinism, and especially of Darwin's theory of sexual selection. What Grottewitz urges against it, was advanced decades ago by other and more eminent men; then people would not listen, to-day they are inclined to listen. Of very special interest is the further admission, that "the principle of gradual development" has been "considerably shaken" and is "certainly untenable." Grottewitz points out that it has been demonstrated that the progeny of the same parents are often entirely dissimilar, and that new organs very suddenly spring up in individuals even when they had had no previous existence. "A slight variation from the parent form is of no utility to the progeny; they must acquire at once a completely developed, new character, if it is to be of any use to them." Quite right! but this one admission is destructive of the entire doctrine of natural selection. If one accepts saltatory evolution, as for instance, Heer, Koelliker, and Wigand did long ago, then, as Grottewitz now discovers, the difficulty arising for Darwinism from the absence of the numerous intermediary forms which it postulates, naturally disappears.

Grottewitz attributes sudden variation to the influence of environment, just as Geoffroy St. Hilaire had already done before Darwin. He likewise repudiates Darwin's doctrine of adaptation and the theory of "chance," which is bound up with all his views. "Darwin's theory of chance seems to me to be especially deserving of rejection." The article closed with these words: "There must evidently be a very definite principle, according to which the frequent and striking development from the homogeneous to the heterogeneous, from the no-longer adapted to the readapted, proceeds. We all of us are far from considering this principle a teleological, mystical or mythical one, but for that matter, Darwin's theory of chance is nothing more than a myth."

He is most certainly in the right. To place this whole wonderful, and so minutely regulated world of organisms at the mercy of chance is utterly monstrous, and for this very reason Darwinism, which is throughout a doctrine of chance, must be rejected; it is indeed a myth. We are grateful to Grottewitz for undertaking to tear the assumed mask of science from this myth and expose it before his associates. He should, however, have done so even more vigorously and unequivocally and should have stated plainly: Darwinism is a complete failure; we believe indeed in a natural development of the organic world, but we are unable to prove it.

In the conclusion of the article quoted there is, of course, again to be found the cloven-hoof: by all means no teleological principle! But why in the world should we not accept a teleological principle, since it is clearly evident that the whole world of life is permeated by teleology, that is, by design and finality? Why not? Forsooth, because then belief in God would again enter and create havoc in the ranks of the "brethren."

But however much men may struggle against the teleologico-theistic principle and secure themselves against it, it is all of no avail, the principle stands at the gate and clamors loudly for admission; and if Grottewitz could but bring himself to undertake a study of Wigand's masterful work, perhaps his heresy would increase and we might perhaps then find another article in the "Sozialistische Monatshefte" tending still more strongly toward the truth.

But what will Brother Bebel with his Haeckelism say to the present article?

All in all, instead of calling his article "Darwinian Myths" Grottewitz might just as well have entitled it "At the Deathbed of Darwinism." May he bring out a series of "deathbed articles" to disclose the truth regarding Darwinism to his associates.

CHAPTER IX.

Professor Fleischmann, zoologist in Erlangen, recently published a book bearing the title, "Die Descendenztheorie," in which he opposes every theory of Descent. The book is made up of lectures delivered by the author before general audiences of professional students, hence is popular in form and of very special apologetic value. Numerous excellent illustrations aid the reader in understanding the text.

One statement in the Introduction characterizes the decided position assumed by the author. He says: "After long and careful investigation I have come to the conclusion that the doctrine of Descent has not been substantiated. I go even farther and maintain that the discussion of the question does not belong to the field of the exact sciences of zoology and botany." At the outset, Fleischmann establishes the fact that in the animal kingdom there are rigidly separated types, which cannot be derived from each other, whereas the doctrine of Descent postulates "one single common model of body-structure" from which all types have been developed. Cuvier in his day, set up four such types of essentially different structure; when Darwin's work appeared two more had been added; R. Hertwig postulates even seven, Boas nine (both 1900); J. Kennel (1893) seventeen, and Fleischmann himself sixteen. In consequence the doctrine of Descent has become more complicated since it now embraces sixteen or seventeen different problems, each of which in turn gives rise to many subordinate problems.

The discussion which the author inaugurates regarding the domain to which the question of Descent belongs, is very well-timed. He forcibly and definitely discountenances the method which transfers it to the domain of religion. The question must be decided by the naturalists themselves according to the strict inductive method; that is, the solution must be based on well ascertained facts, without resorting to conclusions deduced from general principles. "Exact research must show that living organisms actually have overstepped the bounds defining their species, and not merely that they conceivably may have done so." Hence it is absolutely necessary to procure the intermediary forms. This is the foundation on which Fleischmann builds and against which no opponent can prevail. Fleischmann first discusses the differences between the classes of vertebrates; the mammals, birds, reptiles, amphibians and fish. For if the differences of their bodily structure could be shown to be one of degree and not radical, it could be supposed that the lines of demarcation which now delimit the larger types might some day vanish. A single illustration suffices for Fleischmann's purpose, viz., the plan of structure of the limbs of the different classes of vertebrates. The four higher classes are characterized by a common underlying plan of limb structure, whilst fish have one peculiar to themselves. On the other hand it is an inevitable postulate of the doctrine of Descent that fish are the original progenitors of all other vertebrates. Hence the five-joint limbs of the latter must have developed from the fins of fish. This derivation was actually attempted but without success, as Fleischmann points out at considerable length. By means of citations taken from the writings of Darwinian adherents, he illustrates the confusion which even now reigns among them on this matter. The evolution of the remaining vertebrates from the fish is therefore a wholly gratuitous assumption devoid of any foundation in fact.

Fleischmann further discusses the "parade-horse" of the theory of Descent. It has been the common belief, especially fostered by Haeckel, that the history of the Descent of our present horse lies before us in its complete integrity as pictured in the drawings of Marsh. Here Fleischmann again proves at great length the insufficiency of actually available materials. Of special importance is his repeated demand that not only individual parts of the animals but the whole organism as well should be derived from the earlier forms. If, for instance, it be possible to arrange horses and their tertiary kindred in an unbroken line of descent according to the formation of their feet, whilst the other characteristics (teeth, skull-structure, etc.,) do not admit of arrangement in a corresponding series, the first line must be surrendered.

Very similar to this is the case of the "family history of birds," which as all know, has been traced back to reptiles. It is in this matter that the famous Archaeopteryx plays an important part. Unfortunately, however, grave difficulties are again encountered in this connection. This primitive form is a real bird according to Zittel; and according to the same investigator as also according to Marsh, Dames, Vetter, Parker, Tuerbringen, Parlow and Mehnert, it is inadmissible to connect birds with a definite class of reptiles. Haeckel finds his way out of the difficulty by supplying hypothetical forms which no one has ever seen, but which his imagination has admirably depicted as transitional forms. In so doing, however, he abandons the inductive method of natural science.

It is impossible for us to treat at such length all the remaining sections of this important book. We may mention in passing that Fleischmann examines the "roots of the mammal stock," and enters upon a detailed discussion of "the origin of lung-breathing vertebrates," the "real phylo-genetic problem of the mollusks," and "the origin of the echinodermata." It is evident that he boldly takes up the most important problems connected with the theory of Descent, and does not confine himself to a one-sided discussion of individual points. As he did not fear to examine thoroughly the famous, and as it hitherto appeared, invulnerable, "parade-horse," so neither does he hesitate to demolish the other reputed proof for the doctrine of Descent, e. g., the fresh-water snail of Steinheim, the remains of which Hilzendorf and Neumayr examined and were said to have arranged in lines of descent that "would actually stagger one." It is important to call especial attention to this because the adversaries of the book ignore it. He next shows up the so-called "fundamental principle of biogenesis" according to which organisms are supposed to repeat during their individual development the forms of their progenitors (enunciated by Fritz Mueller and Haeckel). Fleischmann points out the exceptions which Haeckel attributes to "Cenogenesis," (that is to falsification) and shows the disagreement among contemporary naturalists regarding this fundamental principle. Even Haeckel's friend and pupil, O. Hertwig sounds the retreat.

The 15th chapter deals with the "Collapse of Haeckel's Doctrine," which is revealed in the fact that "the practical possibility of ascertaining anything regarding the primitive history of the animal kingdom is completely exhausted and the hope of so doing forever frustrated." "Instead of scientists having been able from year to year to produce an increasing abundance of proof for the correctness of the doctrine of Descent, the lack of proofs and the impossibility of procuring evidence is to-day notorious." In the last chapter Fleischmann finally attempts to prove on logical principles the untenableness of the evolutionary idea.

He starts from the fact that philosophers use the word development to designate a definite sequence of ideas, i. e., in a logical order. "Metamorphosis, says Hegel, belongs to the Idea as such since its variation alone is development. Rational speculation must get rid of such nebulous concepts as the evolution of the more highly developed animal organisms from the less developed, etc."

Naturalists use the word in a different sense. Instead of a sequence of grades of being they posit a sequence of transformations; instead of a logical sequence of ideas they posit a transforming and progressive development. Zoology constructs a system of specific and generic concepts, "an animal kingdom with logical relations." Our concepts are derived from natural objects, but in reality do not perfectly correspond to them. The phylogenetic school commits the capital mistake of presenting a transformation which can be realized only in logical concepts, as an actually occurring process, and of confounding an abstract operation with concrete fact. "The logical transformation of the concept ape into the concept man is no genealogical process." The mathematician may logically 'develop' the concept of a circle from that of a polygon, but it by no means follows that the circle is phylo-genetically derived from the polygon.

Because the concept of species is variable, the species themselves, according to Darwin, should be subject to a continual flux; whereas the real cause of the variability which he observed lies in the discrepancy between objective facts and their logical tabulation, in the narrowness of our concepts and in the lack of adequate means of expression. He thus makes natural objects responsible for our logical limitations.

With regard to organisms the Descent-school confounded the purely logical signification of the word "related" with that of blood or family affinity. But surely when they speak of the relation of forms in the crystal systems, they do not refer to genetic connection. To-day this interchange of concepts is so general that one needs to exercise great care if one would avoid it.

The theory which postulates the blood-relationship of individuals of the same species may be correct, but it is utterly incapable of proof, and the same is true in a greater degree when there is question of individuals of the same class but of different species. Since a direct proof is impossible, an attempt was made to construct an indirect proof by a comparison of bodily-organs. But in so doing the Descent theorizers had to relinquish scientific analysis altogether.

In conclusion Fleischmann states that he does not mean to discard every hypothesis of Descent. He simply gives warning against an over-estimation of the theory. In opposition to those who esteem it as the highest achievement of science, he looks upon it as a necessary evil. Its proper sphere is the laboratory of the man of science, and not the thronging market-place.

"The Descent hypothesis will meet the same fate (be cast aside), since its incompatibility with facts of ordinary observation is manifesting itself. At the time of its appearance in a new form, forty years ago, it exercised a beneficial influence on scientific progress and induced a great number of capable minds to devote themselves to the study of anatomical, palaeontological and evolutionary problems. Meanwhile, however, viewed in the light of a constantly increasing wealth of actual materials, the hypothesis has become antiquated and the labors of its industrious advocates makes it obvious to unbiased critics, that it is time to relegate it ad acta."

*　　*　　*　　*　　*　　*　　*

My own views agree with those of Fleischmann as presented above, except in regard to his last chapter. I must, of course, admit that his criticism has discredited the doctrine of Descent as a scientifically established theory. Hence, as I have always asserted, it must be excluded from the realm of exact science. No doubt people will come gradually to see that the theory involves a creed and therefore belongs to the domain of cosmic philosophy. All this I readily admit.

Not so, however, as regards the concept of "development." It seems to me to be incorrect to regard this as a logical concept only, even with reference to organisms. True, the whole zoological system is in reality nothing more than a logical abstraction. And in view of this fact one must be on one's guard against confusing a logical transformation of concepts with a genealogical development.

We must, however, not forget that we possess the wonderful analogy of ontogeny (individual development) and above all, the fact of mutation and of metagenesis. And even if we wish to avoid the error of Haeckel and others who find a necessary connection between ontogeny and phylogeny, nevertheless the analogy will still entitle us to picture to ourselves the development of the whole range of living organisms. Such a representation will, of course, have only a subjective value.

No doubt, it is logically unjustifiable to argue from the variable concept to the variability of the species. Still there is something real in plants and animals which corresponds to our specific concepts. In some cases the corresponding reality may be so well defined that it is not difficult to form the concept accurately; whereas in other cases where the task is more difficult, the difficulty must be due to the object. Under these circumstances we may safely conclude from the lack of definiteness in our concepts to a certain lack of rigid delimitation in the organic forms.

This blending of certain forms suggests the idea of transformation, but does not furnish definite proof of it. Such proof can be had only by the direct observation of a transformation. And no doubt in certain cases a transformation may occur. As regards animals, I may call attention, for instance, to the experiments made with butterflies by Standfuss, and as regards plants, to the experiments of Haberlandt, of which I treated in Chapter III. The limits within which these transformations take place are indeed very narrow as are also the limits of those indisputable varieties which naturally arise within an otherwise rigidly defined species. I am aware that the transformation of one species into another has not yet been effected, but the above-mentioned attempts at transformation have nevertheless demonstrated that certain organic forms when subjected to changed conditions of life, display certain mutations which clearly show that variability is to be attributed, not, certainly, to the specific concepts, but to the corresponding reality. This observation and reflexion, joined with the fact that organisms form a progressive series from the simple to the more complex, and with the observed phenomena of individual development, lead me to regard the concept of Descent as admissible, and in a certain sense, even probable. But I agree with Fleischmann in saying that this is a mere belief, and that all attempts to give it a higher scientific value by inductive proof have signally failed.

My standpoint, moreover, requires me to admit the validity of the hypothesis of Descent as an heuristic maxim of natural science. I believe that we shall be justified in the future, as we were forty years ago, in directing our investigation in the direction of Descent, and I do not consider such investigation so utterly hopeless as Fleischmann represents it. However, I entirely concur with him in the opinion that we are here concerned (and shall be for a long time to come) with a mere hypothesis which belongs not in the market-place, nor among the world views of the multitude, but in the study of the man of science.

Above all it must not be mixed up with religious questions. Whether the hypothesis will ever emerge from the study of the man of science as a well-attested law, is still an open question, incapable of immediate solution.

*　　*　　*　　*　　*　　*　　*

It is of interest for us to inquire what reception Fleischmann's protest against the theory of Descent has been accorded by his associates.

Fleischmann was formerly an advocate of the theory of Descent. He was a pupil and assistant of Selenka, who was then at Erlangen (died in Muenster 1902). He had previously written a number of scientific works from the standpoint of the Descent theory. In the year 1891, investigations regarding rodents led him to oppose that theory. During the winter term of 1891-92 he gave evidence of this change in a public lecture. Not until 1895 was there question of his appointment to the chair of zoology in Erlangen. In 1898 he published a Manual of Zoology based on principles radically opposed to the doctrine of Descent. This manual irritated Haeckel so much that he issued one of his well-known articles, *Ascending and Descending Zoology*, in which, after his usual manner, he casts suspicion on Fleischmann of having received his appointment to the chair at Erlangen by becoming an anti-Darwinian in accordance with a desire expressed at the diet of Bavaria. I am not aware that Haeckel has paid any attention to the work of Fleischmann which we have just reviewed.

By its publication, however, the author disturbed a hornet's nest. Dispassionate, but still entirely adverse is Professor Plate's review in the "Biologisches Zentralblatt," while the "Umschau" publishes two criticisms, one by Professor von Wagner, the other by Dr. Reh, which for want of sense could not well be equalled. It was the former who furnished material for our sixth chapter and who there displayed such utter confusion of thought regarding the inductive method. The same confusion is apparent in his recent utterance in which he observes that Fleischmann's whole aim is to accumulate observational data, meanwhile avoiding speculation as far as possible. His criticism is replete with bitter personal epithets, e. g., "reactionary," "mental incompetency," "dishonest mask of hypercritical exactness," which manifest the writer's inability to enter upon an objective discussion of the question.

A still more reprehensible position is assumed by Dr. Reh, who censures Fleischmann for introducing to the general public the question of Descent which belongs properly to the forum of science. He claims that Fleischmann, by so doing, forfeited his right to an unbiased hearing. Dr. Reh forgets that but a short time ago he had no word of censure for Haeckel's *Weltraetsel* which was intended for a far wider circle of readers. He next appropriates Haeckel's suspicion regarding Fleischmann which we noticed above, and then adds the entirely untrue assertion that the first half of Fleischmann's Manual, written before he took possession of the chair in Erlangen, is written in the spirit of Darwin, whereas the second half which appeared at a later date is written in the contrary spirit. He then takes individual points of Fleischmann's treatise out of their context in order to execute a cheap and nonsensical criticism of them. Haeckel has evidently been giving instructions on the best manner of dealing with adversaries. And very docile disciples they are who imitate his method even to the extent of defaming and abusing their scientific opponents.

But is not this another plain indication of the decay of Darwinism? Of course Haeckel recognized at the very beginning of his career that it was necessary to support the theory by means of personal bitterness, forgeries and misrepresentations. But if the last surviving advocates of Darwinism must needs have recourse to the same disreputable means, to what a low estate, indeed, has it fallen!

Let us hope that these last wild convulsions are really the signs of approaching dissolution.

CHAPTER X.

In order to judge of the present status of Darwinism it is of primary importance to note the position assumed by the few really eminent investigators, who as pupils of Haeckel still seem to have remained true to him. Among these I reckon Oskar Hertwig, the well known Berlin anatomist.

As early as 1899 in an address at the University on, *Die Lehre vom Organismus und ihre Beziehung zur Sozialwissenschaft*, Hertwig gave expression to views which are very little in harmony with the doctrines proceeding from Jena, and which are also put forth in his manual, *The Cell and the Tissue*. In that address we read (p. 8): "With the same right, with which, for the good of scientific progress, an energetic protest has been raised against a certain mysticism which attaches to the word Vitality, I beg to give warning against an opposite extreme which is but too apt to lead to onesided and unreal, and hence also, ultimately to false notions of the vital process, against an extreme which would see in the vital process nothing but a chemico-physical and mechanical problem and thinks to arrive at true scientific knowledge only in so far as it succeeds in tracing back phenomena to the movements of repelling and attracting atoms and in subjecting them to mathematical calculation."

"With right does the physicist Mach, with reference to

such views and tendencies, speak of a 'mechanical mythology in opposition to the animistic mythology of the old religions' and considers both as 'improper and fantastic exaggerations based on a one-sided judgment." "My position on the question just stated becomes apparent from the consideration that the living organism is not only a complex of chemical materials and a bearer of physical forces, but also possesses a special organization, a structure, by means of which it is very essentially differentiated from the inorganic world, and in virtue of which it alone is designated as living."

Here, then, the distinction between living and nonliving nature is clearly and definitely expressed, and Hertwig expresses himself just as definitely when he says (p. 21): "Whereas, but a few decades ago a scientific materialistic conception of the world issuing from a onesided, unhistorical point of view, misjudged the significance of the historic religious and ethical forces in the development of mankind, a change has become apparent in this regard."

To this gratifying testimony against materialism the distinguished naturalist added an equally valuable testimony regarding Darwinism on the occasion of the naturalists' convention in 1900. He there sketched an excellent summary of the "Development of Biology in the Ninteenth Century," in which he decidedly opposes the materialistic-mechanical conception of life. In so doing he also touches upon Haeckel's carbon-hypothesis, to which the latter still clings, and says: "That from the properties of carbon, combined with the properties of oxygen, hydrogen, nitrogen, etc., in certain proportions albumen should result, is a process which in its essence is as incomprehensible as that a living cell should arise from a certain organization of different albumina." Then the speaker is inevitably led to speak of the doctrine of Descent and Darwinism.

In the first place he declares definitely that ontogeny alone, i. e., the development of the individual being, is "capable of a direct scientific investigation." On the other hand we move in the domain of hypotheses in dealing with the further question: "How have the species of organisms living to-day originated in the course of the world's history?" This is a very valuable admission in view of Haeckel's dogmatic assertion that the descent of man from the ape is a "certain historical fact." Very moderate and pertinent are also the further words of the speaker: "Of course, a philosophically trained investigator will regard it as axiomatic that the organisms which inhabit our earth to-day did not exist in their present form in earlier periods of the earth and that they had to pass through a process of development, beginning with the simplest forms."

"But in the attempt to outline in detail the particular form in which a species of animals of our day existed in remote antiquity, we lose the safe ground of experience. For out of the countless millions of organisms, that lived in earlier periods of the earth, the duration of which is measured by millions of years, only scanty skeleton remains have by way of exception been preserved in a fossil state. From these naturally but a very imperfect and hypothetical representation can be formed of the soft bodies with which they were once clothed. And even then it remains forever doubtful whether the progeny of the prehistoric creature, the scant remains of which we study, has not become entirely extinct, so that it can in no way be regarded as the progenitor of any creature living at present." I should like to know wherein this differs radically from Fleischmann's contention in his Descendenztheorie" (p. 10.) For we find stated here what Fleischmann emphasizes so much, viz., that with the problem of Descent we leave the domain of experience. It is worthy of special note in this connection that Hertwig likewise evidently regards as the sole really empirically and inductively serviceable proof of Descent, that which is drawn from palaeontology, from prehistoric animal and plant remains. He makes not the least mention of the indirect proofs taken from ontogenetic development or comparative anatomy, to which the Darwinians and advocates of Descent love so much to appeal, because they feel that the real inductive proof is lacking and totally fails to sustain their position. Hertwig next points out that the problem of Descent stirred scientific as well as lay circles twice during the past century. He then pays Lamarck and Darwin the necessary tribute, at which we cannot take offense since he was reared in the Darwinian atmosphere of Jena. I also willingly admit that Darwinism served science as a "powerful ferment," even if I must emphasize just as decidedly how harmful it was that this "ferment" was introduced into lay circles at an unseasonable time by the apostles of materialism. For while it was very well adapted to bring about in educated circles a fermentation which produced beneficial results, in uncritical lay-circles this ferment produced nothing but a corruption of world-views.

Hertwig then designates "Struggle for Existence," Survival of the Fittest, and Selection, as "very indefinite expressions." "With too general terms, one does not explain the individual case or produces only the appearance of an explanation whereas in every case the true causative relations remain in the dark. But it is the duty of scientific investigation to establish for each observed effect the prevenient cause, or more correctly, since nothing results from a single cause, to discover the various causes."

"The origin of the world of organisms from natural causes, however, is certainly an unusually complicated and difficult problem. It is just as little capable of being solved by a single magic formula as every disease is of yielding to a panacea. By the very act of proclaiming the omnipotence of natural selection, Weismann found he was forced to the admission that: "as a rule we cannot furnish the proof that a definite adaptation has originated through natural selection," in other words: We know nothing in reality of the complexity of causes which has produced the given phenomenon. So we may on the contrary, with Spencer, speak of the "Impotence of Natural Selection."

"In this scientific struggle with which the past century closed, it seems necessary to distinguish between the doctrine of evolution and the theory of selection. They are based on entirely different principles. For with Huxley we can say: "Even if the Darwinian hypothesis were blown away, the doctrine of Evolution would remain standing where it stood." In it we possess an acquisition of our century which rests on facts, and which undoubtedly ranks amongst its greatest."

This last sentence affirms exactly what I have repeatedly asserted: the doctrine of Descent remains, Darwinism passes away. Hertwig then is decidedly of opinion that Darwinism entirely fails in the individual case because in its application the basis of experience vanishes. Indeed, according to him, phylogeny is not at all capable of direct scientific investigation. These are all important admissions which one would certainly have considered impossible twenty years ago; they unequivocally indicate the decline of Darwinian views, and in a certain way also harmonize with Fleischmann's work.

True, Hertwig still clings to the thought of Descent, but apparently no longer as to a conclusion of natural science. This appears from the assertion: "Ontogeny alone is capable of a direct scientific (he evidently speaks of natural science) investigation," and from the other statement that a *philosophically* trained investigator will accept it (Descent) as axiomatic although it belongs to the domain of hypothesis. What else does this mean but that: We have no specific knowledge of Descent but we believe in it. In short, this is not natural science but natural philosophy; it forms no constituent part of our certain knowledge of nature but it is one aspect of our worldview.

All the above-quoted assertions of Hertwig are calm

and well-considered and show a decided deviation from the Darwinian position. Above all we are pleased to note that he appropriates Spencer's phrase regarding the "Impotence of Natural Selection" and that in the citation from Huxley he at least admits the possibility that the Darwinian doctrine will be "wafted away."

It is also proper to mention here the fact that in another place Hertwig no longer recognizes so fully the dogma set up by Fritz Mueller and Haeckel which is so closely bound up with Darwinism. I mean the so-called "biogenetic principle" according to which the individual organism is supposed to repeat in its development the development of the race during the course of ages.

In his book: "The Cell and the Tissue" (Die Zelle und die Gewebe, II. Jena 1898, p. 273) Hertwig says: "We must drop the expression: 'repetition of forms of extinct ancestors' and employ instead: repetition of forms which accord with the laws of organic development and lead from the simple to the complex. We must lay special emphasis on the point that in the embryonic forms even as in the developed animal forms general laws of the development of the organized body-substance find expression."

Any one can subscribe to these statements; in truth they contain something totally different from the "biogenetic principle"; for Haeckel has really no interest in so general a truth, but is intent only upon a proof of Descent.

Hertwig continues: "In order to make our train of thought clear, let us take the egg-cell. Since the development of every organism begins with it. the primitive condition is in no way recapitulated from the time when perhaps only single-celled amoebas existed on our planet. For according to our theory the egg-cell, for instance, of a now extant mammal is no simple and indifferent, purposeless structure, as it is often represented, (as according to Haeckel's "biogenetic principle" it would necessarily be); we see in it, in fact, the extraordinarily complex end-product of a very long historic process of development, through which the organic substance has passed since that hypothetical epoch of single-celled organisms."

"If the eggs of a mammal now differ very essentially from those of a reptile and of an amphibian because in their organization they represent the beginnings only of mammals, even as these represent only the beginnings of reptiles and amphibians, by how much more must they differ from those hypothetical single-celled amoebas which could as yet show no other characteristics than to reproduce amoebas of their own kind."

This is a view which has frequently been clearly expressed by anti-Darwinians: The egg-cells of the various animals are in themselves fundamentally different and can therefore have nothing in common but similarity of structure. In opposition to Hertwig, Haeckel in his superficial way deduces from it an internal similarity as well. After a few polite bows before his old teacher, Haeckel, Hertwig thus summarizes his view: "Ontogenetic (that is, those stages in the individual development) stages therefore give us only a greatly changed picture of the phylogenetic (i. e., genealogical) stages as they may once have existed in primitive ages, but do not correspond to them in their actual content." This is a very resigned position, very far removed from Haeckel's certainty and orthodoxy.

To sum up: O. Hertwig has become a serious heretic in matters Darwinian. Will Haeckel, in his usual manner try to cast suspicion on Hertwig also? For Haeckel himself says (Free Science and Free Doctrine, Stuttgart, 1878, p. 85): "Since I am not bound by fear to the Berlin Tribunal of Science or by anxieties regarding the loss of influential Berlin connections, as are most of my like-minded colleagues, I do not hesitate here as elsewhere to express my honest conviction, frankly and freely, regardless of the anger which perhaps real or pretended privy councillors in Berlin may feel upon hearing the unadorned truth."

Verily, it is a matter of suspense to know whether his school will now pour forth their wrath upon O. Hertwig, or whether finally the discovery will not be made in Jena that Hertwig secretly possessed himself of his position in Berlin, in the same manner as Fleischmann obtained his at Erlangen, viz., by a promise of desertion from Darwinism.

CONCLUSION.

We may conveniently summarize what we have said in the foregoing chapters in the following statement: The theory of Descent is almost universally recognized to-day by naturalists as a working hypothesis. Still, in spite of assertions to the contrary, no conclusive proof of it has as yet been forthcoming. Nevertheless it cannot be denied that the theory provides us with an intelligible explanation of a series of problems and facts which cannot be so well explained on other grounds.

On the other hand, Darwinism, i. e., the theory of Natural Selection by means of the Struggle for Existence, is being pushed to the wall all along the line. The bulk of naturalists no longer recognizes its validity, and even those who have not yet entirely discarded it, are at least forced to admit that the Darwinian explanation now possesses a very subordinate significance.

In the place of Darwinian principles, new ideas are gradually winning general acceptance, which, while they are in harmony with the principles of adaptation and use, (Lamarck) enunciated before the time of Darwin, nevertheless attribute a far-reaching importance to *internal forces of development*. These new conceptions necessarily involve the admission that *Evolution has not been a purely mechanical process*.

THE BOOK OF THE DAY

Science and Christianity
By F. BETTEX

Translated from the German

The author among other things says in the preface: I wish to make clear to my readers how little real science is hidden behind the fine phrases and sounding words ot the infidel, and how little he himself understands of the material creation which he affirms to be the only one . . . The Christian and Biblical conception of the universe is more logical, more harmonious, more in accordance with facts, therefore, more scientific than all philosophies, all systems, materialistic and atheistic.   Contents of the book:

Chapter   I. Progress
Chapter II. Evolution and Modern Science
Chapter III. Christians and Science
Chapter IV. Science
Chapter V. Materialism

One of the many favorable reviews: It is a view of much scope, and so far as it attempts reconciliation between science and christianity, is eminently successful. There can be no doubt that at present, when there is so pronounced a disposition to follow every fad in science, especially if it opposes the Bible, such a book should have a wide reading and is adapted to accomplish much good.

Price $1.50

GERMAN LITERARY BOARD,
Burlington, Iowa

BIBLE LEAGUE, CREDO SERIES, No. 2

Collapse of Evolution

BY

Professor L. T. Townsend, D.D., S.T.D., M.V.I.
Author of "Credo," "God-Man," "Fate
of Republics," etc., etc., etc.

Delivered under the auspices of the American Bible
League, in Boston, December, 1904.

PUBLISHED BY
NATIONAL MAGAZINE COMPANY, BOSTON, MASS.
AND AMERICAN BIBLE LEAGUE
39 BIBLE HOUSE, NEW YORK

COPYRIGHT, 1905,
BY L. T. TOWNSEND.

PRINTED BY
The Arakelyan Press
BOSTON, MASS.

DEDICATION
TO
William Phillips Hall
PRESIDENT OF THE AMERICAN BIBLE LEAGUE, WHOSE BRAIN, HEART AND WEALTH ARE CONSECRATED TO GOD AND ARE BEING USED FOR THE PROMOTION OF BIBLE CHRISTIANITY

CONTENTS

I.
INTRODUCTORY

1. Hypothesis of Evolution Broadly Applied 7
2. Definitions 8
3. History and Triumphs of Evolution 9
4. Naturalists and Supernaturalists 9
5. Indictment 10

II.
LIFE GERMS AND NATURALISTIC EVOLUTION

1. Life Germs said to be a Product of Nature 11
2. Life Germs as yet Unaccounted for by Naturalism . . . 12

III.
EVOLUTION, THEISTIC AND NATURALISTIC: STUDIES IN GEOLOGY

1. No Law of Universal Improvement 15
   (1) Beginnings and Endings 16
   (2) Multitudes of Species, Flora and Fauna, show no Development when Compared with their Earliest Types . . 16
   (3) Man viewed Biologically shows no Improvement . . 18
   (4) Fixedness, Disappearances, Improvements and Reversions . 20
2. No Transmutation of Species by Natural or Artificial Processes 21
   (1) Horse Pedigree 21
   (2) Java Skeleton 23

IV.
EVOLUTION, THEISTIC AND NATURALISTIC; STUDIES IN BIOLOGY, EMBRYOLOGY AND COMPARATIVE ANATOMY

1. Development of the Human Body 25
2. Development of the Human Hand and Eye 26
3. Rudimentary or Useless Members 27
4. Metamorphosis 27
5. Crossing of Species 27
6. Variation of Species 28

7.	Classification of Species	28
8.	Everything after its Kind; Studies in the Floral Kingdom	29
9.	Everything after its Kind; Studies in the Animal Kingdom	30
10.	Wriggling	32
	(1) The Whale Disposed of	32
	(2) Demand for Missing Links pronounced Unreasonable	32
	(3) Explanation of how Links Become Missing	34
	(4) Evolution of Man	35

V.
EMERGENCE OF HUMANITY FROM ITS BRUTE BEGINNINGS

1.	Disclosures of Archaeology and History	36
2.	Decadence among Mankind	38
3.	Philology, Comparative Religion and Codes of Ethics	38

VI.
THE AGE OF HUMANITY

1.	Former Theories Abandoned	40
2.	Man's Appearance and the Ice Age	41
3.	Scientific Mixup	43

VII.
SCHOLARS AND EVOLUTION

1.	All Scholars said to be Evolutionists	45
2.	Scholarship and Narrowness	46
3.	Naturalists are Proposing no Better Scheme than Darwin's	46
4.	The Ablest Scientists and Evolution	47

VIII.
BIBLE CRITICISM AND EVOLUTION

1.	Destructive Intentions of Modern Bible Critics	53
2.	Rejoinder by Professor A. H. Sayce of Oxford	53

IX.
RELIGION AND EVOLUTION

1.	Outcome of Darwinism	54
2.	Recent Evolution and Religion	56

X.
CONCLUSION 59

NOTES 61

I.

INTRODUCTORY.

1. HYPOTHESIS OF EVOLUTION BROADLY APPLIED. — It has been quite the fashion of late years to employ the term evolution with much latitude, and in fields outside those of biology where it began its remarkably popular career.

Herbert Spencer, one of the very much praised pioneers in this broader application of the theory, built his scheme of social economy and government upon the hypothesis of organic evolution. So, too, Professor Drummond's very popular books — " Natural Law in the Spiritual World," and " The Ascent of Man " — adhere throughout to this same hypothesis. The brilliant reasoner and writer, Professor Goldwin Smith, arguing for the Immortality of the Soul, takes occasion to say that, " It has been overwhelmingly demonstrated that man's bodily frame, and its soul, as its outcome and perfection, have been produced by a process of evolution from lower forms of animal, maybe of vegetable life."

Dr. Clifford, a leader among the Non-Conformists of England, in a surprisingly favorable comment on the destructive criticism recently announced by the Dean of Westminster, employs these words: — " We have in the main accepted evolution, and thereby can the better understand the majestic ways of God."

And in almost every field of literature, for a quarter of a century or more, writers of note have been illustrating or enforcing their discussions by appeals to evolution as seen in the world of living things and have been vying with one another in praise of Mr. Darwin and his wonderful discovery. And, too, in American pulpits and in some theological schools, the theory of evolution has been quite as often presented and with about as much reverence and unction as the doctrine of vicarious atonement.

It would seem, therefore, that this theory, in the more recent use made of it, is scarcely less entitled to a place among systems of theology than is the creed formulated by the Nicene Fathers. And perhaps no one will question the further statement that the evolution theory, with its implications, has contributed largely to the vigorous growth of destructive criticism, and that the popularizing of it together with the efforts of higher critics to keep it well advertised have, almost more than anything else, helped to weaken the hold that Christian faith and religious conviction once had upon the minds and hearts of the American people.

2. DEFINITIONS. — A few words at this point by way of definition and explanation may be allowed; perhaps are required.

The leading word in our topic, collapse, describes a thing that has tumbled into such ruin as will not permit of reconstruction. There is, too, suggested by the word the idea that there has not been ample support, as when a poorly-framed house goes to the ground, or that there had been too much inflation, as when an over-blown bladder bursts.

Evolution, the other important word of our topic, in its biological restriction, involves the theory that living things originally came upon the earth in the form of germs, supernaturally created, or imported, or produced by spontaneous generation, and then through natural and orderly processes, long continued, developed into various species of plants and animals, existing and extinct, culminating in man, who is recognized

8

in physical science as the crown and glory of all earthly things.¹ *

3. HISTORY AND TRIUMPH OF EVOLUTION. — In one form or another, the theory of evolution is well on in years, — ancient philosophers, church fathers and scientists for at least twenty centuries have been its advocates, though it did not gain its majorities, nor make what has been termed "its conquest of the world," until Dr. Alfred R. Wallace and Charles Darwin, in 1858, separately announced the hypothesis of the "Origin of the Species by spontaneous variation, and the survival of the fittest through natural selection," in "the struggle for existence." For a while after Mr. Darwin's announcement there was among scientists and philosophers quite a good deal of hesitation in adopting his views, but later they were so generally accepted in Germany, England and America that for one to have questioned them in either of these countries, at any time during a period of twenty years, or more, beginning near 1880, would have been regarded by many as sure evidence of an unphilosophic, unscientific and unscholarly mind.

4. NATURALISTS AND SUPERNATURALISTS. — From the earlier times and on to the present, evolutionists have been divided into two classes, naturalists and supernaturalists. The naturalist, as the term implies, rules God out of the universe from start to finish, the claim being that nature is abundantly able to look after herself and all things committed to her care independent of any antecedent or outside interpositions.

The supernaturalist, on the other hand, admits God into the scheme of the universe and places all nature more or less under his control. In the mind of the extreme supernaturalist, evolution is little other than God's method in world building and furnishing.

* The notes are compiled in the Appendix and are indicated there by the numerals I, II, III, IV, etc.

The naturalist and supernaturalist, however, hold in common, that all developments of living organisms, whether with or without external supervision, are carried on strictly in harmony with processes represented by such scientific terms as natural selection, struggle for existence, survival of the fittest, and transmutation.

The superstructure, builded by advocates of evolution, among whom have been philosophers, scientists, men of literature almost without number, and theologians of the highest repute, appears from some points of view imposing, and its foundations at one time seemed as impregnable as those of any human invention or speculation that ever had a name in science or philosophy.

5. INDICTMENT. — Our topic, the collapse of evolution, implies, therefore, that at the present stage of scientific enquiry, the attractive and stately edifice, built by either the naturalist or supernaturalist, is found to be a poorly constructed affair, supported by not one single well established fact in the whole domain of science, philosophy or religion. Now it must be confessed that this sweeping indictment, unless established beyond reasonable question and by facts that cannot be controverted, would properly be condemned as a piece of ignorant, impertinent and insolent dogmatism.

II.

LIFE GERMS AND NATURALISTIC EVOLUTION.

The issue being now squarely before us, the next step is an examination of certain claims that are made by evolutionists, or that ought to be made, and whose establishment is essential to the successful maintenance of their theory.

1. LIFE GERMS SAID TO BE A PRODUCT OF NATURE. —And first, the naturalistic evolutionist contends that the original germs, from which all life has been developed, came into existence by some unknown natural process but were in no way dependent upon supernatural agency. Dr. Buchner, speaking for this class of evolutionists, clearly states the case thus: — "Matter is the origin of all that exists: all natural and mental forces are inherent in it. Nature, the all-engendering and all-devouring, is its own beginning and end, its birth and death. She produces man by her own power and takes him again."

And it should be added that in exact terms evolution means that "a single protoplasmic cell has, by a process of multiplying forms through an indefinite number of species, produced all the forms of life that have existed on earth, with no supernatural interpositions." For if there were two, or ten, such cells, coming into existence at different times, then there may have been a billion or more, and transmutation would be quite unnecessary.

It may occasion surprise to say that even supernaturalists are of late inclining to the theory that the origin of living germs may also fall within the scope of processes no less natural than those that work out the development of things.

A professor in Wesleyan University, who assuredly would resent being classed among atheists, in a book recently published states the case thus: — "When we trace a continuous evolution from the nebula to the dawn of life and again a continuous evolution from the dawn of life to the varied fauna and flora of to-day, crowned with glory in the appearance of man himself, we can hardly fail to accept the suggestion that the transition from the lifeless to the living was itself a process of evolution."

This conclusion is logically sound, if the premises are correct; that is, if the unaided forces of nature have really evolved from structureless germs the beautiful organisms and mechanisms everywhere met, then those same forces ought to be able, in nature's wonderful laboratory, to manufacture the original germs or germ from which those complex living things are developed.

But it should be observed that the author begs the whole question, his premises being entirely speculative, and, as will appear a little later, entirely without scientific support.

2. LIFE GERMS AS YET UNACCOUNTED FOR BY NATURALISM. — As is well known, the experiments of Dr. Bastian, in 1871, secured for the theory of the spontaneous generation of life germs very decided support. Later there came into use among scientists such terms as "bathmism," "cosmic ether," "cosmic emotion," "germplasm," "pangenesis," "protoplasm," "growth force," "vital fluid" and the like, all suggesting the strenuous efforts that were making to account for the origin of life. It should be said, however, that not for five or ten years have these terms, once potent on the lips of scientists and philosophers, been employed seriously by any reputable writer on these subjects.

Professor Huxley was forced reluctantly and rather mournfully to give up his bioplastic theory.[2] Sir William Thomson, with quick dispatch, surrendered his speculation that life germs came to the earth on a meteorite from some planet or star on which life already had an existence. The chemical origin of life, at one time advocated by Herbert Spencer, was abandoned in the last edition of his "Biology," and the words "spontaneous generation" are mentioned no longer in scientific circles except when classifying it among those theories that have not a particle of scientific or experimental evidence in their support.

"I share Virchow's opinion," said the late Professor Tyndall, "that the theory of evolution, in its complete form, involves the assumption that at some period or other of the earth's history there occurred what would now be called spontaneous generation; but I also agree with him that the proofs of it are still wanting. I also hold with Virchow that the failures have been so lamentable that the doctrine is utterly discredited."

In a word, no cautious and well-informed scientist of whatever school ventures now to go beyond the following statement recently made by a thorough-going naturalist:— " The beginnings of life came upon the earth in some way unknown to science."

We have employed these words, " well-informed scientist," advisedly, being fully aware that men who are to-day holding professorships in American colleges are still asserting the possibility and probability of creating or producing life by chemical agencies, and that all existing life originated by natural processes.

The professor of physiological chemistry in the University of Chicago, for instance, is reported to have used recently in his lecture-room these words: " The divine creation of life is a pure humbug. Life originally happened. Life is made up of certain organic compounds. Certain organic compounds were made by nature. The compounds came together in some manner, and the result was life. I believe that in a short time real life will be created in the laboratory."

For a man who professes to be a scientist to employ such language is surprising and almost incredible. Here is nothing but dogmatic assertion, of which a canting clergyman, or mountebank, not to say scientist and university professor, ought to be ashamed.

Weigh these words that will be a poison in the life blood of the young men who hear and believe them: — " The divine creation of life is a pure humbug "! This sentence challenges the wisdom not only of prophets, apostles and of our Lord himself but also of scientists who have devoted their lives to the investigation of nature's phenomena and who have taken rank in the past and who take rank to-day with those who stand the highest in their departments of study — such men as Agassiz, Beale, Carpenter, Dana, Davy, Dawson, Faraday, Forbes, Gray, Helmholtz, Herschel, Lord Kelvin, Leibnitz, Lotze, Maury, Pasteur, Romanes, Verdt and hundreds of others who ascribe to God and to God alone the power to originate life.

III.

EVOLUTION, THEISTIC AND NATURALISTIC; STUDIES IN GEOLOGY.

At this point some one is waiting to put in a reminder that naturalistic evolution and the origin of life are not at present questions of chief importance, since the popular and more recent view of the theory allows the supernatural to be invoked whenever it suits the convenience of the evolutionist, or whenever natural agencies fail.

But we may be permitted to suggest that the moment a supernatural factor is allowed to take any part in the scheme of the universe, that moment there is a weakening in every timber of any theory of evolution that has been devised. In other words, if God is present and needed in one part of the web of the physical universe, for instance, in the creation of life germs, he is equally needed in every other. His intervention is no more called for when the planet Jupiter begins its mighty revolutions than when a dying sparrow falls to the ground. Unaided natural forces can no more make a hair of the head than they can make the mightiest mammal that ever walked the earth or crushed forests under its feet.

If, however, it is insisted that extreme naturalistic evolution should be taken out of this discussion, we will deal for a few moments with that type called supernatural or theistic, that in some quarters has been received with almost "an intellectual frenzy"; a type, too, that has no hesitation in attacking orthodox views of Bible revelation and primitive Christian dogma, and that announces without apparent misgiving certain claims upon the establishment of which, this popular, but dangerous, illogical and utterly vague scheme of evolution depends.

1. NO LAW OF UNIVERSAL IMPROVEMENT. — And first attention is called to what at one time was thought to be in the world of living things a universal law of development and improvement, of elaboration and progression. And certainly from a biological point of view and from the application that has been made of the theory of evolution to various philosophical and theological subjects, the evolutionist ought to be able to show that both sub-inorganic and organic evolution is such as to secure general progress, more or less pronounced and more or less rapid, the rapidity depending upon surrounding conditions, and that there are among living things continuous and unbroken connections between simple forms and species and those that are the most complex. Without such progress and connections it is obvious that organic evolution rests upon an exceedingly precarious foundation.

Now, while all this is implied in evolution and while a hasty study of the facts may leave an impression that there is in the world of living things what seems to be a continuous elaboration or progression, yet a more careful survey discloses such a mass of evidence pointing in the exact opposite direction that leading scientists are now saying scarcely a word as to continuous and universal progress. On the other hand, they are freely using such words as retrogradation and deterioration.

But as the facts bearing on this point are essential to the

rounding out of the discussion and as they will be suggestive in dealing with other phases of evolution, we shall be pardoned for calling attention to them.

(1) *Beginnings and Endings.* — And one of the first observations made by the student of nature is that all things that have their beginnings and progressions also have their declinings and endings.

> " 'So careful of the type?' but no.
> From scarped cliff and quarried stone
> She cries, 'A thousand types are gone;
> I care for nothing, all shall go.' "

And since the human race began, though all sorts of artificial agencies have been employed and though there has been the closest scrutiny, yet not a single distinctively new type of plant, or animal, on what is called broad lines, has come into existence, but thousands have disappeared, never to return, and many others " are slowly but surely marching to their doom."

And the whole magnificent procession of living things, at the close of which stands the human family, has stopped, nor is there any scientific expectation that it ever again will begin to move. And from present indications and tendencies man has no ground of hope as to continuance or improvement, except for a limited time, and in realms of mind and spirit with which the biologist has nothing to do. Birth, growth, decline and death is one of nature's most exacting laws and is no truer of the insect that lives but a day than of the physical organism of man or of the whole vast material universe.

But this, says the evolutionist, is not what is meant by the law of improvement and progress. Is not? Well, then, let us know definitely what is meant.

We mean this: — that the species, among plants and animals, as the ages pass are on the whole improving.

(2) *Multitudes of Species, Flora and Fauna, show no Development when compared with their Earliest Types.* —

Beginning with what is called "the primordial zone," which covers the earliest stage of biological history, and coming down to more recent times, there will be found numberless species that have shown no improvement since their creation. The *algae* or sea weeds, that appeared in the distant Silurian deposit, millions of years ago, were no less perfect than those of the same class found in our modern seas. The oak, birch, hazel and Scotch fir, easily traced back thousands of years, have remained all this time without the slightest improvement.

And, too, in the animal kingdom the same discoveries are made. Insects that built the coral reefs of Florida, in the three hundred centuries of their existence have shown no improvement.

The crustacean family, especially the crayfish group, that first appeared near the close of the carboniferous period, has gained nothing though geological period after geological period has gone by since its creation.

The highest type of mollusk known to scientists is the one that appeared far back in geological history. The same may be said of the earliest fish, reptilian and mammalian families; they each "appeared fully equipped at the outset in the plenitude of their power," and never since have shown the least elaboration or improvement.

And equally significant and quite as troublesome to the evolutionist are the recent discoveries on the Pacific coast, made by deep sea dredging under the direction of W. E. Ritter, Professor of Zoology, University of California. At a depth of seven and a half miles, where there is almost absolute uniformity of conditions, have been taken living creatures essentially identical with those that lived in deep water in the eocene ages, whose fossils are now found in geological strata, that during terrestrial upheavals were raised from sea depths millions of ages ago.

In comparing these ancient and more recent forms no improvement is discovered; the earliest ones are as absolutely perfect and as marvelously beautiful in color and structure as any living creature, large or small, that came into existence in the later geological ages. While both naturalistic and supernaturalistic evolutionists are acknowledging these facts, yet, as would be expected, it is with some measure of reluctance, for it is evident that every such fact weakens the foundations of evolution, and our friends, therefore, hardly could be blamed if they sincerely wished that all these later discoveries had remained in the depths of the sea.

It is reported of Professor E. D. Cope that on seeing a newly discovered specimen that controverted one of his hypotheses, he quietly said: " If no one were looking I should be glad to throw that fossil out of the window."

Coming to early historic times it is found that mummies of cats, ibises, birds of prey, dogs, crocodiles and heads of bulls discovered in the tombs and temples of upper and lower Egypt, placed there from four to five thousand years ago, are identical with their living representatives.

(3) *Man Viewed Biologically shows no Improvement.*— Passing from these lower forms of living things to the highest, represented by man, there still will be discovered, on biological and physiological grounds, no evidence of improvement.

Professor Pierre Broca, who made a very careful study of the celebrated " Cro-Magnon skull," belonging to the earliest stone age, says: " The great volume of the brain, the development of the frontal region, the fine elliptical profile of the anterior portion of the skull are incontestable evidences of superiority and are characteristics that usually are found only in civilized nations." Professor Huxley, describing one of the oldest existing fossil skulls, says that " so far as size and shape are concerned, it might have been the brain of a philosopher." And what is true of the skull is equally true of other parts of the human body.

A scientist, skilled in these subjects, who has examined statuettes recently discovered in Crete, employs these words: "I spent a long time studying the muscles and veins of the Cretan forearm of four thousand years ago, as shown in some of Dr. Evans' wonderful photographs. Their arrangement is identical to the smallest detail with that of the surface veins and muscles in the arm that writes these words. These statuettes constitute, in my opinion, the oldest exact anatomical records in the world, and my study of them leads to the conclusion that in four thousand years there has been no change in even the minutest details of the forearm of man."

And upon enlarging the field of investigation the evolutionist is confronted with still more serious grounds for embarrassment, for there is not only no universal law of improvement, or elaboration, on which his theory largely depends, but on the other hand in scores of instances there is among things having life a pronounced deterioration of parts and functions.

There is one family of the *ascidia,* a group that begins with backbone, throat and cerebral eye, each of which disappears as the animal matures, and is never restored. Some of the parasite species begin with legs, jaws, eyes and ears, but lose them all, becoming after awhile a mere sac whose life ever after consists in absorbing nourishment and laying eggs.

The fish family began early, and still lives on, but has been in process of degeneration ever since the Devonian period. Likewise none of the modern mammalia equal in size or strength those that flourished during the geological age to which they gave their name.

And from biological and physiological points of view the human race not only has not gained a step since the dawn of history, but on the whole, sometimes slowly, sometimes rapidly, has been deteriorating: and if history warrants any statement, it is that except for a mind endowed at the outset with conscience, with which organic evolution has nothing to do, and had not religion, especially the Jewish and Christian, with their inspiring and uplifting power come to the aid of the human race, mankind long since would have disappeared forever from the face of the earth.

Nothing, therefore, is better established in the realms of science than the conservative announcement of the late Professor Cope, a pronounced evolutionist, at least until just before his death: " Retrogradation in nature is as well established as evolution." [1]

(4) *Fixedness, Disappearances, Degeneration, Improvements and Reversions.* — A fuller statement of the case is, that some forms of animal life in geological history have remained fixed for millions of years and are still living on; others appeared and remained without change for hundreds of thousands of years and then disappeared as suddenly as they came; others began to degenerate as soon as they appeared, and still others in more recent times under domestication, or artificial help, have been much improved, though left to themselves they usually revert to their original condition.

When, therefore, the evolutionist, in support of his theory, says there is in the kingdom of nature anything that can be called a universal law of development and improvement, he most certainly is not telling the truth.

Universal laws do not depend upon circumstances or environments, but were true and operative yesterday, are so to-day, and will be so forever, and everywhere.

We presume no one will question this additional statement that universal and fixed laws are far less numerous in the physical universe than they were once supposed to be.

2. No Transmutation of Species by Natural or Artificial Processes. — Attention is next called to a claim of the evolutionist, held with much tenacity, by both the supernaturalist and naturalist, that by natural processes one species of plant, or animal, may be transformed into another, and that through long continued and progressive transmutations the higher types of animal life, including man, have been evolved from the lower.

It should be said at this point that, if the transmutation of species is not established, then organic evolution can have no scientific standing. And unless it can be shown that man is a transmutation from the ape family, or from some other family back of the ape, from which it and man have both been evolved, then the theory of evolution breaks down at the very point where it is vitally important it should be maintained.

(1) *Horse Pedigree.* — The reader is almost entitled to an apology for the repetition of the so-called proofs of transmutation, some time since overthrown, that are nevertheless the stock in trade of scores of men who appear to be either unpardonably ignorant of facts already established, or else are deliberately trying to fool the public mind.

For instance, there are the fossil bones of the so-called prehistoric horse that from time to time have been paraded as evidence of the transmutation theory.

A Chicago University professor, occupying the chair of paleontology, in reply to an article written by a Boston professor of theology, ventured recently this statement: — "The modern horse can be definitely traced through a series of intermediate stages to a primitive species having four toes on each foot."

Now the only excuse, and it is a poor one, for this statement, is that Professor Huxley, twenty-five or thirty years ago, in a desperate effort to find something to support his

"Demonstrated Evidence of Evolution," made use of these fossils, the earliest species of which are found in the eocene strata. Our Chicago professor may not know, perhaps, that another animal has been discovered having five toes, of which Professor Henry Fairfield Osborn, of the Musuem of Natural History, New York, has recently given an account, and possibly another may yet be discovered having fifteen toes. The facts are, however, that all these fossils differ so entirely from the bones of the modern horse that the animal to which they belonged can not, on strictly scientific grounds, be called a horse at all. And certainly it may be questioned, so far as feet are concerned, to which the evolutionist confines his reasoning, whether the four-toed animal is not of higher order than the one-toed or hoofed animal. Differentiation rather than convolution is nature's method of improving the species if the teaching of the naturalist is to be our guide.

But what makes it all the worse for the paleontological professor is, that the very species that ought to connect those supposed earlier ancestors with the modern horse, thus forming the needed missing links, are entirely unknown in geological history. While there are some resemblances between those four-toed animals and the modern horse, as there are some resemblances between a cow and a crow, a man and a mouse, each having a head with its eyes, nose and ears, and each having feet with which to walk, yet these resemblances furnish no more evidence of organic connections and transmutations in the one case than in the other — that is, no evidence at all. In each instance these differently toed animals lived their geological periods and then forever disappeared, having had neither ancestors nor descendants. Or to make the case a little more specific, and beginning with the orohippus, found in the eocene period, there followed the mesohippus, miohippus, protohippus and so on, to the modern horse. Now, adopting Haeckel's estimate of the "vital era" of the earth, the orohippus lived about three hundred million years ago. Between that animal and the modern horse there are four so-called intermediate species, each of which flourished from twenty to sixty million years. Each species abruptly appeared, remained fixed that length of time and then suddenly disappeared, and where thousands and even millions of the intermediate forms of the different species are demanded by the evolutionist, not one that is assured has yet been discovered. When Mr. Darwin and Professor Huxley were confronted with this, that might well have been regarded as a fatal fact, they met it by saying that the records are imperfect and that the intermediate forms need not be looked for. But may we not ask, why not look for them and why not expect to find them, at least in some numbers, if they ever existed? These are questions that no one should be condemned for asking.

The most of this talk, however, is twenty-five or thirty years old, and our Chicago professor should have known that geologists, on some of these questions, " have changed their views two hundred times in one hundred years," and that no reputable geologist, or paleontologist, at the present time is at all satisfied with the evidence of the horse pedigree derived from those fossils.'

(2) *Java Skeleton.* — Another piece of effete evidence, once generally employed by the advocates of evolution but lately by no scientist of distinction, are the fossil bones of the once famous Java skeleton that for a time had the reputation of being the missing link, or one of them, between man and the monkey family.

The same professor of whom we were just speaking, the Chicago man, recently ventured this announcement: " A few years ago there were discovered in Java the skull and portion of a skeleton of a creature to which the name pithecanthropus erectus was given. Competent paleontologists and anthropologists to-day believe it to be a real connecting link between man and the lower animals."

Now, the facts in this case are of more than ordinary interest, and are these: In the month of September, 1891, Dubois, a Dutch physician, discovered a tooth on the island of Java, about forty-five feet below the surface of the earth; one month later he found the roof of a skull about three feet from where he found the tooth, and in August, 1892, he found a thigh bone forty-five feet further away, and later, another tooth.

That is all that is known of the wonderful pithecanthropus, the link that connects man with the lower animals. A year or two after these discoveries the world's famous zoologists met at Leyden, and among other things examined were the remains of pithecanthropus. Ten of those scientists concluded that they were nothing but the bones of an ape, seven held that they were those of a man, and seven concluded that they were really the missing link connecting man and the ape. So that of twenty-four of the most eminent scientists of Europe, only seven, not one-third, ascribed any importance whatever to this pithecanthropus erectus.

But the amusing thing about this celebrated paleontological affair is a recent explanation that accounts for the different opinions of those Leyden experts, though rather hard on the scientists; it is given by Professor D. C. Cunningham, of Dublin, one of the highest authorities in Great Britain on questions of comparative anatomy. His conclusion is that those different bones do not belong to the same animal at all, some of them being those of a monkey or baboon, the rest human. So that the missing link, pithecanthropus, turns out to be nothing but a few bones of a monkey and fewer of a man found not very far apart on the island of Java. But what seems unpardonable in a Chicago professor is to palm off those bones on the unsuspecting laymen of his town as evidence of the transmutation theory. 24

IV.

EVOLUTION, THEISTIC AND NATURALISTIC; STUDIES IN BIOLOGY, EMBRYOLOGY AND COMPARATIVE ANATOMY.

We may now allow the evolutionist, if he desires, to retreat from the field of geology, where he has met with all sorts of discomfiture, to that of biology and kindred sciences, where he has been thinking he could find more secure entrenchments. From these latter fields, with a show of confidence, he has presented, in support of transmutationism, quite an amount of exceedingly interesting, if not convincing, evidence.

1. DEVELOPMENT OF THE HUMAN BODY. — With assurance and satisfaction the evolutionist calls attention to the fact that the human body, beginning as a single cell, only one hundred and twentieth part of an inch in diameter, develops into a man weighing two hundred pounds. Here, says the evolutionist, is evidence of what nature can do. Certainly, but what has that in common with the evolution of one species into another? From cell to man no mutation takes place. The cell *is* the man. The development of cells and germs is one thing, — evolution by transmutations is another: they are as distinct from each other as day from night.

Again, following out an observation that in the embryonic state man passes through the different stages of worm, fish, reptile and quadruped, the evolutionist has argued that the human race has, therefore, been evolved from the worm, fish, reptile and quadruped. This certainly is a momentous induction from limited data, indeed from almost no data at all.

If we may speak with perfect plainness, an inexcusable blunder in this instance is committed by reason of overlooking, or, what is worse, by reason of a misinterpretation and false application of the prophetic element in nature. That is, the Creator is a prophet and his method has been to anticipate by type, pattern or prophecy what may be expected in his subsequent creations. For illustration the fins of fishes, the wings and feet of birds and the fore and hind feet of brutes, created before man, are prophetic of the arms and feet of man. So, too, the lower forms of life, the worm, fish and reptile, furnish hints of what the higher and later forms are to be.

But from these forecasts or parallels in nature it should no sooner be inferred that there have been transmutations from earlier and lower creations to the higher, than it is to be inferred that a transmutation from quartz crystals to oak trees has taken place, because the root-like base of the crystal resembles the lower parts of a tree. This employment of prophetic anticipations in nature to bolster up the theory of organic connections and transmutations is, to a thoughtful mind, about as flagrant misuse of scientific facts as one can imagine.

2. DEVELOPMENT OF THE HUMAN HAND AND EYE. — And, too, naturalists have given to the world volumes upon the evolution of the fin of a fish or paw of an animal into a human hand.

Sir William Abney, F. R. S., etc., has been writing lately of the evolution of the eye, finding, he thinks, the embryo eye of man in the snail tribe, the approach to an eye being in certain places a slight thinning of the skin that covers the head. The next stage in eye development he finds in a creature of low order where the thin skin gives place to a slight depression; the next advance is found in another low order of life where there is a sac having in it a sort of pinhole. And so the evolution has gone on until the perfect eye is reached. But the trouble with these speculations of Abney and of others who have worked the same field is that nothing has been proved. As a matter of fact there is no more evidence of any organic connection between the thin skin on the head of a snail and the full formed eye of a mammal than there is between the planet Mars and a man.

3. RUDIMENTARY OR USELESS MEMBERS. — In support of evolution and transmutation much has been written about the so-called rudimentary, undeveloped and unused organs and structures of different animals. The range of investigation has been from whales to snails and from men almost to midgets. But in all this writing there can be pointed out not a single sentence bearing on evolution, or transmutation, that can be called a strictly scientific statement; it is ingenious, very ingenious and interesting conjecture; and that is all.

4. METAMORPHOSIS. — And, too, metamorphosis has been forced to pay tribute to transmutation. The so-called evolution of the yolk into the embryo chicken, then into the full formed, or hatched chicken; the so-called evolution of the tadpole into the frog; the evolution of the ovum into the larva, then into the pupa, then into the perfect insect, have been used as evidence of nature's power to transmute one thing into another. But at this late day no scientist who cares for his reputation will make such a plea. From a biological point of view the fecundated yolk and the chicken, the tadpole and the frog, the larva and the butterfly, are in each instance one and the same thing. In these developments there is no more of an evolution than when a bud becomes the full-blown rose.

5. CROSSING OF SPECIES. — And, too, among the twenty thousand species of animals already classified not one instance is known where different species have been crossed that the result has not been sterility in the animal thus begotten; and if this always has been the case, and no reason can be given for thinking otherwise, then there is shut out completely what seems to be the most available agency at nature's command for the production of new species.

6. Variation of Species. — Quite recently Professor Hugo de Vries, of the University of Amsterdam, appears to have developed a mutable species of primrose. California fruit growers are reporting new varieties of berries and plums. Professor Standfus of Zurich, by variations of temperature, claims to have obtained several new species of butterfly.

The pigeon and mice families for a long time have been under experiment. And if it had been possible to produce any new species on what are called "broad lines" it certainly would have been done. But the facts are that nothing has been accomplished in the way of natural or artificial variation outside of "an oscillation around a primitive center." And even in such cases, the "mongrel forms," as has been pointed out by Professor Peschel, of Leipsic, "never have been successfully established nor perpetuated beyond a few generations," and among the sharply defined animal forms "any abandonment of original types is followed by the complete extinction of the family."

It appears, therefore, in all these cases that there is no evidence whatever of a tendency in nature towards the transmutation of species. One might as well argue such tendency when the sweet orange or the Baldwin apple is budded, or grafted, into wild trees, securing thereby a specially rich and luscious fruit. Improvement and variation are vastly different from transmutation.

7. Scientific Classification. — We next call attention to certain matters grouped under what is known as scientific classification. That is, whenever there is discovered in geological deposits the remains of an animal before unknown, the skilled paleontologist finds no difficulty in placing it in its proper class or order. But this would be impossible, as any one can see, if in past ages transmutations had been continually, or even occasionally taking place. And, too, if transmutations

were now going on, the world would be so full of animals in various stages of re-formation and variation that classification would be out of the question. As a matter of fact, however, the scientist is not embarrassed by any such perplexing conditions.

But the difficulties in the way of the transmutationist keep multiplying. It is estimated that organized life has been on earth fifty, perhaps a thousand, million years. It is also estimated that there are at the present time two and a half millions of different species of plants and animals, and that during the entire "vital period" of the earth there have been fifty times as many, or one hundred and twenty-five million species, while an estimate in numbers of the different individuals belonging to these different living and extinct species is beyond comprehension. And yet in the field of geological history and in that of human history not a discovery has been made indicating that among these multitudes of species and billions of individuals there has been a single case of transmutation.

8. EVERYTHING AFTER ITS KIND; STUDIES IN THE FLORAL KINGDOM. — This matter of transmutation is so vital in the discussion and gives such significance to the remarkable words in the Book of Genesis that we may be more specific and dwell upon it a moment longer. In Genesis is this reading: "And God said, Let the earth put forth grass . . . herb . . . tree after its kind. And the earth brought forth grass and herb yielding seed after its kind, and tree bearing fruit, wherein is the seed thereof, after its kind. . . . And God said, Let the earth bring forth the living creature after its kind, cattle, and creeping things and beast of the earth after its kind; and it was so"; and it has been so from the beginning until the present moment. Seaweed for millions, perhaps a thousand million years, until now has "brought forth after its kind."

So, too, the cedar, poplar, willow, oak, fig, tulip, spice-wood, sassafras, walnut, buckthorn, sumac, cinnamon, apple and plum, " from their first appearance thousands of years ago, invariably and unvaryingly, have brought forth after their kind.

To an interesting pamphlet by A. L. Gredley, A. M., entitled, " Thoughts on Evolution," we are indebted for this statement which no scientist will call in question: —

"There are millions of protoplasmic vegetable cells everywhere about us, each one capable of receiving a life principle, but only from its own peculiar source and then its potency is confined to development only along its own peculiar line. The protoplasmic cells on an incipient corn cob cannot be fertilized by the pollen of the rose. They must be fertilized by pollen from the corn tassel and then they will appropriate the nutriment brought to them by the parent stalk and develop into corn and into nothing else. Other flora will receive their life principle from other sources, but each from its own and exclusive source and will develop along its own line and no other."

9. Everything after its Kind; Studies in the Animal Kingdom. — Likewise in the animal kingdom the same phenomena are noticed. There are five hundred species of trilobites that through millions of ages, while the deposits of the paleozoic era were forming, not only brought forth each after its kind, but not a fossil has been found by the paleontologist indicating that a single individual of any of these species ever produced anything but a trilobite.

The same may be said of the nine hundred extinct species of the ammonites, of the four hundred of the nautilus and of the seven hundred of the ganoids; among these species there is not the slightest trace of any deviation from the law that each species shall bring forth " after its kind."

And, too, this law is just as operative now as during any of the millions of ages past. Man, mammals and living things, the most inferior and most minute are equally the subjects of it. From a wiggler gnat germ comes a wiggler gnat and nothing else; this is repeated without deviation over and over again. The same is true of the tadpole and frog; neither one nor the other has ever been known to break from the family line.

And throughout the continuous existence of the deep-sea living things, reaching back perhaps a thousand million years, there has not been discovered, either in the upheaved strata of the past or in the deep-sea dredgings of the present, the slightest deviation from the law announced in Genesis.

But more than this. As is well known the scientific world of late years has become profoundly interested in microscopic disease-producing bacteria. But each species has been found not only to produce the specific disease for which it is named, as bacillus tetanus, bacillus typosi, bacillus xerosis, etc., but each invariably reproduces its own kind. Except for this, medical science to-day would be in direst confusion. And, too, each of the billions of bioplasts that construct the human body, not only attends strictly to its own business, one species forming bone, another muscles, another brain tissue, etc., but no bioplast ever violates the law that like shall produce like. Indeed, if the transmutation of species among bioplasts were possible, there would be no assurance that another normal human body ever would or ever could be brought into existence or be kept alive for a single day.

And what renders the case still more hopeless for the evolutionist is the recent announcement of biological science, that the structureless germ of one species of plant never has been and never can be changed into the structureless germ of another, much less into that of an animal; and that the structureless germ of one species of animal never has been and never can be changed into the structureless germ of another. That is, structureless germs of all life at the very threshold of their creation, or formation, are as immutable as the most highly organized plants and animals known in natural history.

So that from structureless germs up to the most complicated forms of organized life, and from first to last, nature at every turn of the way takes her stand, and as if wielding a drawn sword absolutely forbids the transmutation of species.

Such, therefore, are the facts in the world of living things, flora and fauna, and such the overwhelming evidence arrayed against the theory of the transmutation of the species and in support of the law that clearly marked species forever shall be kept inviolate and distinct.

10. WRIGGLING. — After having fruitlessly searched for missing links of all sorts, and for other evidences of transmutation, it is amusingly interesting to watch the evolutionist in his " wriggling " performances, if we may employ a term Mr. Darwin once applied to Herbert Spencer, who unquestionably was a master in that art.

(1) *The Whale Disposed of.* — This water mammal has been particularly bothersome to the evolutionist because there have been found not only no connecting links but nothing with which to make connections. In fact, the evolutionist is about as much at sea as is the whale, not being able to determine whether it is a land animal developing into a fish or a fish on the way of becoming a land animal; he, therefore, some time ago swallowed the whale and is saying nothing more about it.

This case is cited, as the reader will infer, for the purpose of illustrating the usual method employed by our American evolutionists and college professors when trying to dispose of bothersome facts — they wriggle, gulp, and, whether to the point or not, begin talking about something else.

(2) *Demand for Missing Links pronounced Unreason-*

able. — Links between fin animals and footed animals, between reptiles and mammals, also between reptiles and birds, between apes and men, have been sought with the most untiring and astounding zeal, but none are found. And now that the expectation of finding any is well nigh abandoned, the wriggling of the evolutionist is vigorously resorted to.

The believer in special creations, for instance, asks to be shown the connecting links upon which transmutation depends. The evolutionist replies that the demand is unreasonable and that the one who makes it is not only no scientist, but does not know what evolution is. Such in substance was the complacent announcement made recently by a popular professor of Cornell University before the Twentieth Century Club of Boston.

But without incurring the charge of ignorance, or incompetence, may not one ask why the demand for these links is unreasonable? Or, let the point for a moment be pressed more definitely.

In the eozoon or dawn-of-life period, as we have seen, there were living things that are still extant. Now, if evolution by transmutation is true, it follows that some of those earliest types of life have continued to produce their like, while others, having essentially the same conditions and environments, produced those that are unlike themselves. In other words, we have this remarkable phenomenon, — some eozoon parents have been producing eozoon offspring in unbroken succession for millions of ages, while other eozoon parents gave birth to Polyps, Acalephs, Echinoderms, Acephala, Gasteropoda, Cephalopoda and worms; and some of these in turn kept on, each producing its own kind while others produced in endless variety the Radiates, Mollusks, and Articulates, all existing in the same waters and at the same time. And so upward through the numerous families of the lower vertebrates to the highest. All these varieties, according to the hypothesis of evolution, have taken place in the descendants of some eozoons while others have continued till now without the slightest change, and not a link connecting these different families is anywhere to be found. With these facts clearly before one, is it quite the thing for a college professor when asked to explain these phenomena to wriggle and reply that the question is unreasonable and that the one who asks it is no scientist and does not understand what evolution is?

(3) *Explanation of how Links become Missing.* — The impression should not be left that no attempt has been made by evolutionists and scientists to account for missing links. There are students of nature who frankly acknowledge the validity of the demand for missing links and when questioned offer the following explanation: If species X is transmuted into species Y, then there must have been one or many species Z, that were neither X nor Y. Now these intermediate Z species would be neither normal X species, nor normal Y species. But since all abnormal species, or forms, are less able to survive than normal ones, it follows that there would be an early death of the individual Z forms, and speedily would follow the extinction of the intermediate families and species belonging to the Z group.'

And this is the explanation offered for the disappearance of those connections known as missing links!

To speak with perfect plainness, it is this sort of wriggling that brings science and scientific men into contempt.

But failing in efforts to account for the absence of links, a few naturalists have frankly conceded that there are none and never have been; that new species come from previously existing ones through a rapid, perhaps instantaneous, transformation by processes not yet understood. In other words, all new species are eruptive, hence connecting links are entirely

34

unnecessary. This, however, comes near being a fatal admission, for by it the foundations of evolution through organic connections are not only loosened at every point and from top to bottom, but special creation receives additional support and from a source quite unexpected.

(4) *The Evolution of Man.* — Man is now on earth, but how on earth he got here has bothered the evolutionist perhaps no less than the coming of the whale into the oceans.

That man is a direct or progressive evolution from the monkey, a theory once popular, is no longer held. Professor Osker Peschel, in his " Races of Man," has conclusively shown that the anatomy of the monkey is such that the more it is developed the more of a monkey and the less of a man it becomes.

It is at this point, too, that the evolutionist is able to display his remarkable skill and nimbleness at wriggling.

Professor N. C. Macnamara, for illustration, explains the relation between men and monkeys thus: —

" Man and anthropoid apes we hold to be derived from a common ancestral stock; the former, under the action of natural selection and other causes, including, I think, not only an inherent capacity of cerebral but also of cranial growth, have gradually developed, whereas anthropoid apes, from arrest of cranial and cerebral growth, have not reached the standard attained by human beings; the difference between these two orders of beings, however, is one of degree, and not of kind."

Science ! Is this what is called science, these speculations that may amuse children but have in their support no shadow of fact nor reason. From a clergyman's point of view the foregoing paragraphs are far from being first-class wriggling. They fall considerably below the specimen given by a very estimable professor of Yale, who explains the origin of man thus: —

"Animal life on this continent developed no higher than the South American monkeys. The Old World current developed into the anthropoid ape, and then, by a colossal accident, into Man."

Colossal what? Colossal nonsense!

V.
EMERGENCE OF HUMANITY FROM ITS BRUTE BEGINNING.

Another claim made by the evolutionist, one that is quite essential to the successful maintenance of the most important phase of his theory, is that the human race, after its emergence from lower animals, began its career not much above the level of the brute, and through countless ages has been working its way up ever since to its present state of civilized life.[6]

After having found the previous claims of the evolutionist destitute of scientific support, it cannot be expected that thoughtful men will accept this additional assertion without asking for evidence in support of it. In other words one is justified in demanding facts before accepting this or any other theory on the say-so even of men who hold university professorships and who seem to have vast knowledge and ability to express themselves in exceedingly learned phraseology.

1. DISCLOSURES OF ARCHÆOLOGY AND HISTORY.— It is found as a matter of fact that the peoples of whom there is the earliest historic account were not as has been claimed low down but were high up. The Egyptians builded immense cities, invented systems of astronomy and writing, constructed a time calendar, founded schools of law and medicine, gathered extensive libraries and did other things in ways that people of the present generation are unable to do. And there were other nationalities of equal antiquity, possibly of earlier date, who

were no less civilized, notably those who builded their great cities in the Babylonian valley. The Wolf Expedition, led by Dr. William Hayes Ward, and notably the excavations under Professor Hilprecht in the Nippur region, going back three and four thousand years B. C., have put a complete negative upon all assertions as to the degraded conditions of those primitive people. And, too, other explorations have brought to light hundreds of tablets showing that there were in those Euphrates and Tigris valleys, nearly three thousand years before the founding of Rome and two thousand before Abraham left Ur of the Chaldees, great business activity, peaceful diplomatic, international relations and complicated private life, that afford unassailable evidence of high civilization.

These discoveries impress one especially by reason of the broad range of subjects that engaged the thoughts of the people who lived in those times — the earliest of which there is any record — a range that compares favorably with systems of study now pursued by civilized nations. Aside from mere historical writings there were definite problems of history stated and expounded; there were theories and speculations in astronomy and astrology; there were measurably systematic treatises on geography, jurisprudence and theology; there were treatises on architecture, with plans and ornamentation for buildings, and on applied mechanics and sculpture. And what is especially noteworthy is the fact that these various tablets were arranged, classified and catalogued the same as in modern libraries, as if designed for everyday use and for a large number of readers. It is evident, therefore, that such intellectual enterprise must have had a much earlier background of civilization and knowledge than that of the period when these tablets were written and catalogued. The Augustan age and the Elizabethan era did not shine out from a totally black night that immediately preceded.

Nor are we destitute of other evidences of civilization. In Crete, as early as four thousand years before the Christian era, there were royal palaces having sanitary conditions superior to those in any city of America until within comparatively few years. Indeed, it is gradually dawning upon the minds of well-informed people, that, in the most primitive times of which there is any record, man enjoyed a degree of civilization not surpassed in any period of the world's history earlier than the middle of the last century.

2. DECADENCE AMONG MANKIND. — But what tells even more fatally against the assertion of evolutionists, that man has worked his way up from a savage state in which he is said to have originated, are the almost innumerable and certainly unmistakable proofs of decivilization and decadence rather than progress. Southern Europe, Asia, Africa, Central and South America abound in such evidence. The marble palaces and high attainments of those primitive peoples in the course of centuries have given way to the mud-walled hovels and wretchedness now everywhere met by the traveller. The degraded Fellaheen of Egypt are the descendants of the men who built the gigantic pyramids. If, therefore, progress is the claim, then regress is the counter claim. In other words, the fall downward of these people is more strikingly evident than the fall or climb upward.

3. PHILOLOGY, COMPARATIVE RELIGION, AND CODES OF ETHICS. — Or, taking into view other fields of research, the case against the evolutionist grows stronger and stronger. It is now acknowledged by linguists that if philological science clearly demonstrates anything it is that primitive tongues, in almost every instance, disclose a background of high civilization and bear an unmistakable impress of descent, rather than ascent. By way of illustration, take the name of the beautiful New Hampshire lake, Winnepesaukee, whose meaning is the

Smile of the Great Spirit. Here in this word alone is disclosed the fact that the ancestors of the untutored savage, back somewhere in the family line, had well-defined ideas of the beautiful, were monotheists, believing in a Supreme Being who has a fatherly heart and who at times, with a benignant smile, looks upon his children.

So, too, the science of comparative religion, at almost every point, furnishes damaging evidence against the assumptions of the evolutionist.

Professor Schlegel reached a conclusion that since his day has been concurred in by all workers in this field of research: "The more I investigate ancient history, the more I am convinced that the nations set out from a true worship of the Supreme Being."

And the earliest ethical codes that have been discovered, those of the ancient Egyptians and Babylonians, in loftiness and purity, quite put to blush modern systems of ethics except where Bible revelation has come in touch with the people. In a word, every discovery during the last twenty-five or more years in these different fields of investigation and learning, those of geology, history, archæology, anatomy, philology, ethics, and religion, have demonstrated the fact that so far as is known, the first beings on earth who wore the human form were not brutes, nor even barbarians, as evolutionists tell us, but had bodies just as perfect, brains or intellects just as capable of working and languages just as complete in expressing thought, as those of any people now living. These are conclusions based upon established facts and reached by approved scientific methods rather than that lecture room, platform and pulpit guesswork that for a decade has had full sway — guesswork, boldly venturesome, somewhat ingenuous, but absolutely destitute of any valuable results.

VI.
THE AGE OF HUMANITY.

Nor should the correlated assertion of the evolutionist that the human family has been on earth "countless ages" be received as an established fact until brought under the searchlight of scientific investigation.

There have been, it is true, many speculations as to the long duration of human history. With some show of reason Professor Lyell in his day argued that two hundred thousand years at least should be allowed for human life on earth. Professor Thomas Sterry Hunt, from biological and evolutionary points of view, advanced the opinion that man has been on earth not fewer than nine million years. But M. Lalande, a French astronomer, out-estimated them all, for, not being able to think of any way, scientifically, for starting the human family, he reached the conclusion that man was not started at all and therefore is eternal.

1. FORMER THEORIES ABANDONED. — The facts, however, are now found to be against even the lowest of these estimates.

Within the last decade, as our readers scarcely need be told, the entire drift of reputable scientific opinion is in favor of bringing the origin of the human race within easy hailing distance. Professor H. W. Haynes, a careful investigator, and leading American geologist, within a few months has made this statement: "The evidence for the antiquity of man on the hypothesis of evolution is purely speculative, no human remains having as yet been found in either the miocene or pliocene strata." "The miocene man," says Professor LeConte, "is not at present acknowledged by a single careful geologist." M. Reinach, a specialist in geology and author of "*La Prehistorique*," recently published, affirms that there are no traces of man anywhere in the tertiary period, which brings us to the threshold of historic times.

Twenty or twenty-five years ago it was quite the fashion to assume that human remains and relics found in the west United States, especially those in California and Kansas, are conclusive evidence of the high antiquity of man. But during the year 1903, a thorough reinvestigation, conducted by Professor Holmes, aided by a special grant of money provided by the Carnegie Institution, was made of the caves of Indiana, Kentucky, Tennessee, Alabama, Virginia, Maryland and Pennsylvania. The result of these latest studies is given in the following statement of Professor Holmes: — "There is no evidence at all to prove that man is very ancient on this continent. All ascertained facts seem to point to the conclusion that no human being preceded the Indians in America. Where the Indian came from is uncertain, but their straight black hair, their peculiar physiognomy and other physical traits show that they are surely derived from the same ancestry as the Asiatic Mongols. There is nothing whatever to show that man has been in America longer than four, or five, thousand years at the utmost.

2. MAN'S APPEARANCE AND THE ICE AGE. — Professor Edward Hall, secretary of the Victoria Institute of London, a specialist on these matters, in a recent announcement, June, 1903, says: "Not in one single case in the whole of Europe or America has a trace of man's existence been found below the only deposits which we have a right to assume were developed and produced by the great ice sheets of the early glacial periods." This opinion is concurred in by Professors Haynes, LeConte, Boyd, C. H. Dawkins, Dr. Gandry, John Evans, W. H. Holmes, M. Favre and others. Granting, therefore, that man did not appear until after the climax of the ice age, a fact at present as well established as any other in geology, and following the lead of experts as to the date of that age, there can be fixed pretty accurately the beginning of the human family.

Professor G. F. Wright, who has given almost a lifetime to this and kindred subjects and who has the unchallenged reputation of being one of the ablest glaciologists in this country, has reached the conclusion that it ended not earlier than from seven to ten thousand years ago. Professor Joseph Prestwich collected much evidence showing that the close of the glacial period falls within the limit of twelve thousand years. The opinion of M. Adhemar and Dr. James Croll is that it closed not earlier than eleven thousand years ago. Professor R. D. Salisbury and Dr. Warren Upham, among the most recent of American geologists, think that from seven to ten thousand years is a fair estimate. In a review article (1904), this last-named scientist, speaking of the post-glacial era, says that, "From the studies of Niagara by Wright and myself, coinciding approximately with the estimate of Winchell and with a large number of estimates and computations collected by Hanson from many observers in America and Europe, it certainly seems well demonstrated that this period (postglacial) is between seven and ten thousand years." Dr. William Andrews is of the opinion that the ice age, though lingering still in Alaska, in Greenland and on the mountain plateaus of Norway, was completed nearly as it now is " not further away than from five to seven thousand five hundred years ago."

The words of Professor Winchell are not only confirmatory, but graphic and suggestive: "Man has no place till after the reign of ice. It has been imagined that the close of the reign of ice dates back perhaps a hundred thousand years. There is no evidence of this. The fact is that we ourselves came upon the earth in time to witness the retreat of the glaciers. They still linger in the valleys of the Alps and along the northern shores of Europe and Asia. The fact is we are not so far out of the dust, chaos and barbarism of antiquity as we had supposed. The very beginnings of our race are still almost in sight. Geological events which, from the force of habit in considering them, we had imagined to be located far back in the history of things are found to have transpired at our very doors." [7]

3. SCIENTIFIC MIXUP. — Now, let it be kept in mind that, on this subject, these are not "forty-year-old opinions," but are among the very latest and most indisputable utterances of scientists whose high standing is unquestioned. It turns out, therefore, that in place of the now abandoned estimates of man's great antiquity there stands the absolutely assured fact that his arrival on earth was not much, if any, earlier than the historic dates given in the Bible. If, therefore, a scientific theory ever has been cornered, this of the evolutionist, as to the beginning and development of the human race, is at the present moment in that plight. The case is this: — The biologist requires not fewer than a million years (Haeckel's estimate is a thousand million) to evolve man from the lower forms of organized life, and not fewer than several hundred thousand years to lift him out of the brute condition from which, according to evolutionists, he has been developed. On the other hand, the latest geologists have established the fact that not more than twelve or fifteen thousand years, as an outside limit, can be allowed for the entire life on earth of any being that has worn a human form. Here, therefore, in these two departments of knowledge, those of biology and geology, is a tremendous mixup. But what renders the case still more complicated and hopeless for the evolutionist are those recent archæological finds from Asia, Africa and Southern Europe. They make it clear as daylight, that from six to eight thousand years ago there were already on earth perfectly developed human races living a highly cultivated and social life. So there is left for the development of humanity not a billion, nor a

43

million, nor even two hundred thousand years, but only five thousand at the outside. In other words, the human race, that from biological and physiological points of view has made no perceptible advance in the last six thousand years, and in no other respect has made remarkable gains, except when revealed religion directly or indirectly has been a help and inspiration, did, however, in the preceding five thousand years, though starting on the lowest plane imaginable, become thoroughly civilized. That is, beginning without revealed religion, without science, without philosophy, without art, without literature, without intelligence, without conscience, without God and without anything above a mere animal nature, the human race in those comparatively few years forged ahead from its brute beginnings, if we may believe evolutionists, to the remarkable achievements of those Egyptian, Babylonian, Cretan and other civilizations that are the wonder of all explorers.

What a marvel! In that brief time man developed not only a perfect physical organism, but intellect, conscience, language, literature, codes of law, ethics, religion, art and science.

Talk about miracles! The resurrection of the dead, as a wonder, falls immensely below this speedy upshoot of the human family from the degradation to which the theory of evolutionists has consigned it.

No greater absurdity than such an evolution can be imagined. They are, therefore, these recent scientific investigations and discoveries that have doomed the arrogant edifice of evolution.

The biologist knocks out most of its underpinning, the geologist demolishes the larger remaining part, and the archæologist finishes it.

One is forcibly reminded in all this of what Professor Huxley said about the tragedies of science and philosophy (and he

44

might have added those of history as well), by which he meant the slaying of beautiful and speculative theories by ugly and what he called "provokingly unreasonable facts." And it is questionable if any theory in the history of science has been any more completely and tragically used up by provokingly unreasonable facts than the theory of evolution; and in saying this there is not meant Darwinism, or any given process of evolution, whether that of natural selection, survival of the fittest, or some other, but evolution as taught in our American schools, colleges and universities.*

VII.
SCHOLARS AND EVOLUTION.

1. ALL SCHOLARS SAID TO BE EVOLUTIONISTS. — From what is heard repeated over and over again, one might be led to think that scholarly men, men of science and the world's philosophers, are all evolutionists, and that those who question the hypothesis are afflicted "with leprosy of incompetence," or are "the mental slaves of effete traditions," or, "a howling pack of antediluvians."

The professor already mentioned, the one from Cornell, while criticising in the presence of a Boston audience the American Bible League Convention held in that city (December, 1904), after defining evolution to be "the quest for truth," and after announcing his belief "that all organic life has come from one starting-point, and that every living thing is a modification of the life stem, formed and changed by the ever-increasing struggle for existence," with the utmost assurance and complacency told his hearers that "evolution is accepted by all scientists and publicists," . . . that "attacks upon the theory are made only by persons who are not familiar with either the evolution hypothesis or the facts of natural history,

that they misunderstand and misinterpret what evolution is,"
. . . that "they confuse evolution and Darwinism," and that
"the attacks are made for the purpose of bolstering up dogmas
and beliefs."

Now, all this is very interesting, especially to those who are
pilloried by the professor, and the information given appears
to have been much enjoyed by the Twentieth Century Club,
that is supposed to represent a high degree of culture and
refinement.

2. SCHOLARSHIP AND NARROWNESS. — Now, the trouble
with many of our university professors and their following is
that they are indisposed to look beyond their own window sills
and are either unable or unwilling to make broad, generous
and really scientific inductions. They remind one of a saying
of Martineau: — "The history of knowledge abounds with
instances of men who, with the highest merit in particular
walks of science, have combined a curious incompetency when
attempting a survey of the whole field."

3. NATURALISTS ARE PROPOSING NO BETTER SCHEME THAN
DARWIN'S. — The Twentieth Century Club was also told that
"the Darwinian type of evolution has been abandoned by all
scientific men." This announcement, of course, is pleasing to
orthodox people who never have believed the theory, but one
scarcely can refrain from adding that, so far as the methods
or processes of evolution are concerned, there has been as yet
no better one proposed than that of Mr. Darwin. Is it not
rather ungracious, therefore, for evolutionists to kick and
desert Mr. Darwin, who spent a lifetime of thought and work
in their behalf, especially when they are unable to offer any
substitute for his abandoned theory of descent? And we may
repeat what already has been hinted, that the moment God is
admitted as a working factor in creative processes and the
moment organic connections and transmutations, the survivals

of the fittest and the natural selection of Mr. Darwin, Mr. Spencer and others, are ruled out of the equation, that moment there is left nothing in the theory of evolution that in any sense of the word can be called evolutionary, nor is there anything left that can be recognized as scientific or philosophical. In other words, if Science has no facts, and certainly she has not, to disprove the orthodox view that the first monkey was a monkey and nothing else, and that the last one will be the same; that the first man was a man and nothing else, and that the last one will be the same, and if this is true of other forms of life as well, then what essential or fundamental difference is there between Darwinism and any scheme of evolution that may be or can be proposed?

4. THE ABLEST SCIENTISTS AND EVOLUTION. — But returning to the assertion that scholarly men and others of high standing are all evolutionists, we are compelled to dissent — even to saying that the exact opposite is true. The most thorough scholars, the world's ablest philosophers and scientists, with few exceptions, are not supporters, but assailants of evolution.

We are a little behind the times on these questions in this country as compared with England, France and Germany, though ahead in almost everything else.

But the reactionary ball has been set in motion even among us, and within the next five years the field will be full of kickers, not against Darwinism alone, but against every other theory of evolution that involves ascent or descent through transmutation of species, for the kicking of a thing that is down is easy and always popular. Dr. N. S. Shaler, professor of geology in Harvard University, eminent as a scientist, writing recently for the "International Quarterly," Dec.-March, 1902-1903, has started in with a cautious but fairly good touch-down. "It begins to be evident to naturalists," he says, "that the Darwinian hypothesis is still essentially unverified. Notwithstanding the evidence derived from the study of animals and plants under domestication, it is not yet proved that a single species of the two or three millions now inhabiting the earth had been established solely, or mainly, by the operation of natural selection."

Professor C. C. Everett, also of Harvard, though better drilled in literature than science, is such a careful observer and extensive reader that his late words may be allowed considerable weight. Speaking of evolution he says: — "If in the past those ranks of beings ever rose and moved in procession along the upward slope, each passing, by no matter how slow a step, out of its own limitations, and in itself, or in its posterity entered upon a larger life, it was before the eyes of man were opened to them. No searching of his awakened powers can detect, even among the remains of an unknown antiquity, any glimpse of the great movement while in progress of accomplishment. All, as he looks upon it, is as fixed as the sphinx, that slumbers on the Egyptian sands. All this story of transformation and activity is a dream."

Of earlier date such men as Louis Agassiz, Joseph Henry, John William Dawson and Arnold Guyot pronounced evolution false and unscientific.

Crossing the ocean we hear words that are much more emphatic.

Dr. Etheridge, of the British Museum, one of England's most famous experts in fossilology, has passed the following criticism upon evolution: "In all this great museum there is not a particle of evidence of transmutation of species. Nine-tenths of the talk of evolutionists is sheer nonsense, not founded on observation and wholly unsupported by fact. This museum is full of proofs of the utter falsity of their views."

Professor Lionel S. Beale, physiologist, and professor of

anatomy and pathology in Kings College, London, stands today with Lord Kelvin at the head of English scientists, and in his special field, that of biology, is with one exception, perhaps, without a peer in any country of the world. While addressing the Victoria Institute of London, June, 1903, Professor Beale employed these words: " The idea of any relation having been established between the non-living and living, by a gradual advance from lifeless matter to the lowest forms of life and so onwards to the higher and more complex, has not the slightest evidence from the facts of any section of living nature of which anything is known. There is no evidence that man has descended from, or is, or was, in any way specially related to, any other organism in nature through evolution or by any other process. In support of all naturalistic conjectures concerning man's origin, there is not at this time a shadow of scientific evidence."

It is well known that French scientists as a rule have at no time been captivated by evolutionary theories and especially never have taken kindly to Mr. Darwin's views. As representatives of recent French thought no one will object to the Marquis de Nadaillac, whose articles have appeared in the *Revue des Questions Scientifiques,* or to M. Stanislas Meunier of the Paris Museum. The marquis quite ridicules the many unsupported assumptions employed to support the general theory of evolution, and especially the evolution of man from any lower type of animal life. After admitting that no one can tell what may be the future of evolution he hastens to add that he is entirely unprepared to affirm that there is at present any truth in it.

In the *Revue Scientifiques* (Dec., 1903), Meunier not only antagonizes all theories of the chemical or mechanical origin of life and the transformation of species, but argues in favor of special creations by an infinite power. His paper closes

49

thus: "Doubtless we cannot usefully risk any hypothesis on the mechanism of the production of living things; but it is perhaps a step in advance to come to the conclusion that the cause of life and its manifestations on the earth is exterior to the earth and that it is anterior to our world."

Passing from France to Germany, it is found that the light is dawning fast, though professors in Chicago, a city claiming to stand at the head of all advanced learning, and professors in Boston, a city once thought to be the center of every kind of wisdom, appear to be ignorant of it.

The late Professor Virchow, of Berlin, the highest German authority in physiology, and "the foremost chemist on the globe," at one time a pronounced advocate of Darwin's and Haeckel's views, subsequently, in his famous lecture on "Freedom of Science," while speaking of evolution made this statement: "It is all nonsense. It cannot be proved by science that man descends from the ape or from any other animal. Since the announcement of the theory, all real scientific knowledge has proceeded in the opposite direction." Subsequently, at a convention of anthropologists in Vienna, Virchow confirmed what he previously had said, in these words: "The attempt to find the transition from animal to man has ended in total failure. The middle link has not been found and never will be. It has been proved beyond doubt that during the past five thousand years there has been no noticeable change in mankind." And what seems rather severe, though in keeping with our theme, Virchow, in speaking of certain clubs or circles of evolutionists, called them "bubble companies."

In a recent number of *Beweis des Glaubens,* Professor Zoeckler, of the University of Greifswald, employs these words: "The claim that the hypothesis of descent is secured scientifically must most decidedly be denied. Neither Hartmann's exposition nor the authorities he cites have the force even of moral conviction for the claim for purely mechanical descent. The descent of organisms is not a scientifically demonstrated proposition."

Professor Fleischmann, of Erlangen, one of the several recent converts to anti-Darwinism, in a book just published in Leipsic, *Die Darwin's che Theorie,* reaches this conclusion: "The Darwinian theory of descent has in the realms of nature not a single fact to confirm it. It is not the result of scientific research, but purely the product of the imagination."

The most suggestive words, however, and really the severest criticism on evolution, though not spoken with that intent, are from Professor Ernst Haeckel, of Jena, Germany's greatest biologist, and the rankest naturalistic evolutionist of recent date. In his latest utterances he bewails the fact that he is standing almost alone. "Most modern investigators of science have come to the conclusion," he says, "that the doctrine of evolution and particularly Darwinism is an error and cannot be maintained." Then he enumerates several distinguished men, whom he calls "bold and talented scientists," who, not long since, were advocates of evolution but who lately have abandoned it. The men he mentions are Dr. E. Dennert, author of *Vom Sterbelalager des Darwinismus* (1903); Dr. Goette, the Strasburg professor whose articles have appeared in the *Unchau* (1903); Professor Edward Hoppe, known as "the Hamburg Savant," who in his recent pamphlets takes a pronounced position, in the name of religion, against naturalistic evolution; Professor Paulson, of Berlin, who, among his other criticisms of evolution, has recently declared that Haeckel's theory "is a disgrace to the philosophy of Germany"; Professor Rutemeyer, geologist and paleontologist, of Basel, who charges evolutionists, especially of the Haeckel type, with "playing false with the public and with the natural sciences"; and Professor Wilhelm Max Wundt, of Leipsic, who stands at the head of German psychologists, who wrote books in his earlier days in support of evolution, but who in a late publication characterizes those early writings as "the great crime of his youth that will take him all the rest of his life to expiate"; "and so," adds Haeckel, "he is now writing the other thing."

Such are the men over whom Haeckel is weeping because they have deserted not Darwinism in particular but evolution, and have gone back, as he would say, to the weak and beggarly elements of supernaturalism.

An interesting discussion of late has been going on in Germany between Professor Robert Eduard von Hartmann, the distinguished anti-Christian philosopher, of Berlin, and others, some of whom were classed only a few years ago among evolutionists, but have since gone, almost in a body, over to the ranks of the anti-evolutionists.

Hartmann had published his rather conservative views in these words: "The theory of descent is safe but Darwinism has been weighed and found wanting. Selection cannot in general achieve any positive results, but only negative effects; the origin of species by minimal changes is possible, but has not been demonstrated."

His statements that the "origin of species by minimal changes is possible" and that "thus far the theory of descent is safe" have brought out a small army of scholars and scientists who vigorously oppose Hartmann's naturalistic possibilities, and who are taking the position held by those eminent English and French scientists who believe in special creation. These recent recruits are such men as Eimer, Gustav Wolf, De Vries, Hoocke, von Wellstein, Fleischmann and Reinke.[52]

Now the surprising thing, notwithstanding these facts, is that American university professors, on the lecture platform, assure the people that "evolution is accepted by all scientists," and that "those who oppose it are not familiar with either the evolution hypothesis or the facts of natural history." Were these professors clergymen would it be discourteous to characterize such an exhibition as a piece of superb ignorance or insolence?

And if these facts as to the attitude of leading scientists, and if this revolution of opinion in Germany are known, and certainly they ought to be, then can the silence of our American evolutionists be looked upon as honest and manly? So far as anything can be gathered from what these men are saying, one would not know that there is an eminent anti-evolutionist anywhere in Christendom.

VIII.
BIBLE CRITICISM AND EVOLUTION.

1. DESTRUCTIVE INTENTIONS OF MODERN BIBLE CRITICS. — A recent announcement of what higher criticism proposes to do under the guidance of evolution is from the pen of one of its advocates: "We intend, First, to reconstruct Bible history in harmony with the theory of evolution. Second, to eliminate by this process all that is supernatural in the record. Third, to unite scholars in support of sweeping changes in the orthodox view of the Holy Scriptures."

What trumpery! "We intend to reconstruct Bible history in harmony with the theory of evolution," — a theory discredited and abandoned by the best scholarship of the world! One gets thoroughly out of patience with the conceit and pretence of these belated higher and destructive critics.

2. REJOINDER BY PROFESSOR A. H. SAYCE OF OXFORD. — This matter is admirably put by Dr. A. H. Sayce, professor of Assyriology in the university of Oxford, who, besides being

one of the world's ablest archæologists, takes rank in Bible studies with the most distinguished scholars of recent date: "The whole application of the supposed law of evolution to the religious and secular history of the ancient world is founded on what we know to have been a huge mistake. The actual condition of the oriental world in the age of Moses, as it has been revealed to us by archæology, leaves little room for the particular kind of evolution of which higher criticism has dreamed. But in truth the archaeological discoveries of the last dozen years in Egypt and Crete have once for all discredited the claim of 'criticism' to apply its theories of development to the settlement of chronological or historical questions. The scepticism of the critic has been proved to have been but the measure of his own ignorance, and the want of evidence to have been merely his own ignorance of it. The spade of the excavator in Crete has effected more in three or four years than the labors and canons of the 'critic' in half a century. The whole fabric he had raised has gone down like a house of cards and with it the theories of development of which he felt so confident."[10]

If, therefore, higher critics have not lost their wits completely, they will henceforth hesitate in the presence of thinking people to make use of this defunct theory in their discussions of Biblical criticism, religious faith, and systems of ethics.

X.

RELIGION AND EVOLUTION.

1. OUTCOME OF DARWINISM. — There remains one other point of view, the ethical and religious. First of all there should be an acknowledgment of indebtedness to evolutionists, beginning especially with Mr. Darwin, for a vast amount of

information and for awakening general interest in the study of nature's phenomena. And the discredit, almost disrespect, now heaped upon Mr. Darwin's scheme awakens one's orthodox pity, especially when recalling the imperial sway his hypothesis held for years over a world of scholars.

But now, after only twenty-three years have passed, reverence, even by the poorest of our scientists, is no longer shown the once famous man's theory, and every leading naturalist is echoing the words of one of the most accomplished naturalists in Great Britain, St. George Mivart: "I cannot call it (Darwin's theory) anything but a puerile hypothesis." And yet even this dirge is far from being the saddest feature of Mr. Darwin's funeral, for his hypothesis not only paved the way for making every kind of assault upon the Christian religion, but destroyed his own early faith, leaving him at last in mazes of doubt and disappointment.

The mischievous tendencies of his teaching were pointed out on the year of his death, in a country (France) where least expected. *L'Univers* (1882) published the following severe criticism upon Mr. Darwin at the very time a wellnigh universal and certainly extravagant homage was being paid him: —

"When hypotheses tend to nothing less than the shutting out of God from the thoughts and hearts of men and the diffusion of the leprosy of materialism the *savant* who invents and propagates them is either a criminal or a fool."

Herbert Spencer, too, has suffered scarcely less in postmortem judgment than Mr. Darwin. In his unification of knowledge he found no place for God in the universe, and already the day of retribution has come; those who are masters of scientific processes and are capable of broad generalizations almost to a man have pronounced their condemnation upon the scientific pretensions of Mr. Spencer.

2. RECENT EVOLUTION AND RELIGION. — But the point we are making is this, that there is every reason for thinking that our later evolutionists who have abandoned Mr. Darwin and Spencer, and are now offering to the world a new scheme of naturalism, will be overtaken by a doom no less utter than that which has befallen these distinguished predecessors. What else could be expected? Any theory that tends to dethrone God, elevate monkeys and degrade men (every scheme of evolution points that way) is sure, if followed, to end in disaster. Supernatural evolution as now taught, no less than naturalistic, antagonizes traditional Christianity. Bible cosmogony never can be harmonized with any possible theory of evolution. This late " hybrid product " that contends for the creation of a few germs and from them the evolution of the world's flora and fauna is neither Biblical nor scientific. What hope, therefore, for it or for those who advocate it? Scientists and theologians of the new school already have parted company with nearly every phase of the Christian faith, and are leading their followers where no anchorage nor peace can be found. An undenominational paper recently has put the matter thus: —

" Not only have these men abandoned faith in the supernatural, but they have sown the seed of unbelief in thousands of hearts, so that it is even now getting to sound somewhat old-fashioned to assert belief in the supernatural. They have presumed to apply even to the infinite God Himself the puny measuring-rod of their scientific dicta, and demand proof of the supernatural where the very nature of that proof is itself denied. The very essence of religion is sublimized into airy nothingness by these intellectual iconoclasts, and yet they are received into the bosom of the church which claims to be above all others the residuary legatee of the faith once delivered to the saints."

It cannot be otherwise than fatally disastrous when speculation is substituted for revelation, and evolution for creation; when the immanence of God takes the place of his transcendence; when the Bible is treated as the record merely of the development of the religious ideas of the people of Israel, instead of being the inspired word of God; when everything supernatural is eliminated from the birth, life and resurrection of Christ, and he is classed simply as a high and unusual development of humanity; when conversion and regeneration are spoken of as evolutions in life and character instead of being a revolution of man's spiritual nature. Under these destructive teachings the world may continue to mark time, but in matters most vital to human interests and happiness there will be an end of all progress. And if the day ever comes when these so-called advanced views in science and religion generally shall prevail, theological schools will have no students, and why should they? Christian churches will be emptied of hearers, and why should they not? The command, "Go ye into all the world, and preach the gospel," will lose its authority, and why should it not, if Christ is only human? Mission fields will be abandoned, family worship will be silenced, the consolations and inspirations of Christian faith will no longer be felt in the hearts and homes of men. Such will be the inevitable and woeful fruitage of an evolution and theology that does away with the essential doctrines of the early Christian faith.

In 1900, on the assembling of the International Peace Congress in Paris, *L'Univers* published these forceful and significant words: —

"The spirit of peace has fled the earth because evolution has taken possession of it. The plea for peace in past years has been inspired by faith in the divine nature and in the divine origin of man; men were then looked upon as children of one Father and war, therefore, was fratricide. But now that men are looked upon as children of apes, what matters it whether they are slaughtered or not!"

Well is it for the world, however, that amid this dangerous drift of modern speculative science and theology the hearts of those who know what and whom they have believed are held to the ancient faith with cables stronger than steel. Advocates of these new, rather revived theories, ought to know that this faith, as interpreted by Christian consciousness, stands not in the breath of any given generation. It is independent of accidents, incidents, of anything historic or transitory.

This primitive faith is like the productions by Michael Angelo, Raphael, Mozart, and Beethoven, old but new. The beauty of a mild sunset, the sublimity of a midnight heaven, the dazzle of lightnings playing across the sky, the repose of a lily clad in raiment surpassing that of any present or future Solomon, have been repeated for millions of years, but they will never be outgrown though society should exist in a state of constant progress for ten thousand years.

And thus the primitive faith of Christendom will endure, because it is a revelation from heaven; because the more it is studied and experienced the more highly it is prized; because the path it opens is one of elevation, emancipation, knowledge, peace and salvation; because it gives strength to the weak, hope to the discouraged and stimulus to the sluggish; because it promises reward to the good and pardon to the penitent, though holding threats of woe over those who do not repent; because it can enter all dark places and leave them full of light; because it can satisfy all desires that human want awakens; because it can stand by the bedside of the dying, quell every misgiving, wipe away the death-sweat, and leave the brow calm and serene as heaven; and because it places before the human soul inducements for leading a better life and for engaging in those philanthropies whose object is to save mankind from distress and despair, — inducements that evolution and the new theology never can offer or make effective; inducements that have given to the world the most splendid types of manhood that have adorned the pages of the world's history — these are the reasons why the faith of the fathers will be found standing and undisturbed· when every theory opposed to it, or that deviates from it, shall be both dishonored and forgotten. The foundations of this faith are impregnable. Its fortified home is in the wants and depths of human souls. And human nature, in her better moments and conditions, will endow it with her last dollar, and will defend it with her last strength. Evolution and its new theology may bring into play every piece of their artillery — the Alps remain.

IX.

CONCLUSION.

As a result of these investigations there are before us the following facts: — The failure of evolutionists to establish the claim that original life-germs came into existence by natural processes; their inability to show that, in the world of living things, there exists a law of development and improvement; the complete breakdown of their claim that, by natural processes, lower species of plants and animals may be transmuted into higher; the fact that in all early and late excavations and researches not one connecting link between any of the millions of different species has been found; the fact that mental science and all the physical sciences have not yet discovered a particle of evidence showing, or even suggesting, that any animal ever has reached or ever can reach a point where, slowly or suddenly, it can come into possession of a human soul, a human mind, or a human body; the fact that biologists, geologists and archæologists have overwhelmingly silenced the assertion that the human race began low down and through countless ages has worked itself up to its present civilized state; the downfall of the scarecrow and utterly false though continually repeated assertion that scholarly men, men of science and the world's great philosophers are all evolutionists; the recent abandonment of evolution by those who once held the theory and who at the present moment are making vigorous assaults upon it; the absolute incompetence of evolutionists and of " advanced theologians " to formulate any system of ethics or religion that at all approaches those made known by ancient Jewish prophets and New Testament evangelists — in view, therefore, of this majestic array of facts, need there be a moment's hesitation in saying that the hypothesis of evolution, together with all other speculations so far as they are attached to it, new theology, higher and destructive criticism included, has collapsed beyond any hope of restoration?

NOTES.

I. (Page 9.)

Suborganic evolution, treating of the formation of worlds; organic evolution, treating of things having life, and superorganic evolution, having to do with the constitution and operations of mind, are terms now in use, but the present discussion is confined chiefly to organic evolution.

II. (Page 12.)

The story of Professor Huxley's protoplasm, since called "the bathybius delusion," is interesting and ought to be instructive if not a warning to our speculative evolutionists.

Professor Huxley claimed that he had discovered the substratum of all life, which he believed covered the whole bed of the world's oceans. The discovery was hailed with enthusiasm in almost every scientific circle. By casting into the ocean a deep-water dredge any one could draw up a muddy substance from which all living things, including Adam and Eve, have been evolved.

Mr. Huxley's confession of faith was this:—" Protoplasm is the origin of all life . . . it is a molecular machine, all-powerful and all-sufficient."

The Challenger, a vessel sent out by the United States Government to make deep-sea soundings, with Professor Murray, the scientist, on board, was commissioned to secure with other things some of this suboceanic ooze or mud. A quantity was gathered sufficient to preclude the possibility of mistake, carefully preserved and brought home. But in his experiments with it the professor discovered that sea water and alcohol mingled gave a flocculent precipitate which, separated from the liquid, was identical with Huxley's protoplasm.

He showed the experiment to Professor Huxley and the delusion vanished. The all-powerful and all-sufficient protoplasm was merely a precipitated sulphate, which any chemist can make for himself.

It was a rude shock to the complacent materialistic biologist, who had built extended theoretical edifices and written learned treatises on the wonders of this protoplasm found on the sea bottom.

III. (Page 20.)

Should our readers desire to pursue this line of thought further they will find interesting facts in a treatise on "Degeneration" by Dr. Dohon, of Naples, and in another, on the same subject, by Edwin Ray Lankester, professor of comparative anatomy, Oxford.

IV. (Page 23.)

The following instance showing the changes that have taken place in geological science is vouched for by the eminent geologist, Professor Charles Lyell. "In the year 1806," he says, "the French Institute enumerated not less than eighty geological theories which were hostile to the Scriptures; but not one of those theories is held to-day."

V. (Page 34.)

A fuller discussion of this point may be found in the Geological Magazine, London, Jan., 1905.

VI. (Page 36.)

In one of the earliest editions of the "Descent of Man" Mr. Darwin thus describes the primitive human race: —

"The early progenitors of man were, no doubt, covered with hair, both sexes having beards. Their ears were pointed and capable of movement, and their bodies were provided with a tail. . . . The foot . . . was prehensile and our progenitors, no doubt, were arboreal in their habits, frequenting some warm, forest-clad land. . . . At an earlier period the progenitors of man must have been aquatic in their habits."

In justice to Mr. Darwin, however, it should be said that he was wise enough to expunge this and some other unscientific speculations from the later editions of his works.

VII. (Page 43.)

Professor Winchell's words as to the recent chaos of the ice age will seem entirely reasonable if we bear in mind that the waning glaciers of the Pleistocene era are still found in many quarters of the globe. British Columbia abounds with them.

In this note attention is also called to the fact that some of our glaciologists and paleontologists have thought that human remains found in the later glacial times, notably those in the Delaware deposits, furnish evidence of man's great antiquity. But no one now insists that these fossils are pre-glacial, if the climax of that age is meant.

The later glaciations, though holding New England in their grip, left no marks of their presence in Maryland, few in Pennsylvania, none in Virginia, Kentucky, Tennessee nor Missouri; they probably belong to the close of what Professor W. L. Elkin, of Yale, calls the astronomical winter of ten thousand five hundred years ago, when the annual winters were longer and colder than now, and when the summers were shorter and hotter. It is not improbable that bold navigators from Tyre, or from some European or African port crossed the Atlantic and, following the icy shores of New England, landed in the Delaware Bay and perished on those shores with the coming of the severe winter seasons of those primitive times. Or colonies coming from old Mexico, Yucatan or Central America, where are many evidences of the earliest civilization on this continent, one that appears to be of Asiatic origin, and on reaching the Delaware glaciers, may have been overtaken by one of those winters of the

62

later ice age, and perished, as do the modern Arctic explorers sometimes, before a retreat could be made.

At least, judging from a large number of facts, it is quite certain that the human fossils in the Delaware deposits are not those of men who came from the northwest, as did the later immigrants. Professor Holmes has clearly shown this in the following statements: — "The great ice sheet of the glacial epoch spread itself over the northern part of Asia and America 300,000 years ago, and was not withdrawn until 10,000 years ago," approximately. The ice sheet covered Wisconsin 10,000 years ago and glacial ice was everywhere in our northern and western states. It would seem to have been impossible, therefore, for primitive human beings, without houses or means of keeping themselves warm, to make the journey by way of Behring Strait and down the Pacific coast to warmer latitudes."

VIII. (Page 45.)

Adopting the theory of supernatural creation as revealed in the Bible, and admitting the attainments, and especially the mechanical skill, of the immediate descendants of Adam (Gen. ii, 19; iv, 17, 21, 22), difficulties as to the early and rapid civilization of Babylon and Egypt disappear.

IX. (Page 52.)

Hartmann's history of Darwinism is discriminating. Under the title, "The Passing of Darwinism," Hartmann gives an outline of the history of evolution. After tracing its career, beginning in the sixties, and passing through the seventies and eighties, he says: — "In the nineties, for the first time, a few timid expressions of doubt and opposition were heard, but these gradually swelled into a great chorus of voices, aiming at the overthrow of the Darwinian theory. In the first decade of the twentieth century it has become apparent that the days of Darwinism are numbered."

X. (Page 54.)

It is of interest to note that M. Halévy, the distinguished Orientalist, who outdistances even the ablest German Assyriologists, not only stands by Professor Sayce, but has spoken words that ought to hold in check our American theological professors and clergymen who have been in haste to worship at the shrine of destructive criticism. The case is this, —

When the younger Delitzsch gave his lecture on Babel and Bible, and when our secular, and, in many instances, our religious, press, and perhaps the larger number of our theological schools, surrendered without firing a gun (perhaps they had no desire to fire one), it was M. Halévy who made the earliest and perhaps the keenest reply to the somewhat arrogant and unsupported assertions of Delitzsch.

After saying a few words complimentary of the address, as is the way of a cultivated Frenchman, M. Halévy then charges him with a "predisposition to rest content with only superficial appearances" and adds: — "Sincerity compels me to point out certain inapt, inaccurate and redundant statements that disfigure the whole lecture." And this is done to the entire satisfaction of the friends of the Bible.

ANNOUNCEMENT

"Collapse of Evolution" will be found aggressive and only incidentally apologetic.

The author's other writings, for the larger part, have been in defence of the primitive Christian faith.

His publications of recent date that discuss questions now of special interest are, "Evolution or Creation," 318 pages, sold at .75; "Story of Jonah and Higher Criticism," 119 pages, .25; "Satan and Demons," 131 pages, .25; "God's Goodness and Severity," 165 pages, .25; "Adam and Eve: History or Myth," 130 pages, paper cover, .25; cloth, .50.

The following is a list of Professor Townsend's other books: —

Credo (444 pages), **Lost Forever** (448 pages), **Arena and Throne** (264 pages), **God-Man** (446 pages), **Intermediate World, Sword and Garment** (238 pages), **Supernatural Factor in Revivals** (311 pages), and **Fate of Republics** (297 pages), .60 per volume.
Bible Theology and Modern Thought (332 pages), .50. **Art of Speech,** two vols., .40 each.
Faith Work, Christian Science and Other Cures, .30.
The Bible and other Ancient Literature (205 pages), .25.
What Noted Men Think of the Bible and **What Noted Men Think of Christ,** .10 each.

These books can be ordered after May 1, 1905, through the American Bible League, 82 Bible House, New York.

AMERICAN BIBLE LEAGUE is an organization for the banding together of "the friends of the Bible, to promote a more thorough reverential and constructive study of the Sacred volume, and to maintain the historic faith of the Church in its divine inspiration and supreme authority as the Word of God."

THE BIBLE STUDENT AND TEACHER is the organ of the Bible League, containing nearly a thousand pages. Among its contributors are some of the ablest men in the United States and Europe. One dollar per year secures membership in the League and the Magazine.

Address AMERICAN BIBLE LEAGUE,
82 Bible House, New York.

THE FUNDAMENTALS
VOLUME VII

CHAPTER I
THE PASSING OF EVOLUTION

BY PROFESSOR GEORGE FREDERICK WRIGHT, D. D., LL. D.,
OBERLIN COLLEGE, OBERLIN, OHIO

The word evolution is in itself innocent enough, and has a large range of legitimate use. The Bible, indeed, teaches a system of evolution. The world was not made in an instant, or even in one day (whatever period day may signify) but in six days. Throughout the whole process there was an orderly progress from lower to higher forms of matter and life. In short there is an established *order* in all the Creator's work. Even the Kingdom of Heaven is like a grain of mustard seed which being planted grew from the smallest beginnings to be a tree in which the fowls of heaven could take refuge. So everywhere there is "first the blade, then the ear, then the full corn in the ear."

But recently the word has come into much deserved disrepute by the injection into it of erroneous and harmful theological and philosophical implications. The widely current doctrine of evolution which we are now compelled to combat is one which practically eliminates God from the whole creative process and relegates mankind to the tender mercies of a mechanical universe the wheels of whose machinery are left to move on without any immediate Divine direction.

This doctrine of evolution received such an impulse from Darwinism and has been so often confounded with it that it is important at the outset to discriminate the two. Darwinism was not, in the mind of its author, a theory of universal evolution, and Darwin rarely used the word. The title of Darwin's great work was, "The Origin of Species by Means of Natural Selection." The problem which he set out to solve touched but a small part of the field of evolution. His proposition was simply that species may reasonably be supposed to be nothing more than enlarged or accentuated varieties, which all admit are descendants from a common ancestry. For example, there are a great many varieties of oak trees. But it is supposed by all botanists that these have originated from a common ancestor. Some chestnut trees, however, differ less from some oak trees than the extreme varieties of both do from each other. Nevertheless, the oak and the chestnut are reckoned not as varieties, but as different species. But the dividing line between them is so uncertain that it is impossible to define it in language; hence, some botanists have set up an independent species between the two, which they call "chestnut oak."

WHAT IS A "SPECIES"?

This, however, is but a single illustration of the great difficulty which scientific men have had in getting a satisfactory definition of species. That most generally accepted is "a collection of individual plants and animals which resemble each other so closely that they can *reasonably be supposed* to have descended from a common ancestor." It is easy to see, however, that this definition begs the whole question at issue. For we have no certain means of knowing how widely the progeny may in some cases differ from the parent; and we do not know but that resemblances may result from the action of other causes than that of parental connection. The definition is far from being one that would be accepted in the exact sciences.

It may be "reasonably supposed" that such small differences as separate species have resulted through variations of individuals descended from a common ancestry, yet it is a long leap to assert that, therefore, it may be reasonably supposed that all the differences between animals or between plants may have arisen in a similar manner.

A characteristic difference between the African elephant and the Indian elephant, for example, is that the African elephant has three toes on his hinder feet and the Indian has four. While, therefore, it may not be a great stretch of imagination to suppose that this difference has arisen by a natural process, without any outside intervention, it is an indefinitely larger stretch of the imagination to suppose that all the members of the general family to which they belong have originated in a like manner; for, this family, or order, includes not only the elephant, but the rhinoceros, hippopotamus, tapir, wild boar and horse.

But many of Darwin's followers and expounders have gone to extreme lengths in their assertions, and have announced far more astonishing conclusions than these. Not only do they assert, with a positiveness of which Darwin was never guilty, that species have had a common origin through natural causes, but that all organic beings had been equally independent of supernatural forces. It is a small thing that the two species of elephant should have descended from a common stock. Nothing will satisfy them but to assert that the elephant, the lion, the bear, the mouse, the kangaroo, the whale, the shark, the shad, birds of every description—indeed, all forms of animal life, including the oyster and the snail—have arisen by strictly natural processes from some minute speck of life, which originated in far distant time.

ORIGIN OF LIFE

It need not be said that such conclusions must rest upon very attenuated evidence, such as is not permitted to have weight in the ordinary affairs of life. But even this is only the beginning with thoroughgoing evolutionists. To be consistent they must not only have all species of animals or plants, but all animals *and* plants descending from a common origin, which they assert to be an almost formless protoplasm, which is supposed to have appeared in the earliest geological ages. Nor does this by any means bring them to their final goal, for to carry out their theory they must leap to the conclusion that life itself has originated, spontaneously, by a natural process, from inorganic matter.

But of this they have confessedly no scientific proof. For, so far as is yet known, life springs only from antecedent life. The first chapter of Genesis, to which reference has already been made, furnishes as perfect a definition of plant life as has ever been given. Plant life, which is the earliest form of living matter, is described "as that which has seed in itself" and "yields seed after his kind." A half century ago the theory of spontaneous generation had many supporters. It was believed that minute forms of plant life had sprung up from certain conditions of inorganic matter without the intervention of seeds or spores. Bottles of water, which were supposed to have been shut off from all access of living germs, were found, after standing a sufficient length of time, to swarm with minute living organisms.

But experiments showed that germs must have been in the water before it was set aside. For, on subjecting it to a higher degree of temperature, so as apparently to kill the germs, no life was ever developed in it. All positive basis for bridging the chasm between living matter and lifeless matter has thus been removed from the realm of science.

THE MYSTERY OF FIRST BEGINNINGS

This brings us to the important conclusion that the origin of life, and we may add of variations, is to finite minds an insoluble problem; and so Darwin regarded it. At the very outset of his speculation, he rested on the supposition that the Creator in the beginning breathed the forces of life into several forms of plants and animals, and at the same time endowed them with the marvelous capacity for variation which we know they possess.

This mysterious capacity for variation lies at the basis of his theory. If anything is to be *evolved* in an orderly manner from the resident forces of primordial matter it must first have been *involved* through the creative act of the Divine Being. But no one knows what causes variation in plants or animals. Like the wind it comes, but we know not whence it cometh or whither it goeth. Breeders and gardeners do not attempt to produce varieties directly. They simply observe the variations which occur, and select for propagation those which will best serve their purposes. They are well aware that variations which they perpetuate are not only mysterious in their origin, but superficial in their character.

In Darwinism the changing conditions of life, to which every individual is subjected, are made to take the place of the breeder and secure what is called natural selection. In this case, however, the peculiarities selected and preserved must always be positively advantageous to the life of the individuals preserved. But to be of advantage a variation must both be considerable in amount, and correlated to other variations so that they shall not be antagonistic to one another. For example, if a deer were born with the capability of growing antlers so large that they would be a decided advantage to him in his struggle for existence, he must at the same time have a neck strong enough to support its weight, and other portions of his frame capable of bearing the increased strain. Otherwise his antlers would be the ruin of all his hopes instead of an advantage. It is impossible to conceive of this *combination* of advantageous variations without bringing in the hand and the designing mind of the Original Creator.

Of this, as of every other variety of evolution, it can be truly said in the words of one of the most distinguished physicists, Clerk Maxwell: "I have examined all that have come within my reach, and have found that every one must have a

God to make it work." By no stretch of legitimate reasoning can Darwinism be made to exclude design. Indeed, if it should be proved that species have developed from others of a lower order, as varieties are supposed to have done, it would strengthen rather than weaken the standard argument from design.

But the proof of Darwinism even is by no means altogether convincing, and its votaries are split up into as many warring sects as are the theologians. New schools of evolutionists arise as rapidly as do new schools of Biblical critics. Strangely enough the "Neo Darwinians" go back to the theory of Lamarck that variations are the result of effort and use on the part of the animal; whereas Darwin denied the inheritance of acquired characteristics; while Weissmann goes to the extreme of holding that natural selection must be carried back to the ultimate atoms of primordial matter, where he would set up his competitive struggle for existence. Romanes and Gulick, however, insist that specific variations often occur from "segregation," entirely independent of natural selection.

Nor do the champions of evolution have a very exalted estimate of each other's opinions. In a letter to Sir Joseph Hooker in 1866, referring to Spencer, Darwin wrote: "I feel rather mean when I read him: I could bear and rather enjoy feeling that he was twice as ingenious and clever as myself, but when I feel that he is about a dozen times my superior, even in the master art of wriggling, I feel aggrieved. If he had trained himself to observe more, even at the expense, by a law of balancement, of some loss of thinking power, he would have been a wonderful man." ("Life and Letters," Vol. ii., p. 239.)

To account for heredity, Darwin, in his theory of "pangenesis," suggested that infinitesimal "gemmules" were thrown off from every part of the body or plant, and that they had "a mutual affinity for each other leading to their aggregation either into buds or into the sexual elements." But when he ventured the opinion that these were the same as Spencer's "vitalized molecules" in which dwelt an "intrinsic aptitude to aggregate into the forms" of the species, Spencer came out at once and said that it was no such thing. They were not at all alike. Darwin, in reply, said he was sorry for the mistake. But he had feared that as he did not know exactly what Spencer meant by his "vitalized molecules," a charge of plagiarism might be brought against him if he did not give Spencer due credit. But others seemed to find it as hard to understand what Darwin meant by his "gemmules" with their marvelous mutual "affinity" for each other, as he did what Spencer meant by "vitalized molecules." Bates wrote him that after reading the chapter twice he failed to understand it; and Sir H. Holland set it down as "very tough," while Hooker and Huxley thought the language was mere tautology, and both failed "to gain a distinct idea" from it. ("Letters of Darwin," Vol. ii., p. 262.)

Indeed, thoroughgoing evolution has no such universal acceptance as is frequently represented to be the case. Few naturalists are willing to project the theory beyond the narrow limits of their own province. Such naturalists as Asa Gray and Alfred Russel Wallace, who in a general way accepted the main propositions of Darwinism, both insisted that natural selection could attain its ends only as giving effect to the designs of the Creator. Agassiz, Owen, Mivart, Sir William Dawson, and Weissmann either rejected the hypothesis altogether or so modified it that it bore little resemblance to the original. Professor Shaler declared, shortly before his death, "that the Darwinian hypothesis is still unverified." Dr. Etheride of the British Museum says that "in all this great museum there is not a particle of evidence of transmutation of species." Professor Virchow of Berlin declared that "the attempt to find the transition from the animal to man has ended in total failure." The list could be extended indefinitely. Haeckel, indeed, had from his imagination supplied the missing link between man and the apes, calling it *Pithecanthropus*. While, a few years after, Du Bois discovered in recent volcanic deposits in Java a small incomplete skull in one place, and near by a diseased femur (thigh bone), and not far away two molar teeth. These were hailed as remains of the missing link, and it was forthwith dubbed *Pithecanthropus Erectus*. The skull was indeed small, being only two-thirds the size of that of the average man. But Professor Cope, one of our most competent comparative anatomists, concluded that as the "femur is that of a man, it is in no sense a connecting link." The erect form carries with it all the anatomical characteristics of a perfect man. ("Primary Factors," 1896, pt. 1, chap. vi.)

But the Darwinians themselves have made their full share of erroneous assumptions of facts, and of illogical conclusions. It will suffice for our present purpose to refer to a few of these.

Darwin himself made two great mistakes which in the eyes of discerning students vitiate his whole theory.

1. *As to Geological Time.* The establishment of Darwin's theory as he originally proposed it involved the existence of the earth in substantially its present condition for an indefinite, not to say infinite, period of time. In one of his calculations in the first edition of "Origin of Species," he arrived at the startling conclusion that 306,662,400 years is "a mere trifle" of geological time. It was not long, however, before his son, Sir George H. Darwin, demonstrated to the general satisfaction of physicists and astronomers that life could not have begun on earth more than 100 million years ago, and probably not more than 50 million; while Lord Kelvin would reduce the period to less than 30 million years, which Alfred Russel Wallace affirms is sufficient time for the deposition of all the geological strata. Evolutionists are now fighting hard and against great odds to be allowed 100 million years for the development of the present drama of life upon the earth.

The difference between 306,662,400 years, regarded as "a mere trifle," and 24,000,000, or even 100,000,000 years, as constituting the *whole sum*, is tremendous. For, it necessitates a rapidity in the development of species which must be regarded as by leaps and bounds, and so would well accord with the theory of creation by special Divine intervention.

If a critic of Darwinism had made so egregious an error as this which Darwin introduced into the very foundation of his theory, he would have been the subject of an immense amount of ridicule. The only excuse which Darwin could make was that at the time no one knew any better. But that excuse shows the folly of building such an enormous theory upon an unknown foundation.

2. *As to the Minuteness of Beneficial Variations.* The unlimited geological time required by Darwin's original theory is closely bound up with his view of the minuteness of the steps through which progress has been made. The words which he constantly uses when speaking of variations are "slight," "small," "extremely gradual," "insensible gradations." But early in the discussion it was shown by Mivart that "minute incipient variations in any special direction" would be valueless; since, to be of advantage in any case, they must be considerable in amount. And furthermore, in order to be of permanent advantage, a variation of one organ must be accompanied with numerous other variations in other parts of the organism.

The absurdity in supposing the acquisition of advantageous qualities by chance variations is shown in the pertinent illustration adduced by Herbert Spencer from the anatomy of the cat. To give the cat power of leaping to any advantageous height, there must be a simultaneous variation in all the bones, sinews, and muscles of the hinder extremities; and, at the same time, to save the cat from disaster when it descends from an elevation, there must be variation of a totally different character in all the bones and tendons and muscles of the fore limbs. To learn the character of these changes, one has but to "contrast the markedly bent hind limbs of a cat with its almost straight fore limbs, or contrast the silence of the upward spring on to the table with the thud which the fore paws make as it jumps off the table." So numerous are the simultaneous changes necessary to secure any advantage here, that the probabilities against their arising fortuitously run up into billions, if not into infinity; so that they are outside of any rational recognition.

THE ORIGIN OF MAN

The failure of evolution to account for man is conspicuous. Early in the Darwinian discussion, Alfred Russel Wallace, Darwin's most distinguished co-worker, instanced various physical peculiarities in man which could not have originated through natural selection alone, but which necessitated the interference of a superior directing power.

Among these are (a) *the absence in man of any natural protective covering.* The nakedness of man which exposes him to the inclemency of the weather could never in itself have been an advantage which natural selection could take hold of. It could have been of use only when his intelligence was so developed that he could construct tools for skinning animals and for weaving and sewing garments. And that practically involves all essential human attributes.

(b) *The size of the human brain.* Man's brain is out of all proportion to the mental needs of the highest of the animal creation below him. Without man's intelligence such a brain would be an incumbrance rather than an advantage. The weight of the largest brain of a gorilla is considerably less than half that of the average man, and only one third that of the best developed of the human race.

(c) This increase in the size of the brain is connected also with *a number of other special adaptations of the bodily frame to the wants of the human mind.* For example, the thumb of the hind limb of the ape becomes a big toe in man, which is a most important member for a being which would walk in an upright position, but a disadvantage to one who walks on all fours. The fore limbs of the ape are shortened into the arms of a man, thus adapting them to his upright position and to the various uses which are advantageous in that position. Furthermore, to make it possible to maintain the erect position of man there has to be a special construction of the ball and socket joints in the hip bones and in the adjustment of all the vertebra of the back and neck. All these would be disadvantageous to an ape-like creature devoid of man's intelligence.

(d) *Man's intellectual capacity* belongs to a different order from that of the lower animals. Naturalists do indeed classify men and apes together in the same genus anatomically. But to denote the human species they add the word "sapiens." That is, they must regard his intelligence as a specific characteristic. The lower animals do indeed have many common instincts with man, and in many cases their instincts are far superior to those of man. But in his reasoning powers man is apparently separated from the lower animals, one and all, by an impassable gulf.

Romanes, after collecting the manifestations of intelligent reasoning from every known species of the lower animals, found that they only equalled, altogether, the intelligence of a child 15 months old. He could find no such boundless outlook of intelligence in the lower animals as there is in man. As any one can see, it would be absurd to try to teach an elephant geology, an eagle astronomy, or a dog theology. *Yet there is no race of human beings but has capacity to comprehend these sciences.*

Again, man is sometimes, and not improperly, defined as a "tool using animal." *No animal ever uses, much less makes, a tool.* But the lowest races of men show great ingenuity in making tools, while even the rudest flint implement bears indubitable evidence of a power to adapt means to ends which places its maker in a category by himself.

Again, man is sometimes, and properly, defined as a "fire using animal." *No animal ever makes a fire.* Monkeys do indeed gather round a fire when it is made. But the making of one is utterly beyond their capacity. Man, however, even in his lowest stages knows how to make fire at his will. So great is this accomplishment, that it is no wonder the Greeks looked upon it as a direct gift from heaven.

Again, man may properly be described as a "speaking animal." *No other animal uses articulate language.* But man not only uses it in speech but in writing. How absurd it would be to try to teach a learned pig to translate and understand the cuneiform inscriptions unearthed from the deserted mounds of Babylonia.

Finally, man may properly be described as a *"religious animal,"* but who would ever think of improving the nature of the lower animals by delivering sermons in their presence or distributing Bibles among them? Yet, the Bible—a Book composed of every species of literature, containing the highest flights of poetry and eloquence ever written, and presenting the sublimest conceptions of God and of the future life ever entertained—has been translated into every language under heaven, and has found in those languages the appropriate figures of speech for effectually presenting its ideas.

THE CUMULATIVE ARGUMENT

Now, all these peculiarities both in the body and the mind of man, to have been advantageous, must have taken place *simultaneously* and at the same time have been *considerable in amount*. To suppose all this to occur without the intervention of the Supreme Designing Mind is to commit logical "hara-kiri." Such chance combinations are beyond all possibility of rational belief.

It is fair to add, however, that Darwin never supposed

that man was descended from any species of existing apes; but he always spoke of our supposed ancestor as "ape-like," a form, from which the apes were supposed to have varied in one direction as far as man had in another. All efforts, however, to find traces of such connecting links as this theory supposes have failed. The Neanderthal skull was, according to Huxley, capacious enough to hold the brain of a philosopher. The *Pithecanthropus Erectus of Du Bois* had, as already remarked, the erect form of a man; in fact, was a man. The skeletons of prehistoric man so far as yet unearthed, differ no more from present races of men than existing races and individuals differ from each other.

In short, everything points to the unity of the human race, and to the fact that, while built on the general pattern of the higher animals associated with him in the later geological ages, he differs from them in so many all-important particulars, that it is necessary to suppose that he came into existence as the Bible represents, by the special creation of a single pair, from whom all the varieties of the race have sprung.

It is important to observe, furthermore, in this connection, that the progress of the human race has not been uniformly upward. In fact the *degeneration* of races has been more conspicuous than their advancement; while the advancement has chiefly been through the influence of outside forces. The early art of Babylonia and Egypt was better than the later. The religious conceptions of the first dynasties of Egypt were higher than those of the last. All the later forms of civilization shine principally by borrowed light. Our own age excels, indeed, in material advancement. But for art and literature we fall far below the past, and for our best religion we still go back to the Psalm Singers and Prophets of Judaea, and to the words of Him who spake "as never man spake." Democracy has no guides whom it dares trust implicitly. We have much reason to fear that those we are following are blind guides leading on to an end which it is not pleasant to contemplate, and from which we can be delivered only by the coming of the Son of Man.

CONCLUSION

The title of this paper is perhaps a misnomer. For, doubtless, the passing of the present phase of evolution is not final. Theories of evolution have chased each other off the field in rapid succession for thousands of years. Evolution is not a new thing in philosophy, and such is the frailty of human nature that it is not likely to disappear suddenly from among men. The craze of the last half century is little more than the recrudesence of a philosophy which has divided the opinion of men from the earliest ages. In both the Egyptian and the East Indian mythology, the world and all things in it were evolved from an egg; and so in the Polynesian myths. But the Polynesians had to have a bird to lay the egg, and the Egyptians and the Brahmans had to have some sort of a deity to create theirs. The Greek philosophers struggled with the problem without coming to any more satisfactory conclusion. Aniximander, like Professor Huxley, traced everything back to an "infinity" which gradually worked itself into a sort of pristine "mud" (something like Huxley's exploded "bathybius"), out of which everything else evolved; while Thales of Miletus tried to think of water as the mother of everything, and Aneximenes practically deified the air. Diogenes imagined a "mind stuff" (something like Weissmann's "biophores," Darwin's "gemmules possessed with affinity for each other," and Spencer's "vitalized molecules") which acted *as if* it had intelligence; while Heraclitus thought that fire was the only element pure enough to produce the soul of man. These speculations culminated in the great poem of Lucretius entitled, *De Rerum Natura*, written shortly before the beginning of the Christian era. His atomic theory was something like that which prevails at the present time among physicists. Amid the unceasing motion of these atoms there somehow appeared, according to him, the orderly forms and the living processes of nature.

Modern evolutionary speculations have not made much real progress over those of the ancients. As already remarked, they are, in their bolder forms atheistic; while in their milder forms they are "deistic"—admitting, indeed, the agency of God at the beginning, but nowhere else. The attempt, however, to give the doctrine standing through Darwin's theory of the Origin of Species by Means of Natural Selection has not been successful; for at best, that theory can enlarge but little our comprehension of the adequacy of resident forces to produce and conserve variations of species, and cannot in the least degree banish the idea of design from the process.

It is, therefore, impossible to get any such proof of evolution as shall seriously modify our conception of Christianity. The mechanism of the universe is so complicated that no man can say that it is closed to Divine interference. Especially is this seen to be the case since we know that the *free will of man does pierce the joints of nature's harness and interfere with its order* to a limited extent. Man, by cultivation, makes fruits and flowers grow where otherwise weeds would cover the ground. Man makes ten thousand combinations of natural forces which would not occur without his agency. The regular course of nature is interfered with every time a savage chips a flint implement or builds a canoe, or by friction makes a fire. We cannot banish God from the universe without first stultifying ourselves and reducing man's free will to the level of a mere mechanical force. But man is more than that; and this everyone knows.

Furthermore, a great mistake is made when the dicta of specialists in scientific investigation are accepted in religious matters as of any particular value. Indeed, the concentration of specialists on narrow lines of investigation really unfits them for duly weighing religious evidence.

Spiritual things are not to be discovered by material instruments nor detected by the material senses. Physical science cannot penetrate to the *origin* of anything, but must content itself to deal with processes already begun. Profound mystery hangs over the birth of every human soul. Who can tell when it becomes a free personality, reflecting the image of its Creator? Is the soul, as well as the body, begotten by the parent? This question has divided theologians from the time of Augustine to the present day.

The worst foes of Christianity are not physicists but metaphysicians. Hume is more dangerous than Darwin; the agnosticism of Hamilton and Mansel is harder to meet than that of Tyndall and Huxley; the fatalism of the philosophers is more to be dreaded than the materialism of any scientific men. The sophistries of the Socratic philosophy touching the freedom of the will are more subtile than those of the Spencerian school. Christianity, being a religion of fact and history, is a free-born son in the family of the inductive sciences, and is not specially hampered by the paradoxes inevitably connected with all attempts to give expression to ultimate conceptions of truth. The field is now as free as it has ever been to those who are content to act upon such positive evidence of the truth of Christianity as the Creator has been pleased to afford them. The evidence for evolution, even in its milder form, does not begin to be as strong as that for the revelation of God in the Bible.

ACKNOWLEDGMENTS

Patterson, Alexander. *The Other Side of Evolution.* (1903): 1–153. Courtesy of Ronald L. Numbers.

Dennert, Eberhard. *At the Deathbed of Darwinism.* (1904): 1–146. Courtesy of Holy Cross College Library.

Townsend, Luther Tracy. *Collapse of Evolution.* (1905): 1–64. Courtesy of Ronald L. Numbers.

Wright, George Frederick. "The Passing of Evolution." *The Fundamentals* 7(1910–15): 5–20. Courtesy of Yale University Sterling Memorial Library.

For Product Safety Concerns and Information please contact our EU representative GPSR@taylorandfrancis.com
Taylor & Francis Verlag GmbH, Kaufingerstraße 24, 80331 München, Germany

www.ingramcontent.com/pod-product-compliance
Lightning Source LLC
Chambersburg PA
CBHW071140300426
44113CB00009B/1034